D1132307

LIVING ARTFULLY

REFLECTIONS FROM THE FAR WEST COAST

2012 © ANITA SINNER & CHRISTINE LOWTHER
The Key Publishing House Inc.

First Edition 2012
The Key Publishing House Inc.
Toronto, Canada
Website: www.thekeypublish.com
E-mail: info@thekeypublish.com
Print ISBN 978-1-926780-14-6
E-book ISBN 978-1-926780-36-8

Copyediting & proof reading Caroline Macomber
Cover design David Stevenson
Typesetting Narinder Singh
Library and Archives Canada Cataloguing in Publication is available.

Published by a grant and in association with The Key Research Center (www.thekeyresearch.org). The Key promotes freedom of thought and expression and peaceful coexistence among human societies.

KPH

The Key Publishing House Inc.
www.thekeypublish.com
www.thekeyresearch.org

LIVING ARTFULLY
REFLECTIONS FROM THE FAR WEST COAST

EDITED BY

ANITA SINNER & CHRISTINE LOWTHER

The Key Publishing House Inc.

TABLE OF CONTENTS

INTRODUCTION

EARTH   **1**

48° 37' N   123° 68' W *Anita Sinner*   3

CREATIVE GEOGRAPHY *Karen Charleson*   8

FROM BADLANDS TO TIDE POOLS: FINDING MY
PLACE *Robert Dalton*   12

UP AND OUT: ISLAND TREES AND STORYMAKING
Margaret Murphy   23

MY CLAYOQUOT SAMPLER *Michael Scott Curnes*   26

STRAIGHT TO HERE *Jan Janzen*   30

SACRED GROUND, SACRED HEART: A VIEW FROM
WHALER BAY *Kit Grauer*   34

THE TAO OF TOFINO: IN BETWEEN ARTIST AND
COMMUNITY *David Floody*   40

FORMATIVE YEARS *Sharon McInnes*   43

MY VICTORIA *Robert Amos*   46

. . . AND TOPOGRAPHY *Wanda Hurren*   49

WIND   **55**

WEATHERGRAMS *Kim Goldberg*   57

FINDING HOME, FINDING ART *Peter Cressey*   62

WHO I AM, HERE *Mary Ann Moore*   66

THINGS THE CITY NEVER GAVE ME *Bernice Lever*   72

THE BOOGEYMAN, FIRST COMPOSITION, THE SPELLING
QUIZ, AND THE PLAGIARIST *Keith Harrison*   74

THESE WORDS, THIS FARM, MY HEART: A JOURNEY OF
LOVING INQUIRY *Ahava Shira*   78

FROM TORONTO TO BULL HARBOUR *Libbie Morin*   81

THE FINE ART OF TAKING ONE'S TIME *Johanna Vanderpol*   85

MOUNTAIN, SKY AND SEA: THE ART OF GAZING AND
IMAGINING *Bill Zuk*   87

ISLAND RHYTHMS *Sandra Gwynne Martin*   97

FIRE   **101**

ART OF THE SOAPBOX *Greg Blanchette*   103

A TREMOR AT MY FEET *Janine Wood*   108

LETTERS TO DAD: YOU SET THE BAR HIGH, DON'T
BE DISAPPOINTED *Keven Drews*   112

THE AWAKENING OF THE ARTIST IN A YOUNG MAN
Adrian Dorst   120

COLOURS *Marla Thirsk*   129

ROOFING *Michael Elcock*   147

HEART SONG *Gael Duchene*   152

A POET'S RETURN *Lisa Shatzky*   153

GETTING IN TUNE *Shirley Langer*   160

WATER   **167**

THE ART OF NOTICING *Mark Hobson*   169

S E A F L E S H *Celeste Snowber*   177

ART IS A GHOST *Janet Marie Rogers*   183

MYSTERY ELEMENT *Joanna Streetly*   186

RETURN *Mike Emme*   189

A PAINTER'S TRAJECTORY *Avis Rasmussen*   204

THEY SAY THAT SEEING IS BELIEVING *Roland Rasmussen*   209

WAKING UP IN CLAYOQUOT SOUND *Susan Kammerzell*   212

UNDERWATER STARS *Velcrow Ripper and Heather Frise*   214

THE CORTES CURE *Melody Hessing*   221

LIVING AND WRITING ON THE EDGE *Heather Kellerhals-Stewart*   225

THE WET AND ROTTING REALM OF NANG SDINS,
SGANG GWAAY LLNAGAAY, HAIDA GWAII *Susan Musgrave*   227

A BEAUTIFUL IMPOSITION *Christine Lowther*   231

CONTRIBUTOR BIOGRAPHIES   237

INTRODUCTION

In this anthology we enter into a conversation about living artfully on the margins of Canada's west coast. Living artfully is a form of practice as well as a forum for reflection, debates and critiques with visual, performative and literary artists. We explore experiences formed in the spaces between physical, social and cultural geographies by bringing together wide-ranging professional and emerging artists who share their understandings of identity and place through everyday moments in their lives. From their reflections we may begin to cultivate awareness of how the far west coast can offer a renewed understanding of place within contemporary Canadian art and culture.

In this collection of forty-three chapters, artists explore how place shapes the sometimes contested but ever-evolving fabric of our west coast communities. We define the far west coast as all points west of the mainland, where numerous islands stretch from our southern-most tip along the US border, from the Gulf Islands to Vancouver Island, up to Haida Gwaii and, eventually, to the northern border, forming a chain of land masses separated by waters from the vast expanse of this nation.

By asking artists to excavate their turning points and critical life moments, we begin to extend Jack Hodgins' description of Vancouver Island to encompass this far west coast as a region that is "self-consciously on the edge of the continent" (Hutcheon, 1988). Physical geography is a point of departure for a host of artists with diverse interests, perspectives, purposes and backgrounds to consider what it means to live here. Artists provide insights to living artfully in ways that honour both traditional and alternative modes of expression, from fine art to craft practices. With diverse ways of being artists, we share in the embodied experiences of authors through their exemplars of life writing. Exploring the far west coast in this way brings a lens to how and why art is often tied to our geographies. The far west coast is a sort of artful microcosm and through this dialogue, authors bring forward an inspiring mix of stories about creativity.

We asked artists: How does geography influence artistic expression? How do creative people prevail and thrive in a not-so-creatively oriented culture? Why is this place meaningful for so many artists? Writers, painters, journalists, poets, photographers, dancers, carvers, singers and others responded by sharing their experiences in creative non-fictions, memoirs, letters, journal entries, and photo essays, offering exemplars of practice that provide a way to think about what it means to live artfully. In their responses we discover the landscape as a character in art-making that is always present, resulting in broad definitions and interpretations of art, artwork, and artist.

At the heart of these chapters are private spaces – the inner worlds of struggles and challenges as well as joys and rewards of pursuing expression – and the public spaces of communities and natural environments. Many writers express being in between here and elsewhere; in between past and present; in between social contexts, as artists and workers of regular jobs; in between forms of artful expression, like painter *and* writer, writer *and* dancer, dancer *and* singer. Some artists dreamed of the far west coast, and like a pilgrimage, chose to uproot and relocate to be part of a perceived lifestyle. Some artists are discovering a new mythology of the far west coast. And some envision and purposely shape their lives within nature. Each chapter invites readers to navigate how artists understand living in the places they call home. As a result, this collection is organized around elements of nature combined with art practice: earth, wind, fire and water. Elements are both literal and metaphoric, and elements converge and intersect, bringing artists of many genres together to discuss what constitutes the qualities of their ways of living, their ways of meaning-making in art, and how their lives are deeply entwined with place.

Earth

The landscape as a habitat defining the artist and his or her artistic vision is understood physically in terms of territories or towns, and metaphorically, as a dwelling place for memory, emotion, and the heart. Here artists explore questions of our life cycle through the element of Earth, sharing notions of being born of Earth, and returning to the earth. This is a contemplative and meditative approach to thinking about creativity and physical movement, and the relationships that make being an artist and living artfully possible on the far west coast.

Opening our collection from Sooke, longitude and latitude are the points for Anita Sinner, where becoming an artist is a response to the physical landscape and a community of caring. Karen Charleson of Hesquiaht questions notions of creative geography in relation to her husband's First Nation heritage and western paradigms, and her experience of convergence within both. Robert Dalton shifts the conversation to focus on art practice as a way of knowing, drawing on intertidal zones in greater Victoria and beyond to open a dynamic conversation about belonging. Margaret Murphy of Nanaimo is an oral storyteller actively involved in establishing this tradition in her community. For Margaret, it is all about the trees; they become characters in her storytelling. From Tofino, Michael Curnes lets rip his hilarious tale of moving with his partner to run a tourist resort and how doing so quickly drains the cultured gayness out of the couple. In a back-to-the-land adventure, Jan Janzen of Tofino weaves together nature, relationships and creative experimentation in his art practice. As a writer, Kit Grauer shares her reflections on how life and death are symbolised in her multiple landscapes, making Galiano Island both the centre and margin for living with grief. David Floody observes social and cultural dynamics in Tofino, and in his chapter, he poses the question: What is community? Moving to Gabriola Island, Sharon McInnes charts her life path with nature, and how after retirement, she finally claimed her profession as a writer. Back on Vancouver Island, Robert Amos of Victoria describes why he has chosen this place as his home, rather than the major art centres across the continent, and how in his Victoria, the arts are nurtured to create community. Drawn by light, Victoria photographer Wanda Hurren concludes this section with a description of the far west coast as a liminal space through her art practice of contemplative photography. In a triptych, Wanda expresses the idea that geography and identity are cumulative events and never mutually exclusive.

Wind

Wind brings us to the ephemeral qualities of living artfully, where an instant in the everyday lives of artists suggests a direction, a movement, a response and a flow, like an idea carried by the wind. Artists invoke this element to express their presence and proximity on the far west coast. Sometimes they drift. Sometimes the wind fills the body with breaths of hope and vulnerability to reveal unexpected moments. Wind exposes artists and their opinions, weaving, curving, and turning in response to changing perceptions of place.

In Nanaimo, Kim Goldberg situates her role as one of encouraging the creative process through her art interventions – in this case, weathergrams – and she purposely leaves her work open to interpretation for viewers and readers. Peter Cressey's wood sculptures serve as a metaphoric extension of his own life journey that took him to Sooke. He meditates on what is often unacknowledged in the Canadian context: social and economic classism. Mary Ann Moore infuses us with insights into becoming an artist by layering Canadian places, generational identities, sexual orientation and women's genealogies. Bernice Lever offers an affirming account of life on Bowen Island, and the dynamics of community life. A humorous life sketch drawn from his imaginative childhood situates Keith Harrison in Port McNeill, where the unknown and strange landscape created the perfect conditions for a child's anticipation of the 'boogeyman.' In a comic book style of storying, Keith recalls an earlier time on the far west coast, and how familial love sustained the challenges of living in a remote location. Ahava Shira's chapter is about love as a form of inquiry, and how she has come to live artfully in the intricate realms of Salt Spring Island. The remote

Hope Island, off northern Vancouver Island, becomes a character in Libbie Morin's account of learning to live with the land, in contrast to her city life. A Cowichan Bay perspective is brought to us by Johanna Vanderpol, in a descriptive reflection that brings forward an aura of peacefulness as she maps the views that inspire her writing. Bill Zuk of Victoria invites us to join his art practice in nature, where we learn more about how he renders mountains, sky and sea. Sandra Gwynne Martin of Galiano Island writes of the rhythms of the island, like a generous lover that gives to and demands of the artist within. It is in the beauty of island life beyond the surface landscape that we discover the place shaping Sandra's experience as a writer.

Fire

A sensual, passionate approach to living artfully, artists express their practice through the element of fire as active, shifting and sometimes rupturing accounts of their emotional and spiritual experiences. Through fire, artists set us alight with their enthusiasm, imagination, inspiration, critique and even anger, in compositions that explore the forces driving them on to make an impact in the places they call home. We discover the cracks that push the boundaries of art, and how art can kindle different kinds of lifestyles.

Tofino resident Greg Blanchette delivers a soapbox rant to his townspeople against limiting their artistic expression to the cult of Supernatural British Columbia. Janine Wood furthers notions of living artfully through flamenco dance, a journey that crosses continents and forms of art-making. Journalist Keven Drews writes a series of letters of mourning to his father in the style of a news story. This is a deeply intimate and courageous expression of the father-son relationship and what it is to witness the passing of life to death. Becoming an artist is a theme also taken up by Adrian Dorst, who began as a carver. In this humorous tale of happenstance, Adrian delves into the spaces between formal and informal art practice, and what art and culture mean to him in centres like Vancouver and the margins of the far west coast. From Ucluelet, painter Marla Thirsk turns to her palette of colours to etch her life story, and through colour, charts her difficult journey to become an artist. In a character sketch, Michael Elcock shares an experience of roofing in Haida Gwaii, demonstrating his art practice in story. Gael Duchene, long-time resident of Clayoquot Sound, shares a narrative of the mysteries of mudflats by night. In "A Poet's Return," Lisa Shatzky brings us into a conversation about bruised silences as traumas of childhood, detailing how the Clayoquot geography can contribute to healing and reclaiming self. And an inspiration to us all, Tofino's Shirley Langer fulfils a life-long dream to become a jazz singer at age seventy-one, just one more achievement in a dynamic life as a mother, nurse, reporter, mayor and writer.

Water

Water represents mirroring and memory, and the reflective qualities generated by flowing water and waves that are so much a part of life along shores. On the far west coast, artists express how water stirs in them what it means to belong, and not belong, like a fish out of water, and how water is the essence of life: deep, heavy, sacred, shallow, strong, calm. Water is an element in which to submerge and emerge as an artist, always a precarious balance to remain afloat in the midst of uncertainty.

In Mark Hobson's memoir of becoming an artist, we discover how his passionate embrace of nature changed his life, and how art is a continuous practice that records the environment of Clayoquot Sound in minute detail, as an interrelationship of many ecosystems. Celeste Snowber, a lover of Galiano Island, expresses how the island is flesh embodied in dance, where we read nature and at the same time, nature reads us. She longs for island time, receiving the island like a mentor that teaches how to live well. Responding to petroglyphs in Nanaimo, Janet Marie Rogers interprets art as female, like a ghost that is everywhere, leading to the element and energies you need, if you trust in art. Joanna Streetly describes living artfully as the "mystery element," where she writes through her embodiment of nature and the many geographies she has known. Mike Emme in turn explores the importance of water in his life, evoking a sense of buoyancy in a chapter written like a graphic novel. Shifting our attention to the south coast, Avis Rasmussen describes her life as a painter in Sidney that requires her being away, both metaphorically and physically, in order to look back and make art that is meaningful. Extending Avis' account, her son Roland Rasmussen writes a response to his mother, and in this way we are granted an unusual opportunity to enter the life story of an artist from multiple perspectives. Susan Kammerzell's life-long love of nature has been the catalyst for her poetry. Velcrow Ripper and Heather Frise offer a split-text-style account of their efforts to film their journey to Sgang Gwaay, where they discover transformative creatures, have an unexpected encounter with a whale and meet eccentric people. Cortes Island becomes Melody Hessing's "cure." Written as a series of journal entries, Melody temporarily enters into spaces of the far west coast to hone artistic skills and to find inspiration. From Quadra Island, Heather Kellerhals-Stewart unfolds the edges between land and water as the edges of living as an artist on the margins. In her relationships with the natural world, in particular with animals and birds, Heather reminds us to enter nature with sensitivity and awareness that extends beyond convention. From Haida Gwaii, Susan Musgrave relates a pilgrimage to Sgang Gwaay, a UNESCO World Heritage Site, where she enters a supernatural realm that stuns visitors into silence. Closing this collection,Christine Lowther explores how living artfully is a beautiful imposition, where beneath the romantic images of the far west coast there are deep tensions, disappointments and doubts. She explores creativity and the burden to write, wondering if living artfully is freeing or imprisoning for the artist.

By inviting artists to reflect on what it means to live artfully, we consider how we might come to new understandings about place on the far west coast. Artists, it may be argued, are continually rethinking geography in terms of expression, and perhaps most importantly, artists seek to recognize and preserve these often 'unseen' spaces, rather than focus solely on the end products of art – books, paintings, exhibitions, photographs, final performances. This anthology is an exchange with the people behind the arts, and their insights on what inspires and influences, and what sustains and nurtures creativity.

From emerging artists and novices, to well-established professionals to community artists, and those who observe with appreciation, we all share a common want: to contribute to and help shape meaning through the act of creative expression. This is not to suggest we do not attend to broader issues, such as the politics of representation, or that we are setting out to erase or inadvertently contribute to a singular vision for the far west coast. Instead, these accounts are broad and full of possibilities – speculative, mythic, reactive and discursive – and all are open to multiple interpretations. Yes, art brings hopefulness, even though many of the artists have worked for endless years and in some cases for a lifetime without what is traditionally defined as 'success.' But artists forge ahead, despite periods of ambiguity and ambivalence. By sharing their stories, artists provoke questions and offer alternate points of view on art and how we understand art and culture in Canada from perspectives of the far west coast. This is a beginning.

Anita Sinner & Christine Lowther, September, 2012

References:

Hutcheon, L. (1988). *The Canadian Postmodern: A Study of Contemporary English-Canadian Fiction.* Toronto: Oxford University Press.

Note on place names:

Haida Gwaii is also known as the Queen Charlotte Islands.
Sgang Gwaii has been commonly referred to as Ninstints. Accepted spellings include SGang Gwaay, Sgang Gwaay, S̲Gang Gwaay. For this book, we have adopted Sgang Gwaay.

EARTH

48° 37' N 123° 68' W

ANITA SINNER

I revisit my scrapbook to find inspiration for this essay, remembering moments recorded in this archive of newspaper cuttings, exhibition announcements, juried scores and all sorts. I often wonder if becoming an artist would have been possible if I had been elsewhere, if I had remained in the 'big city,' where more structured concepts of what art is can prevail. Living artfully involves decades of expression, intersecting life's challenges, events of loss, hope and all emotions in between. In my mid-twenties, I thought my formal pursuit of the arts was very late for a serious artist, but now I wonder at my boldness. Perhaps becoming an artist in a small town like Sooke, situated in the world at latitude 48° 37' N and longitude 123° 68' W, on the far west coast of Canada, has had its advantages. I embraced and was embraced in what I perceived to be an atmosphere of nurturing, belonging to community, forming landscapes that were and remain creative, emotive and above all, geographic.

My art and writing remain improvisational. Perhaps that is why my 'studio' is found in every room, with supplies for varied activities filling the closets, under the beds, behind the chairs, anywhere there are unused spaces. Our cottage's sitting room converts to a place to paint, with a drop sheet and easel, allowing that particular odour of oils and paint thinner to fill the air. The 'study' is where I write, but this space is often not navigable, with stacks of books here and there, and boxes of resources for more planned projects than time allows lining the walls. I express in ink and pencil sketches and watercolours too. But despite the years and many mediums, I have no formal dedicated space, and now I am not sure I would like the permanence. I wonder if temporality is integral to the spontaneousness and impulsiveness that overtakes my body, mind and heart in creative moments when I gladly linger in my hermitage.

After twenty years in the rainforest, we have lived change: changing landscapes, changing faces, changing degrees of friendliness, a changing small town. We arrived on the cusp of the decline of two contradictory cultures: the hippies and the loggers. These seemingly divergent groups lived side by side, making homes in the recesses of the forest. I recall fondly a sense of rural kinship with women in long skirts accompanying barefoot kids running along the road after the chickens; the old black Hearse with a grizzly-bearded driver still brings a warm smile as I remember. But they are gone now. The commune next door, with once funky west coast shacks and a glass blowing shed, among other unique attributes, has returned to the forest. We still hear stories of the days when a flute could be heard in the afternoon, its soft notes drifting along with the meandering creek. But I also recall the community's trauma over the prolonged closing of the local mill, and how, despite a sense of loss, many felt relieved when the stench of sulphur that choked every breath of air on those misty last days of November finally came to an end.

After a long legacy of logging, there were a number of years before new directions were possible. Change was in hindsight both sudden and slow, but this place did change, and into this social gap came a different kind of resident. It was the catalyst of community development that helped the arts emerge, with more and more people moving to what was then a relatively inexpensive location – a familiar narrative – finding ways to be both urban and rural as weekend farmers and weekend artists, as I too was destined to become. My impulse was for creative expression: to paint, to sketch, to photograph, to write, to do all that I desired in an idyllic place, a cottage under grand fir, spruce and cedar trees where all is mossy green and vibrant in the long grey winters. I began collecting stories, and to take seriously art as a lifelong practice, attending to the intricate moods of light and shadow that camber and curve between the layers of this landscape.

Like most artists, I have lived mixed vocations in my life, including teaching art, but through these incarnations, art-making remains my singular constant, weaving the experiences of different life contexts and life locations into thinking, expressing and creating. Perhaps the most beautiful renderings artists offer the world require more considered and deliberate readings for what is behind the art, as belonging to both the past and present, where aesthetic works can also embody derivative moments; negative critiques in pleasing forms; and emptiness, banality and even measures of inertia in rich colours. Living artfully amplifies such suspended states of knowing and being.

To situate myself as an artist, I must begin by situating myself in community, by recognizing those who have made my journey so rich and inspiring. The art I enjoy in my home bears witness to this place, with most of the works made by local artists. These works are also stories of friendship and in some cases are treasured foremost because of friendship. In fact, in my home and in the pages of my archive there are three key women who have facilitated an artful way of life: Barb, Mrs. Dixie and Elizabeth. They are and were unconventional women, each teaching me about the arts in ways that have become life lessons where community is central in art making, and art reflects our shared love of the natural world. Art is also a social practice in relation to this place. Art is friendship, and it is through our friendships that creative expression becomes ever more meaningful to me.

Long ago I joined the local arts council, attending meetings in search of like-minded artists wanting to work together. For the most part, I found a highly-charged space, with many talented people competing for limited opportunities, especially during the time of transition. Becoming part of the community fabric was not as idyllic as I had imagined. The arts were often precarious, responding to social, economic and political shifts, where over time necessity caused many locals to shift to other communities, other life stages and occupations. But I did meet people who were to become long-standing influences, and through this experience I came to understand that emergence and sustainment of art and culture are due not only to artists, but to those who support the arts. In my experience, in this small town, women like Barb, Mrs. Dixie and Elizabeth, among many others, have and continue to take up roles of leadership, investing themselves in community, and nurturing and encouraging art practice. I cannot remember who I met first or under what circumstances, I simply know today we are still artful friends, and although we lost Mrs. Dixie a number of years ago now, I find her influence continues to emerge in my photographs, in the contours, colours and perspectives. Our conversations remain threaded into who I am.

Years ago Barb was a member of a women's craft collective in Sooke, with a storefront and time-share arrangement where each woman took shifts running the store while working on her art projects on-site. After sheering her sheep, Barb skirted, washed, and hand-carded fleece, and spun and plied wool during the winter. The shop afforded Barb time to practice her craft in between operating her farm with her husband, Bill, raising five children and many more foster kids, and eventually building and operating the only store in East Sooke. In addition to all these responsibilities, Barb was also among several women who helped Mrs. Dixie in her senior years, caretaking a large property and keeping the elderly lady company. In casual conversation with me, Barb mentioned that Mrs. Dixie and I would make a great team, so she facilitated a meeting over afternoon tea. I recall feelings of excitement and nervousness, for there was a great local mystique surrounding Mrs. Dixie. The artist was well known but seen only by a select few, and I think she preferred it that way. Nevertheless, upon our first meeting, we quickly discovered we were kindred spirits.

From her wheelchair she would command her audience at the kitchen table. Mrs. Dixie still held the imprint of Edwardian social manners while living bohemian in a house secluded deep in the forest overlooking the Sooke harbour. Often in her artist frock, spattered with many colours, we discussed the arts, planned our collaborative shows, and organized our entries for upcoming juried exhibitions. In her late eighties at the time, Mrs. Dixie was actively painting in a style uniquely her own, dominated by bold line work, unconventional elements such as adding birds' nests to paintings, and signature methods like never painting eyes. In some ways Mrs. Dixie was an emerging artist throughout her career. Her innovative approach meant her art was continually renewed as an ongoing practice that few artists seem to achieve. She steadfastly refused to date her work, stating that once dated, interest in the work diminished, and her purpose was to advocate art, not art history. Despite her many successes in the formal art world, she firmly believed in making art accessible, in bringing art to people, rather than waiting for people to attend galleries.

When we were invited to join a local studio tour, Barb made our first exhibit possible, offering an empty office space next to the grocery store. It became our place for several years. And so Mrs. D and I embarked on a productive and rewarding artistic journey that bridged the sixty-two years between us. Our exhibits, under the banner of *Canvas and Film*, were a blend of paintings, woodcut prints and photography, with complementary contrasts in form and expression. And Barb always collected a few pieces for her own home, helping in the ways that make creating possible for artists.

Our last collaboration was held at Elizabeth's South Shore Gallery, and as we prepared, there was a sudden turn. Mrs. Dixie became unwell and had to be hospitalized. Her spirit remained strong, and she shone in front of the camera, giving interviews from her hospital bed. But when the exhibit ended, her will faded somehow. Mrs. Dixie passed away when she was ninety-two. She was my mentor, my art partner and most importantly, my friend. An independent, free-spirited, candid and adventurous woman, Mrs. D remains a great inspiration. I can still hear her say of art practice, "You must do a line a day!"

The South Shore Gallery is centrally located in town and it is a key site of affirmation for many local artists. In a recent conversation, Elizabeth described the gallery as a place "important to a number of people for the creative energy it holds and nurtures, and I feel very fortunate to spend my time here surrounded by that energy." When I visit Elizabeth's, I experience an art infusion, entering a conversation with the artworks of many. Such exchanges with self and art serve as a means to influence and change processes and practices, highlighting for me how art continually enriches our emotional and intellectual lives. I always return home inspired to pick up my brushes and get busy, to make art part of this ongoing community conversation.

Elizabeth studied art history and design at universities in Victoria and Manitoba, and after travelling the world for a time, found her way back to the island, looking for new artistic ventures. With interludes from the arts, including building several homes herself which garnered the nickname "the lady tin-basher," and working with plant and garden design, Elizabeth opened the gallery and art supply store in 1993. As an artist as well as gallery curator, she works in mediums of painting, paper, fibre and more. Her stylish and wearable fibre creations are with me when I travel, making wearable art a source of conversation and compliment. Elizabeth is also an active member of a remarkable group of women fibre artists who hold biannual exhibitions with a strong following in the region. I especially enjoy the spring exhibit, held in a turn-of-the-century church, surrounded by a cemetery, amidst daffodils, blue bells, irises and lilies, in a spiritual coming-together of art and heart. Early on Elizabeth held art courses in the gallery, where conversations and learning facilitated creative interests. Her support of the arts now extends to volunteering time at numerous art events, like *Sooke Fine Arts,* which attracts upwards of 10,000 visitors, making it the largest art exhibition on the island. Elizabeth's commitment to building the gallery as part of the community means she is also creating opportunities and encouragement for both novice and established artists, helping artists grow by nurturing and supporting their evolving directions. Her gallery showcases the visual arts as well as the efforts of local writers and musicians, carrying DVDs and books alongside paintings and prints. The pulse of what is happening artfully can always be found at Elizabeth's place.

She welcomes ideas, projects and possibilities, and is remarkably generous in facilitating connections and opening spaces. I have never known her to judge an artist or their work critically; instead, Elizabeth's independent spirit influences her selection of art for originality, not only formal training. The gallery is a site in which artists can dialogue with and about art as a social practice of people, of our town and our region, profiling diverse representations and perceptions of place. In this way, a consciousness of art is promoted that is uniquely tied to community, a way of seeing that is indicative of the far west coast.

My understandings have evolved in relation to Barb, Mrs. Dixie, and Elizabeth. And in relation to the cumulative moments of the many days residing here, on the edges of Vancouver Island, where I have become like the symbolic representation of an Arbutus tree in one of my photographs, like a *Woman in Repose,* contemplating art, community, friendship, time and perhaps most importantly, place.

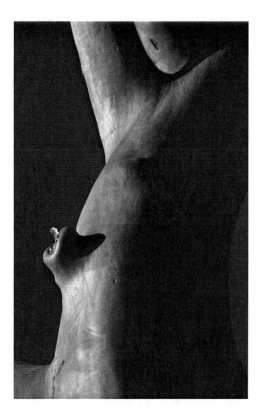

Woman in Repose (See page 131 Colour Insert)

CREATIVE GEOGRAPHY
KAREN CHARLESON

My husband tells me a story about a two-headed squirrel. The squirrel – as squirrels usually do – lives in the forest. It holds a rattle. The story my husband tells is an explanation of sorts, a description of what to do if one ever encounters this squirrel with its rattle.

Not too many years ago a story circulated around the Nuu-chah-nulth communities here on the west coast of Vancouver Island. According to this story, from inside a floatplane a Nuu-chah-nulth Tribal Council worker witnessed a killer whale transforming into a wolf. Killer Whale left the water and strode up the beach as Wolf. In the version I heard, this happened in Hesquiaht territories – near Hesquiaht Point. The beach is steep here. It is easy for me to imagine a killer whale approaching close to shore, and a wolf walking up the pebble and stone beach. I never heard more of the story, who the worker was, anything like that, anything that the Western world would interpret as resembling 'factual' evidence. It was enough to have just heard as much as I did, and to know that it had happened here.

I am not especially knowledgeable about squirrels, but I know something about their habits in this part of the world. In the springs, summers, and early falls I see the squirrel that lives closest to us almost daily. I listen to the cones falling from the spruce and hemlock trees and know that Squirrel is knocking them off their branches. I walk in the forest and see the piles of cones Squirrel has made for the winter. In another season, I see the piles of cone remnants that Squirrel has finished. On sunny winter afternoons, when squirrels – according to the books – are supposed to be hibernating, I hear its chatter.

I don't know a lot about killer whales either. Like many other residents along the coast, I marvel at seeing them, their massive, yet subtly sleek bodies gliding gracefully through the ocean. Any encounter is a highlight, an unplanned gift. Similarly I do not know a lot about wolves. I most often see their tracks, their footprints, left on the beach. I sometimes hear their howls in the evenings, night-times and early mornings. Less often, I actually see a wolf far down the low tide beach or barely visible in the distance. Occasionally we spot one along the road between Hesquiaht Harbour and Hot Springs Cove, or we see one travelling along the shoreline from our boat.

So, I listen to the stories about Two-Headed Squirrel and Killer Whale/Wolf carefully. I want to learn more about Squirrel, Killer Whale and Wolf, these creatures I encounter here. More than that though, in listening to the stories, in reflecting upon the stories, I want to expand upon what I know about the reality that these beings inhabit.

Posing questions about creativity and geography, and thinking about this suggested interrelationship, I cannot help but be reminded of the old children's riddle asking: Which comes first – the chicken or the egg? Does geography feed my creativity? Does creativity influence my choice of geography? Which comes first – creativity or geography? As though it were possible to separate and to surgically excise the two areas. As though creativity and geography were somehow separate entities, existing apart in their own distinct realms.

Western knowledge is adept at categorizing, at tucking things into neat and tidy labelled boxes. The Western academy attempts to thoroughly dissect knowledge and knowing within specific boundaries that they call disciplines. This is science; this is art; this is mathematics; this is literature; this is history, and this is anthropology. The boundary-making is seemingly infinite. Within each of its categories, its disciplines, are yet further boundaries. This is literature, but it is specifically narrative; it is specifically fiction; it is specifically drama.

It is from this mindset of Western knowledge that the separation between creativity and geography comes. The two exist there in different spaces. Separated, I'll venture, by a huge gap. Creativity lives in the world of art. Geography lives in the world of science, the world of 'fact' where Two-headed Squirrel does not exist and Killer Whale does not transform into Wolf. They cannot. They can exist only apart from the 'truth' of scientific physical evidence. They can be known only in realms like fiction or magic, in the fantasy world of creativity.

But in my reality, in my daily reality here of waking up to the sun rising over the mountain, its rays separated as they find their path through the forest to reach the open beach, are creativity and geography apart? Are Two-Headed Squirrel and Killer Whale/Wolf merely figments of the imagination, characters in some make-believe fantasy story? The categories imposed by Western knowledge, with their rigid divisions between fact and fiction, are of little use to me here.

Questions about the interrelationship of creativity and geography lead me to my dictionary. The word 'creative' is related to words like 'creation' and 'Creator,' sharing the same root word 'create.' My dictionary tells me this is derived from the Latin term *creatus,* akin to the Latin term *crescere* meaning to grow. The word 'create' and the words that have sprung from it are about bringing into existence. *Create* is a very spiritual term for a very spiritual concept and action: Creation. As the Creator created the world. As we continue to create. The concept brings me images of light blossoming, spreading and flowing, an unfolding of the universe.

I look in my dictionary again for the meaning of the term 'geography' and find that the word is derived from the Greek word *geographein* meaning to describe the

Earth's surface. It's as though geography is a tool with which to articulate creation. Creation is described, explained, and illuminated, through geography.

In my mind, the two once distinct words merge into a single term – creative geography. Not an interrelationship between the creative and geography so much as a binding together, a blending of the spirituality of creation with the physical descriptiveness of geography.

Heshook-ish tsawalk is the Nuu-chah-nulth concept that roughly translates into English as "everything is one." It is used often in discussions, policy-making and the like, in connection to the physical world. It makes perfect sense in the field of ecology. When we look at questions of sustainable environments, for example, it becomes quickly evident that what happens in one section of the ecosystem affects other parts and the whole of the ecosystem. Clear-cutting the forest at the headwaters of a stream impacts the health of that stream, which impacts the health of numerous creatures that live in that stream and the quality of the habitat that stream provides, which impacts the survival rates of fish that return to that stream to spawn, which impacts the people and bears and wolves and so on who feed on the salmon. In thinking about healthy ecosystems, *heshook-ish tsawalk* is easy to understand. Everything in an ecosystem, including people, is connected or 'one.'

What is more difficult to understand from a Western perspective is that *heshook-ish tsawalk* is about more than physical connections. It is also about spiritual connections. It is about the unity of the physical and the spiritual – the whole of the physical and metaphysical worlds. The physical of geography is in co-existence and co-reliance with the spiritual of creation. Not only are we a part of the physical world, we are also a part of the spiritual world. We are a part of them at the same time, in unity and in one reality.

I have led a rich life. I have been blessed by nurturing family, relationships and places. What I know comes out of these blessings, from my experiences learning within this human, spiritual, and physical space I know as my home. What I can say I know comes from passages in books, trips on the ocean, stories of ancestors I have never met, conversations, and days spent on the beach. It comes from a plenitude of different teachings, experiences, and moments of realization. What I write here is the result of the ongoing, steady, sustained teachings of my husband and family, and my ancestors and relatives. It is also the result of the people and places that are Hesquiaht traditional territories – from the tiny *hyshtoop* that cling to the low tide rocks, to the mountains and cedar trees that tower above us, to the community members who ask, "How are you?" My memories, my reflections, my thoughts, and my creativity are continuously nurtured by my physical and metaphysical surrounding relationships. My creativity is fed by my geography; it also feeds that geography, that human, physical, and spiritual space I call home.

Living here in this particular place allows me to continue to explore its reality, to know it as my world. Here is the place where I can see Hesquiaht traditional territories spread out to the horizon. Where I can walk endlessly on the beach, watch the sea birds, the seals and sea lions and grey whales and humpback whales, trace the bear trails through the forest, watch the sun rise over the trees every morning and set behind the mountain across the harbour every evening. It is a place full of life and activity too diverse to even begin to detail. Here is the place where my family has roots, where my children have grown up and return, where my memories are alive in a thousand particular locations, people, tides, and weather systems. Here is also the place where I can connect to the Creator, where I can most easily and readily give thanks for all that encompasses us. And here are also the hints, the portions of reality I only have to open myself to understanding, of Two-Headed Squirrel, Killer Whale/Wolf, of transformation, of an infinitely deep and vast world. It is a creative geography, a unified reality. It is where I want to be.

FROM BADLANDS TO TIDE POOLS: FINDING MY PLACE

ROBERT DALTON

The West Coast's west coast

Casting my eye around this small and wonderfully cluttered character home, I discover such marvels as a whale vertebra footstool, woven baskets, glass globe fishing net floats borne on the Japanese current to local waters, and a coffee table that is a cross section of a spruce tree with rough bark edges. Artwork is everywhere, on every wall, and stacked up against the wall waiting a turn in the rotation. There are screen prints by Bill Reid and Robert Davidson, pastels by Joe Plaskett, and intaglio prints, photographs, and watercolours by local artist friends. Retired teacher and now world traveller, Fran has filled any remaining corners and counters with treasures acquired in markets abroad: a weaving from Bolivia, a puppet from India and more.

Our host's rustic home in Haida Gwaii looks across Skidegate Inlet offering a stunning view of natural beauty. I haven't felt this relaxed in some time. A serpentine stack wall borders her small backyard lawn; stack walls are a common sight in this area, made of short logs stacked one on top of another and held together with concrete as mortar. The drop from lawn level to shoreline is considerable. Below are the mud flats, which at low tide are alive with scavenging shorebirds. During high tides and winter storms, the stack wall will resist the assault of the sea and its pounding waves. But mostly this is a sheltered stretch of water, about as idyllic as any place I know. There is barely a breath of breeze on this crisp February morning. Small tree-covered islands rise out of the sea and dip back into the silver waters without a ripple. With low clouds nesting in the mountain valleys of Moresby Island, time seems to stand still. In this magical space, my thoughts reach back to our move from Alberta's badlands to Victoria on Vancouver Island seventeen years ago, and more immediately to the last few days of our visit to Haida Gwaii. Time to pause and reflect is something of a rarity these days.

This is as far west within Canada as I've ever been. Earlier in the day we travelled through Skidegate, up the coast to Tlell and beyond to the northernmost part of the island to Old Masset where a number of Haida homes have clan poles to honour ancestors and commemorate their accomplishments. A short drive to the east, I could make out the mountainous islands of the Alaska panhandle. What was it that brought my wife and me to Haida Gwaii? It is certainly a place we've always wanted to visit. The opportunity came with an invitation to serve as adjudicator for the *All Islands Art Exhibition* and to conduct workshops for local artists. The opening, held in the beautiful Haida Heritage Centre, featured song and dance by native performers dressed in splendid black capes with bright red trim and traditional designs. Native and non-native communities appear to co-exist successfully, sharing a deep attachment to this remarkable place.

Photographing the west coast: Getting acquainted

My first order of business when we moved to Vancouver Island was orienting myself as an artist. In advance of going somewhere, people like me will pour over maps and photographs in order to get acquainted. What does this place look like and where is it in relation to prominent geographic features such as rivers, lakes, mountains, and shoreline? What is it about culture and history that makes this region distinctive? Others before me have asked those questions and found their own answers. When I walk among the trees of Goldstream Provincial Park or look out across the Strait of Juan de Fuca, I see many of the sights that inspired Emily Carr.

Where to begin? Being in nature is far too stimulating to sit in one place for hours patiently stroking a canvas. Who has that kind of discipline? Besides, I rationalize, the light is constantly changing; I would need to continually revise the work throughout the day. I'm not at all objective about a good composition when seduced by the fragrance of conifers, enchanted by the rustle of leaves or the music of songbirds while basking in the warmth of a summer breeze. Being in nature stimulates me to wander and to explore. The camera has always been my 'sketching' tool. It allows me to take away those memories and gives me distance and perspective for later work. And so I began recording the landscape as David Hockney and countless others before him have done.

This is taking a photo then moving the camera to the left, to the right, above, and below, building a composite image through as many as twenty photographs that can later be assembled on a piece of matt board. Shingled and at times not lining up, the result seems to capture what I am looking for without being precious or obsessive. The process is dynamic for me. It admits to the fact that this is a composite image with gaps and overlaps, a series of individual views that suggests the land is *not* viewed through a window but is rather a visual experience much like scanning. A dense overlapping of photos indicates areas of high interest for me as viewer, while the sparsely populated periphery shows gaps in a way that seems natural to my experience.

Garry Oak on Mount Douglas, photo montage (See page 132 Colour Insert)

A power place: The contested boundary of the intertidal zone

The intertidal zone holds great fascination for me. It is difficult to imagine a place more inhospitable to life forms, submerged by cold and churning saltwater for parts of each day and exposed to air and sun at other times. The forces of pounding surf and wave action are clearly visible on battered driftwood logs, once enormous trees that have had their bark stripped from them and in many cases are in various stages of being reduced to splinters. And yet life not only survives, it *thrives* in the intertidal. I can't recall anywhere else feeling so inspired to examine and record nature close up.

I began a series of pastel drawings on black Arches paper, using photographs I had taken at China Beach as my reference material. Here, it was the light and texture that caught my interest. From rough white barnacles to black polished boulders, still wet and gleaming in the sunlight, each rounded rock seemed to provide shelter for many small ones and for thumbnail-sized crabs and other marine life. The drawings were more about form than colour. And they were also about wonder. It is difficult to create such works without reflecting upon the life lessons of the stone. The Apostle Paul wrote: "…we glory in tribulations also: knowing that tribulation worketh patience; and patience, experience; and experience, hope." (Romans 5: 3-4, KJV). The beauty and character of these rounded stones are the result of endurance in the extraordinary forces of nature.

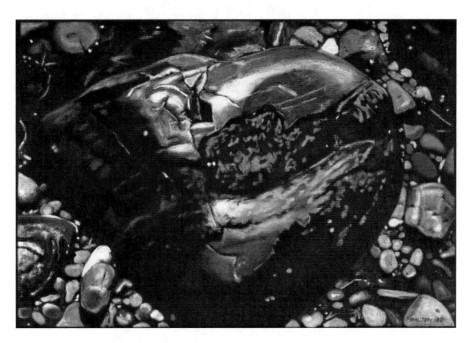

Emerald Stone, pastel drawing (See page 132 Colour Insert)

Change over time and space

In the forest it is easy to recognize evidence of burgeoning growth. A rotting tree stump or fallen tree often becomes a nursery for new plants. In some cases a young tree may appear to be standing on its tiptoes, with its roots entirely exposed, the nurse log that nourished it for its first years of life having now completely rotted away. A world of growth occurs underground too, where seeds germinate and sprouts push upwards, erupting from the soil. In the next series of artworks I wanted to represent that change. One of the simplest and most direct ways of showing this is by means of a diptych or two-panelled work. Change may be a matter of *time* – before and after; night and day; seasons. It may also represent *space* – above and below; inside and out. In this series of works I laid down a pale wash of watercolour and then began exploratory gestures and strokes with coloured pencil. The work emerged as I intuitively blended, layered, erased, and developed form while thinking about and being reminded of aspects of plant life observed on my walks.

Germination, Coloured pencil drawing (See page 133 Colour Insert)

As the process unfolded, I would discover something recognizable and the paired image would emerge. My role at that point would be 'to guide it into shore.' Germination is one such image where seeds, emerging roots, and stalks became the discovered image.

West Coast icons: Earth, water and air
Earth and the rose

In a fourth series, I began to reflect on some of the symbols that define my sense of place. These exist as figures within a ground, like residents setting down roots and living out their lives. I identified subjects such as the eagle, the salmon, and the rose, and developed these into several simple, identifiable symbols. The ground symbolizes place as a colour field or atmosphere, and it is both fluid and spontaneous. It evolved from watercolour washes applied loosely with a broad brush. For me, the layers of wash represent nature through gestures and movements, having qualities of luminosity, like water and air. I want the backgrounds to seem natural, as though not created by human hands but by nature itself. After developing representative images for each, the image was used over and over again with new painterly contexts. *Blushing Rose* is representative of the rose paintings. Beginning with a ground of flowing washes, the icon was then masked before applying further washes. Being a city of gardens and having a strong British colonial history, the rose seemed a fitting icon for Victoria.

Blushing Rose, Watercolour painting (See page 134 Colour Insert)

Water and the salmon

Salmon is another icon. Thousands of people living in and around Victoria visit Goldstream Park each year to observe the salmon run. It never ceases to amaze me that these magnificent creatures return after years at sea, at the same time and to the same place they were hatched in order to spawn, leaving their decaying bodies to add nutrients to the sediment in the streambed. In the late fall the area is often under grey skies with damp moss hanging from tree limbs. The shores of the small stream are strewn with dead and dying fish, many bearing the scars of their journey. Eagles and gulls feast on the carcasses while newly arriving salmon press upstream in search of a nesting place to lay their eggs or to fertilize them. There may be times when the fish are difficult to see, either because of reflected light on the water's surface or because of ripples that distort what lies below. Close-cropped and crowded, these fish are yellows and greys, much like Goldstream itself, effectively camouflaging them. In these acrylic paintings on paper, viewers may not at first notice the salmon because they are mottled and may be mistaken for the ground rather than the figure. The cycle of life is there for all to witness.

Creating a salmon silhouette, I applied it over an area already spattered or stained with acrylic paint. The image repeated over again provided the sense of vast numbers of salmon, all responding to the same ancient call. *Ekklesia* uses the salmon run as a metaphor, not just for the lifecycle but also as a spiritual reference. *Ekklesia* is the ancient Greek word that is the root of our term "ecclesiastical." It is a Biblical term referring to the gathering of the New Testament saints to worship. Weary from their spiritual journey, there is comfort, encouragement, and a strengthened sense of mission in coming together.

Ekklesia, acrylic painting (See page 134 Colour Insert)

Sky and the eagle

Salmon seem to defy gravity in water. Seemingly weightless, they can effortlessly rise to the surface and just as effortlessly submerge to the depths. Even more remarkable are their athletic leaps up waterfalls. Eagles also seem to move with ease. For millennia, humanity has yearned to fly. Only in the past century have we developed the technology to accomplish that feat. Flight is a common metaphor for freedom; *earth bounds* marvel at the sight of the eagle wheeling at incredible heights, circling with barely so much as a wing beat as it rides the updrafts. Another iconic west coast image I developed involved several silhouette images of the eagle in flight, and I used them in a series of acrylic and collage paintings on a square format. Fabric references began to enter these pieces as well, with western traditions of quilting and First Nations traditions of button blankets. The eagle can be a nurturing parent, building a nest, feeding and caring for its chicks. *Coastline* is one representative image from that series. The large-scale eagle wing shape is cut …

Coastline, collage (See page 135 Colour Insert)

… from a sheet of paper that has been painted and then turned around. Placed on a blue field, the shape vaguely resembles Vancouver Island with the mainland just a short distance away. The blue strait is also an eagle wing shape. Quilting is suggested by squares superimposed, and a clearly recognizable eagle in profile appears on the right side of the painting. The idea of a quilt represents the comfort of a handmade blanket, while the square speaks of regularity, or the rational and logical control humankind exerts over the land through surveying and planning.

Though the eagle is often thought to symbolize fierce independence, biologists and environmentalists are coming to see it as vulnerable and endangered. With population depleted by pesticide use, hunting, and habitat loss, the eagle's decline, like so many other species, is a sobering reminder that we must develop an ethic of care for one another and for all creatures that share the planet. In my watercolour and collage works, the landscape is represented by the forces of nature in the form of diffusions and stains that appear as a result of wet-on-wet and spatters of paint, all giving up control to the accidents of media. In mixed media and collage works such as *Approach* the eagle advances directly towards the viewer in an open space between sky and land. Below is a quadrangle that once again suggests the presence of human habitation or presence, yet it has a vibrant blue colour that may also symbolize both sky and sea. The juxtaposition of raptor and quadrangle is one of equality and contrast – a tension that questions the possibility of coexistence. Holding these two images is a fiery background that may be romantic or apocalyptic. The choice is ours.

Looking back

My first impulse as an artist is to observe and to marvel. During and following that response there is inevitably a period of thoughtful consideration. Reflection looks outward and also inward to ask some essential questions: What is it about *the object* that I find so arresting? And what is it about the object that *I* find so interesting? How can this aesthetic quality be identified and intensified? Even more ambitiously, can I extend that frame to work towards a level of poetic distillation, embodying in material form some of the other sensory experiences that are just as much a part of my recollections? With sustained investigation around these questions, the expressive and communicative element of art can increase.

But there is a further step for me, one that reaches deeper still. This has to do with the integration of self and subject to the point where working draws heavily upon intuition and intrinsic motivations that involve, dare I say it – *play*. As children our sense of place was not so much a matter of knowing coordinates on a map or recognizing prominent places shown on flash cards; it came about as a natural process of curiosity and embodied experiences. What strategies can we as adult artists employ to recover some of that motivation to learn? One method that works for me is to call upon media and processes that are full of surprises and rich with character. Spilling, squeezing, staining with paint, cutting up magazine images as colour and texture for collage, mixing media and layering them are some of the methods that hold the promise of entirely new challenges and the hope of unexpected discoveries. Setting aside my insecurities, my need to plan everything and know in advance what form the image will take, I prefer to commit to a process and trust myself to navigate uncharted waters. I remind myself that it is okay to live with the prospect of getting hopelessly lost.

Approach, mixed media (See page 136 Colour Insert)

Moving towards an authentic expression of place, I want my art making to be motivated by something other than a sense of duty. And I want my art to achieve higher goals than that of replication (acknowledging that this may be a worthy introduction to something new). Among my broader artistic goals, I search for ways to invite invention and discovery, and to allow the media to take a greater role in the emerging composition. I don't *want* to control every aspect of an image. When I have finished a work of art I want it to look like it was a collaborative activity. My media and I put our ideas together and the end result is full of twists and turns that neither of us could have predicted.

My journey continues, of course. This wonderful place could not begin to exhaust the possibilities for me. Through my art I have come to know the west coast in a way that would not have been possible elsewhere. More than anywhere else I have lived and visited, the west coast has always felt like home, a place of extraordinary power and beauty, a beauty not confined to corridors and pockets but a beauty that seems surrounding and limitless. My wife and our three sons were eager for this place and the adventures that would surely follow. And I knew it would be gratifyingly challenging to find a way of responding to my chosen surroundings through art, from the wonder of discovery in all that the natural environment had to offer, to deeper and more intimate attachments to particular places like the intertidal zone.

With familiarity, it became possible for me to begin to interpret and express what it is about this place that so deeply affects me. Here the processes of nature, its moods and its seasons became the real subject matter. And finally through the use of symbols, it became easier for me to speak to others about relationships that range from spiritual to cultural, and to find meaning that moves the question from *where* I am to *who* I am.

Note:

On June 3, 2010, the Queen Charlotte Islands officially became Haida Gwaii ("Islands of the People") as part of a reconciliation protocol between British Columbia and the Haida people.

UP AND OUT: ISLAND TREES
AND STORYMAKING
MARGARET MURPHY

After I married Noel on Sadie Hawkins Day, February 29th, 2008, we decided on a quiet holiday: Long Beach, for no other place would do. We walked the beach and the forest paths in blissful, beautiful sunshine, rare and wonderful in early March.

My yearning for the west coast of Vancouver Island began in the hustle and bustle of Ontario cities years earlier. An Ottawa native, I also lived for years in the thrum of Toronto. I was a city woman, thriving on cafés, bookstores, theatre and dance. I studied and taught and shared stories in schools and festivals, surrounding myself with people. Water was important. Kayaking and swimming in the deep jelly waters of Georgian Bay nourished me each summer. It was in the mid-seventies when I first came to the far west, to Long Beach, and I was never really the same after that.

It took some time to move here. We settled mid-island, in Nanaimo, the Harbour City, minutes from the water. Friends and family flocked to us, less for our company and more for the fishing, the whales, the sailing and kayaking.

"I could never live here," said Linda from Toronto. "It's all far too pretty for me, too much like…well, Disneyland."

My brother thought the island too small and too quiet. My dear friend Dana found it boring. As for me, I loved the pace as much as the space, the quiet routine and the openness of islanders.

I once saw an interview with Eckhart Tolle, where he spoke about how he could not write in the United Kingdom. He described a great pull to British Columbia, a place in which the words flowed out of him. An "energy shift" he called it. I, too, sat on many stories for years. My Ontario life was filled with the great distractions of work, family and friends. I never had time to finish a writing project. Mother was ill, then my brother, then my father, and I had my teaching . . . I was always busy. Others wrote, and I waited. Like Tolle, that changed when I moved to British Columbia. The words came flooding out through stories, so many stories. Sharing others' stories helped me get my own stories out. Telling folk and fairy tales, myths and legends allowed me to go deeper and plumb my own story well. And then, I met the trees.

"Look, Dad, that girl is walking backwards," said the young boy as he watched me gaze up at the great fir trees.

Yes, I was walking backwards, looking at the tall giants of the island. The trees continue to inspire and thrill me. Like the sea, they comfort me in an old, old way. I believe the trees on Vancouver Island are the foundation of this place. The great Red Cedar, the Douglas Fir, Garry Oak and Arbutus proudly proclaim their space. When asked how geography and place influence artistic expression, I answer: in providing the stillness, the silence. The trees, old and young, listen brilliantly. The trees provide strength, with branch-arms reaching out, opening and enfolding.

There is an old flowering maple tree in our Nanaimo backyard. I love that tree. I grew up with two great maples on our front lawn in Ottawa; the Nanaimo maple takes me back there and quiets me here at the same time. It provides shade and shelter, and houses the songbirds and the robins. Yesterday the pileated woodpecker tapped a message on it. Such moments remind me just how much trees influence my writing. I'm drawn to another tree here on the island: the craggy, twisty, windy Garry Oak. At Neck Point Park wild old oaks gather in clusters on the hill, in conference, endlessly deliberating. This attraction to trees is surprising to me. I love the ocean and yet just now, the trees speak even more candidly to me. They also listen to heartbeat and heartbreak, and hold space and time. For me, they are the ultimate caregivers of the west coast.

Vancouver Island is a beautiful space for artists for many reasons. It provides the quiet and the whirl, the community and the solitude. Many of us gather to write, speak and paint, dance, plant and sew, play and build, photograph and create. There is a sharing and support within the community but, at the heart of it all, it is the place and space which inspire. Yet I am more than aware of the fragility of this space. As Nanaimo grows in size and volume I feel an increasing need to seek the quieter space of path or park to preserve my stories. I believe others may feel the same, because storytelling has reclaimed a place in Nanaimo. Islanders are proud of their history and celebrate stories through music, dance and storytelling at numerous festivals and gatherings. In January 2007, storytelling formally returned to the Harbour City as seventy-five people jammed into a local café, and from that first gathering, a storytelling community quickly re-emerged. The challenge was to provide a welcome space for stories, tellers and listeners, "to collect the energy," I kept saying. This remains my mantra.

And the people gathered. They continue to gather every month with a very loyal following. Magically, story draws in new listeners and tellers. Our storytelling group, *The Around Town Tellers*, has moved to a larger venue, opening into the wider community. We share stories in schools and festivals, in hospices and seniors' residences. One of our members initiated a radio program celebrating stories and music. Ongoing courses and workshops allow both the new and seasoned teller to hone his or her skills. Personally, I am thrilled to witness this surge of story-sharing in Nanaimo. This is story in action. Mostly I am in awe, whether listening to a new teller bravely sharing a story for the first time, or wrapped in the story blanket of a master teller. The circle widens. The need to share who we are, where we came from and how we connect to one another is most welcome on the island, and this sense of community unites our hearts.

As a result of sharing stories here, I have started to write. My stories tell of courageous women who prepared the way for all of us. Their passion calls to me: Canadian writer/poet Pauline Johnson, peace activist Muriel Duckworth, gardener/entrepreneur Cougar Annie, and Salt Spring Island pioneer Sylvia Stark. Great Canadian women, strong and stalwart, like the trees. I research, write and share these stories of noble women. In turn, I continue to hear the stories of the loggers, fishermen and miners and their families, and the traditions of the First Nations people who celebrate through a legacy of story. But there is another side to this. When the coin is flipped, artists are anxious and concerned, seeking support and funding to pursue their plans and dreams. I am awake to the frustration and challenge of creating art, yet I need to continue to create and be at peace in a world where support is often measured by financial gain.

The island produces great bounty. Artists, like farmers, passionately tend their crops and gently offer their produce. We continue to gather and celebrate the gift that it is to live in this place and time. As we come together to share our stories, songs and art, let us reflect each other's vision and bravery, and remember and honour the trees.

MY CLAYOQUOT SAMPLER
MICHAEL SCOTT CURNES

Between the *bookending* years of 1995 and 2003, I never lived farther away than ten metres from the gravitationally-determined Pacific high tide mark, during a period I now refer to as the Prolific Phase of my Creative Moon. Whether perched obtrusively on MacKenzie Beach, tucked in the shore forest of Chesterman, all-but-camouflaged at the sticky edge of the Tofino Mud-flats or braced on a storm-side cliff above Salamander Cove on Wickaninnish Island, I was tugged and compelled by this place to undertake a body of written work that eventually included oh-at-least-a-dozen letters to the *Westerly* News Editor, an anonymous Tofino travel book that enjoyed eight reprints, a handful of feature essays for the *The Sound* Magazine, two screenplays, a stage play, the concepts and lyrics for two musicals plus two complete novels.

To this day, risking identification and perhaps even dismissal as a hippie wan-nabe or worse, a hippie impostor, I still freely make the claim that the lunar lifecycle of my Creative Moon, when it completes its one and perhaps its only revolution, began at birth and will end on the occasion of my death. But surely it waxed, waned and peaked prolific during this truly tidal eclipse in Tofino when my creativity streaked like a comet through a galaxy of trivialities.

The piece from this written legacy that I am most proud of is a story that appeared in the *The Globe and Mail* on Tuesday, June 25, 1996 as a *Facts & Arguments* feature. I remember this day distinctly, as the out-of-town owners of the resort that I was managing and the target of my rather damning exposé had made a surprise visit to the resort the night prior, prompting me and my partner to dash around Tofino snatching up every copy of that day's *The Globe and Mail* from the stands so it wouldn't fall into their hands and we wouldn't lose our jobs—jobs that we loathed, at least according to the article, reprinted here by permission of *The Globe and Mail.*

Heterosexuality as a Last Resort

I am a gay man. My lifetime, same-sex partner is also a gay man. I disclose this, knowing all too well how very crucial it is to espouse certain, undeniable (though at times alienating) facts about my particular situation. So that established, you may now feel free to embrace your generalizations, rev up your biases and grit your ever-loving hetero-teeth because I honestly believe I can guarantee that during the course of this essay, my gayness will not go away – at least not completely. I offer this preamble as a matter of reader preparedness – yes, but I write it down also to reassure myself.

Two months ago, having allowed the ultra-cosmopolitan and ferociously competitive sprawl of Vancouver to sucker-zap me of all but my basic chromosomal identity, I persuaded my somewhat reticent and equally entrenched West End partner, during a sleepy literature and Barbara Streisand-filled Sunday afternoon that we pick up and relocate permanently to the rugged west coast of Vancouver Island.

You may not appreciate the achievement in successfully luring a homosexual away from the centre of his self-defined, 24-hour culture injected, over-caffeinated, health club pumped, richly nouveau appointed, and of course, track-lighted universe for – let's face it – the raw, backwater groin of our pristine but scarcely inhabitable national inseam. For fun now, we ask ourselves what diabolical force could have ever provoked us to slash at our culturally nourished roots with such self-mutilating determination, knowing full well that the answer to this rhetorical question lies in an advertisement that appeared roughly three months prior in the *Vancouver Sun*, seeking an experienced hotel-management couple to oversee all aspects of a *quaint, oceanfront cottage resort.* So experienced and qualified were we that we applied for the post, were hired, crammed our well-appointed lives into an axle-strained U-haul and headed for the literal and figurative end of the road, where, I can accurately proclaim, we had been duped. (Okay, so we fell for the quaint, oceanfront cottage spiel, but by the look of the *ABSOLUTELY NO VACANCY* sign and the owner's bulging cash register, I can at least say with a smidgeon of dignity that we certainly were not the only ones).

Still, it seemed we had been sentenced to become real men at this oceanside penitentiary that we have sadistically come to revere as *The Last Resort.* After an ever-so-brief arrival celebration where a scarcely half-drained wine bottle had been re-corked, the slyly liberated owners made their hasty departure just as the antiquated sewer cistern backed up, blowing nearly as high as Yellowstone's Old Faithful, sending chunks of madness into the atmosphere and streams of churning filth toward the heretofore unspoiled seashore. Being penthouse-bound environmentalists to the core, we all but threw our bodies into a human levy to contain the raw sewage, only to later learn the local village pumps its untreated bio-waste directly into the ocean anyway just a few kilometres away. Two saturated and condemned pairs of Italian leather loafers later, we began to mutate – crudely at first, using banal euphemisms and sinking to childish name-calling when referring to the owners in absentia. But the many physical changes, none of which can be pleasantly described here, quickly followed. Formerly manicured hands chapped, cracked, stained then bled in the days to come. Almost overnight, the smalls of our backs hunched and then ballooned into a host of new and unflattering muscles sure to destroy the v-shaped illusions we had devoted years to sculpting in the health club where we had met. Our eyes, once crowned by carefully tweezed brows and enhanced by age-concealing lenses and imported wrinkle creams, narrowed cynically then turned bloodshot as we began to take a passing interest in the latest hockey scores in the normally discarded sports page of our *Globe and Mail*.

I didn't say anything when our teeth began to yellow (surely a result of the local grocery store's inability to stock replacement filters for our *Britta*) and I merely bit my lip when I began to detect the advent of halitosis (no, we can't find spare polishing pads for our big-city dental-hygienist-recommended *Roda-dent* either).

Perhaps it is in keeping with the land's rich cultural heritage that words here are often imbued with more than one significance. Take the word *resort*, for instance. It's curious, but when you stand in the middle of what was once old-growth ancestral forest at the edge of the Pacific Ocean, up to your formerly pierced left nipple in the primordial mud of a Walmart-sized parking lot dotted with a dozen barrack-type cottages, accented by a chlorinated duck pond (because the swimming pool overflows into it when it more-than-occasionally rains here) that feeds a wild Coho breeding stream-turned-latrine (because the electrical pumps designed to carry sewage back to the mainline running under the highway won't function in any of the 147 unplanned power outages this winter storm season alone) you would have thought the resort trademark police would have somehow swooped in with their citation book a long time ago.

One recent, rainy afternoon, my once-gay lover and I, ever committed to biological restoration, set about unearthing overcrowded evergreen survivors from along the highway for transplantation around our slashed-and-burned resort. Family car after recreational vehicle hurried by pointing at us in our matching orange rain slickers, surely explaining to bewildered children in the back seat how we must be hardened criminals serving time in a strenuous work-release program under the watchful eye of a heavily armed guard. The explanation wouldn't have been that far off the mark. We were certainly being held against our normally sensible wills.

I can offer you no medical explanation nor credit some soon-to-be famous institution for our remarkable recovery from a life of tasteful living and civility. But we are unequivocally cured of our addictions to musical theatre and fine wine. Our clothes no longer match and our hair has gone un-styled and un-cut for 90 consecutive days and counting. We have gained proficiency with every power tool known to man and commune daily with the slugs and spiders that share our personal space. Perhaps the most conclusive proof of our conversion lies haphazardly tossed on top of our unmade bed: two flannel shirts for this Friday night's local Legion Hall dance.

So, my now-fellow Reformers, say "no more" to behaviour-modification Bible camps where *our type* eventually beds down with our same-sex counsellors anyway. Rather, I say create jobs in the British Columbian outback and then offer "West Enders" and "Church and Wellesleyites" and "East Sherbrook-esters" employment incentives to GO STRAIGHT WEST.

The next time the rest of you find yourselves travelling along the very last kilometres of Highway 4 on a particularly congested July evening, after inquiries at every motel, campground, hostel and B&B have yielded absolutely no vacancy and suddenly you recognize what you think must be the northern lights ahead, take heart. The lights are always burning at *The Last Resort*. Of course, this celestial illumination is nothing more spectacular than the residual glow of the Agent Orange used to deforest this swath of land for maximum revenue-earning potential; but you'll find a pillow, a credit-card transaction terminal and two burly innkeepers guaranteed to smell like real men and likely to leer at your shapely wife and statuesque daughters. Welcome to the end of the road – evidently our last resort, too.

STRAIGHT TO HERE
JAN JANZEN

In the noise and the business we're drawn away from our spirits. But in the stillness, when we're absolutely alone in the world, we can sometimes find a vision of justice and beauty that will ever afterwards infuse our lives with purpose.

Soren Kierkegaard

Part of me, deep inside, secretly *knew* I'd live on the west coast of Vancouver Island. Somehow, I must have sensed that I could unfold here as an artist and as a more complete human being. Looking back to a time before I'd consciously considered living here, I see signs of foreknowledge. On a door I made I painted drift logs piled high atop a long sweeping curve of beach with the waves morphing into smoky flames, morphing into black knots echoing the shape of the gnarly driftwood handle. One night I dreamt of nature spirits pulling me on a raft "to a better location," predicting in detail the shape and fate of a cabin I would build years after the dream. Then there was the afternoon I accompanied a friend to the University of British Columbia. He was researching aerial photographs of his neighbourhood, so I passed the time browsing through bird's-eye-view photos of other areas. I came across an old one of Chesterman Beach before houses, and I imagined building a cabin near the midpoint where the land juts out towards Frank Island, almost exactly where I would indeed build one years later. Perhaps that deeper part of me, the part that *knew*, existed here already as an element of some larger, timeless life expression that includes myself and others who live here. Sometimes it feels like I've always been here, like I belong, as if molecules of my being mesh with those of this environment, both physically and at deeper, subtler levels.

I'd lived in the Greater Vancouver area for most of my life, with family, friends or lovers in shared households. Whenever I felt bored or empty there was always consolation in the distraction of company, but I felt stifled in my creative expression. I knew from past experience that solitude revealed inner resources, that the fountain of inspiration released its creative juices when I was open to receive them. I needed a hermitage. Failing to find a suitable retreat on the mainland, I considered the west coast of Vancouver Island. I'd camped at Long Beach years ago, buying supplies in the nearby village of Tofino. Surely I could find discreet lodging there for a couple of months, maybe bang up a little plastic shack, or even rent the back of a store or a small cabin. I didn't realize vacancies in Tofino were as scarce as my moments of solitude in the city.

I left for the coast with a friend in late February of 1986, staying at Greenpoint in the national park. It was a good week. We set up a comfortably dry camp and hiked around in the rain. I bought a local newspaper, checked the bulletin boards, and then we went back to the mainland. Pulling into our driveway, I realized my blunder. What was I doing *here*? I'd gone away to find a place to hide out, and now I was back inside the social vortex! I returned to Greenpoint the next day to set up my prospector's tent, two large tarps and an oil-stove we'd salvaged from the dump and converted into a wood-heater.

The following morning I drove into town to put up 'wanted to rent, cheap housing' notices. This, I know now, is the height of optimism in Tofino. However, there on the board was a small scrap of paper advertising a cabin for rent. Unaware of the highly competitive rental situation, I nonchalantly called the number. A gravelly voice gave me directions and I went to see "Ratso" to check out "the cabin at the sand pit." There I met a man whose appearance fit the voice: Ratso was a grizzled, disgruntled Vietnam veteran with (I learned later) an unsavoury reputation. And there also, in a small clearing that had once been a tree-covered sand dune (sold to local contractors), sat a funky little cabin: one room with a sleeping loft, a collage of windows in the south wall, rainwater collected off the moss-covered shake roof, a 'hippy killer' woodstove, and even electricity and a telephone hook-up. A plastic-covered outhouse completed the amenities. I looked it over and, imagining I could do better, declined the offering saying that I'd think about it!

Twenty minutes later, back at my campsite, puffing on a smoke and sipping a scotch, watching with bemusement the torrential rainfall soaking into the lower canvas walls of my tent, I realized I'd made another blunder. *What was I thinking?* I rushed to the pay phone at the campground entrance and called Ratso. The cabin had not been rented yet, so I told him I'd be right over with the money. When I got there, he said I was lucky, that after I'd phoned and agreed to take it, four other people had answered his ad, willing to rent it sight unseen. I paid him the rent and stepped inside my new home. It was beautiful, perfect in every way.

So began a transition period in my life, comparable in effect and intensity to adolescence or leaving the familial home. My plan was to stay for a few weeks to get a kick in the creative butt, but what happened was a complete shift in my worldview, my inner processes and my creative expression. Within a year I was a very different person from the one who'd come blithely unaware of the challenges and opportunities of life at the end of the road.

To maintain solitude during that time I limited town trips to once per week, strictly business, barely speaking with anyone. Each day I'd rise before dawn, get a fire going, and then set out for a walk on the beach. Returning to a warm cabin, I'd have breakfast, read and often enjoy a little nap in the armchair facing the woodstove. The rest of my time was spent carving, painting, and writing. The paintings I attempted during that time were forced and stiff; but my carvings were whimsical, charming and enjoyable to create. That lifestyle may sound idyllic, but sometimes it was painful, both emotionally and spiritually. My inner and outer lives were struggling for common ground, some place I hoped existed, but had no idea where or how. I worked with wood and searched within, driven by a feeling that *something* was waiting to be born.

What began as a kick-start to my stalled creativity became an exploration of my inner universe. Fewer distractions allowed me to notice personality quirks and patterns that were counterproductive. I dropped some old habits and utilized discipline and meditation for self-nurturing and growth. One meditation I did sitting at home was to imagine travelling up a straight path to the *Godhead*, a spiritual journey into the source of being. Sometimes I'd do it while walking, visualizing that path stretching out before me. Early one spring morning I was walking from the south end of the beach, heading north. I pressed my palms together in front of my chest, bowed my head and closed my eyes, visualizing the path before me. When I had that route firmly envisioned, I lifted my head and looked to see where it lay in the physical world. Across the expanse of flat hard-packed sand, it went straight out in front of me between tangled heaps of kelp, over scattered seashells and bits of driftwood up to the horizon line. There at the 'T' intersection of those lines, on the tombolo that joins Frank Island to the shore, was a dot. It was too far away to identify, but I enjoyed the coincidence of having a solid object as a goal. Drawing nearer, I was at first surprised and then amazed. There on the sand was a twelve inch diameter sphere of blue-green glass: an errant fishnet float from Asia, a physical manifestation of perfection. At least that's what I took it to be. I bent down, picked it up, and with a huge smile of gratitude gave thanks for the generosity of that which was my heart's goal.

Later that spring I felt ready to rejoin society. I sold most of my carvings through a gallery, and took a job. It was a wonderful time, becoming socially active and feeling so at home I never once considered leaving. Two people in particular intrigued me: an older woman with long grey hair who walked the beach early each morning with the graceful power of a dancer, and one around my age with wild curly black locks, whose beauty and energy moved and fascinated me. To my delight I discovered they were friends, living on the same property; one of them in the house I admired the most in Tofino. Soon we three were compatriots: Ann became my friend and benevolent landlady when I moved onto her property, and Thérèse and I fell in love.

Living beside Ann and Thérèse provided unique opportunities for creativity. Ann needed a woodshed. Beauty being a priority for her, I designed and built a little jewel of a shed. Thérèse wanted to rebuild her plastic greenhouse as a glass addition to her tiny A-frame. It was my good fortune and great pleasure to build it for her. That project was a labour of love, and its visibility provided my work with good exposure to the community. Ann gave me a spot to build my own little cabin. Unfortunately it turned out to be on the neighbours' property. Fortunately they liked my work, later hiring me to build their house.

For the first time in my life, I was blending carpentry with the wilder wood sculpturing I'd previously done separately. The fabulous materials available here and local resonance with the style allowed me to explore an aesthetic that marries the extravagant beauty of driftwood with the more lineal requirements of daily living. I discovered that the sheer immensity of the natural environment here dwarfs me, reduces my experience of the 'civilized' technological world to a pin point. Conventions of normalcy become (to me) aberrations in this world of towering trees, tangles of vegetation, and a tempestuous coastline. Wild inhabitants, the truest locals, the birds, bears, and animals of every size and sort, wander past my cabin and whatever art I create is meant to please *them* first, or at least not offend them. My work is often described as "organic" and so it is: I attempt to let my entire experience of this place, both inner and outer, past and present, flow through me, through the elements of whatever I'm creating, and come into being as if it grew here in this wild and magical place at the edge of the world.

Now twenty-two years after arriving here as a refugee from the crush of society, I look back with a kind of wonderment and outright gratitude. Ratso turned out to be a good (if roguish, by some standards) man, the cabin at the sand pit was my delightful home for over a year. Ann moved away but remains a dear friend. Thérèse and I are ever more deeply in love. I successfully moved my cabin "to a better location" and creative work has fed my stomach and my soul. I still endeavour to more fully realize awareness of the fountain of inspiration. Encouraged by the immense power of the natural environment, by fortunate circumstances and the fellowship of other refugees, I continue on the path of creativity and love, and if I were to choose something to symbolize my life here, a glistening blue-green glass ball on this sandy shore would be perfect.

SACRED GROUND, SACRED HEART: A VIEW FROM WHALER BAY

KIT GRAUER

I feel the heat rising from the words, and the human relief of having shared a story and thereby mitigating its power. By getting such stories "off our chests," we are lightened and enabled. Frequently we discover that what we believe to be singular is, in fact, universally experienced. No wonder Holocaust survivors seek each other out. No wonder those who have lost a child turn to others who have endured the same loss. We need these conversations desperately.

Carol Shields

I live with my family on bays on both sides of the Gulf of Georgia. We have always lived on the west coast, generations rooted into the soft earth of deltas, where the shoreline offers many variations of contact with the water and the ecology of coastal living. Our "permanent" residence on Boundary Bay, a block from the American border, is a retreat from the everyday world of work. There, the pull of the tide is strong, bringing eagles and herons to reside with us. This is not city living but it does keep us connected to the responsibilities and burdens of contemporary life. Across the Gulf, only forty-five minutes by ferry, is our island home. Here is another world, another kind of contemporary living, another way of being, as anyone who has resided on an island can attest. It is more than a *get-away*; it is a connection to place. We are tied even more intimately with the land and sea, with our artist selves and our spirits. Life revolves around relationships of our own choosing: family, friends and the creatures that inhabit the forest, stream and shore. Stepping onto the ferry is like stepping away from the responsibilities set by occupation and into a rhythm rooted by location.

On Galiano the forest and seashore that surround our home provide a welcome sanctuary, a place to enact the rituals of cottage life, a life not defined by built-in appliances, ubiquitous Internet, and the mad minutia of life in the 'fast lane.' On the island, our dishwasher does not wash dishes; it makes a near-perfect mouse-proof cupboard for food staples. We prefer to hand-wash the cups and plates and sweep the floor as simple acts of living that are a slow meditation, a contemplation of the commonplace. Life slows down to heartbeats. We are on Island Time. But for us, the most important ritual of all is to reflect on Whaler Bay.

Whaler Bay cuts into the island from the Gulf of Georgia. We have taken hundreds of photos of this view over the years, and we are not the only ones captivated by it. Galiano's main road passes between the cottage and the boathouse, splitting our land. Like the name of the small café that borders us, we are Grand Central: the place where cars slow down, hikers and bikers stop to pull out their cameras and local painters ask to set up their easels. In our observations of the movements along this roadway and the adjacent waterway, we have found sources of inspiration, emerging between the layers of our own stories and the stories of those who linger with us in these spaces.

Whaler Bay is a safe harbour to a small fleet of fishing vessels, a few sailboats and a variety of power boats and row boats that ferry their owners to the smaller islands nearby. Occasionally river otters, harbour seals and humans can be seen swimming; a canoe ventures down the bay to watch the birds or the deer along the shores. The local boat builder moors one of his wooden masterpieces in the open for all to enjoy. The movement of the tides and the reflections on the water inspire hours of contemplation.

My husband and I are both art teachers. With almost seventy years of teaching between us, in classrooms from kindergarten to university, and across a number of media from fibre to photography, art making and teaching are inseparable from our lives. We have worked both independently and together and presented our ideas and work at local, national and international venues. After much time working in the Vancouver Art Gallery and the Museum of Anthropology, we find ourselves curators of our own places of residence. We see the spaces of our home as integral to our art-making practice. Our setting is ever-evolving and always in movement, a canvas that can only be read over many decades of living. Here we enjoy freedom of expression in ways we cannot undertake in our mainland, mainstream lives. We draw, photograph and sculpt in response to our environment, looking for the nuances and relationships that bring aesthetic delight. Our property on Galiano is an art installation. For example, renovations revolve around incorporating the spiral staircase that was used in a now defunct beauty pageant, or the bridge from the demolished children's garden. We are collectors of the neglected and the whimsical. A row of Chinese bamboo bird houses; "Loonie" banks, made to hold the Canadian dollar coin and shaped like the loons that swim outside the window; table cloths lovingly embroidered and then abandoned in thrift shops; all are rescued and brought to life again in our gallery-home.

And we collect odd signs for fun. Large wooden letters that spell out "Something Different" adorn our studio, and provoke questions from passers-by. The "Paradise Care Home" is a weathered, white-lettered sign, found by friends when an old-age facility was torn down. Each is a symbol, a story, an imprint of living through creative expression, for our delight, and we hope, the amusement of those who share artful points of view. Like the outside walls of the cottage where a rusted rack to hold BBQ tools is juxtaposed against several painted wooden fish and a folk art piece from our travels. Everywhere are my husband's lanterns and my baskets of seashells and sea glass. We are bound to this place in these objects, the marks we make on the land, and the found treasures from the forest, seashore or shops. The play between art making and our lives as makers of art is intimately tied to the flora and fauna, tides and tributaries. But this wondrous island life is also a life marked with sadness, both personal and communal.

The summer my mother was dying, my husband, two sons and I retreated to our cottage on Whaler Bay. Everything became more poignant. Tears came unbidden at the birth of a fawn in our woods, at the reflections of boats and trees on the water, at the chattering sounds of a kingfisher. An image, a sound, a touch could unleash a torrent of emotion. Back and forth we went between the mainland and the island, my mother insisting that nothing was wrong with her health. My children watched me and worried: Why was I fighting with Nana? Why was I so upset? Why could I not allow Nana to follow her own path? I could not learn the lessons she was teaching me. I took pictures of Whaler Bay, attempting to ground myself in images of a place where reflections of light on water shaped meaning. It was a time when I lost myself, wholly, in a whirlpool of anguish for what I could not control.

Grievous events converged that summer to shift our understandings of the island beneath our feet. It began when we took a trip to Steveston, a small fishing village near our mainland home. On that day in this otherwise peaceful village, it was announced on the radio that a fish boat loaded with salmon had overturned on the way to the docks. Coast guard and divers were called. Fishermen spoke anxiously to each other of friends. We felt the apprehension in those who make their livelihood on the coast. We decided to return to Galiano. The afternoon ferry took us across the Gulf. The same stretch of water that somehow had been treacherous that morning was now calm and serene. My fascination of water is lifelong, its mirages and enchantment, danger and death. Whole worlds lie beneath the surface, unseen, unknown. Motion is constant; the surface always varied. The secrets of the sea felt sinister that afternoon. On the ferry rumours swirled about the accident: the boat's big catch of fish had shifted, causing the boat to capsize; the boat might be from one of the Gulf Islands; it was feared that a family was on board; the divers were not allowed to dive because of new coast guard regulations.

"It might be the *Cap Rouge*," my husband said. One of the trio of fishing boats that moored at the dock in Whaler Bay. A boat we knew well. People we knew well.

By the time we arrived, makeshift shrines of flowers and school pictures of the children met us as we walked from the ferry to the cottage. A wreath hung on the crossbeams of the wharf. A large heart-shaped rock lay surrounded by candles. These objects confirmed the worst of the rumours. Even as I shuddered in grasping their meaning, I pulled out my camera, driven to capture these mementos of mourning. We continued on to the cottage but our need to understand took precedence over shutting out the larger world. We switched on the radio and waited to hear the official story.

A mother and her two children had been caught in the overturned wheelhouse and drowned as the captain, their father, watched helplessly from the rescue boat. The close-knit island community was in shock. I held my children tight. Looking up Whaler Bay, all I could see was absence. The *Cap Rouge* would never again be in her rightful place on the wharf. Beyond the view was an unseen ocean of grief and sorrow.

* * *

I printed my pictures, tore them apart, and wove them together, placed images of the old view within images of a new view – all ways of expressing my distress. My husband looked through his negatives and found a series of details of the *Cap Rouge* he had taken the previous summer in black and white. We made frames from the painted wood that washed up on the shore of our bay; creating shadow boxes to frame images of loss. It was through our art making we attempted to come to grips with this sea of change.

We had long been members of the Galiano Artist Guild, and we exhibited our creations in the September show. For the most part, our work was accepted as it was given: a personal response to a community in mourning. But there were some who felt that as "weekenders" we were acting insensitively to the "islanders" in their grief. I was taken aback. I had believed we were part of the community, but now, part of that community saw us as outsiders. Even here, community was a concept delineated by multiple meanings, rooted in the politics of insider and outsider, us and them.

Later that fall, my mother died of cancer. For my children, it was not only the loss of their much-loved Nana but also the realization that their own mother would also someday die. At Mum's funeral, the minister talked about our many family photographs, but I could only dwell on the fact that my mother would no longer appear in pictures surrounded by we who had loved her.

Like the water that ebbs and flows in our tidal bay revealing and concealing the shifting sandy ground, so my emotions continue to ebb and flow. Sometimes what is revealed is so transitory and elusive that only the next tide will provide clarity. It has taken me a long time to finally get to a place where I can give words to these memories, although I have been making art around them for many years.

Our studio sits at the base of Whaler Bay on consecrated ground. The building's foundations were part of the first Mission House on Galiano. This was the place where births and deaths were celebrated by the community. Also on this ground is another sign pointing the way to a new church up the hill: St Margaret's of Scotland. Margaret was my mother's name, and Scotland her ancestral home. Last summer, we decided that such serendipity begged an opportunity to commemorate my mother. On a bench we built overlooking the bay a plaque reads, "Welcome to Paradise." To this we added a newly-carved wooden sign that simply reads, "Saint Margaret of Scotland." From it we hang baskets of flowers in the summer, with pots of "mums" in the fall. The hidden meanings would have pleased my mother. She didn't want a big memorial but she would have loved the flowers, and would have smiled to know about those who make use of her bench: children as they wait for the bus on their way to the water taxi; older women as they pause from picking blackberries; little girls dressed in pink having a tea party with their dolls; the fishermen returning from a day on the rocks at Bell House Park; an elderly man walking his aging dog. The bench is situated so that those who stop to rest have the best view of Whaler Bay. And we can see the bench from the cottage as we look to the view beyond.

A new ritual has developed in our life on Galiano. Everyone is watchful for visitors to the bench. When travellers take rest there, my husband or children call and I reach for the camera. My mother has a visitor. Even the deer are photographed, eating the lowest hanging flowers. I come to Galiano to find my centre. In the process, I take pictures of the view and ask to photograph those who rest on the bench. Inevitably we get to talking, sharing stories of how we are in this place, at this time. Mostly I listen. Everyone has a story, and everyone is pleased to be acknowledged, pleased to have his or her picture taken on the bench. Sometimes they are "islanders" and we really talk for the first time. Sometimes this leads to a jar of Blackberry jam appearing on our deck, and new smiles from familiar faces on the ferry. And sometimes this is a first visit to Galiano by someone who just wants to admire the view.

I read fiction on Galiano. Often it provides me with resonance and truth that I find lacking in my mainland life. Lately I have been reading Canadian writer Camilla Gibb, who left her academic career to become a novelist. From *Sweetness in the Belly*:

> *It is his absence that is part of me and has been for years. This is who I am, perhaps who we all are, keepers of the absent and the dead. It is the blessing and burden of being alive.*
>
> CAMILLA GIBB

Recently I decided to exhibit my pictures, expressing my homage to absence. It is the absence in the photographs that gives them their poignancy. The memorial is in the continued everyday lives of those who follow. The images are about the moment of their taking and about those who came before. They represent a counter-monument to loss. It was difficult to select from my hundreds of images of strangers and new friends sitting on the bench at Whaler Bay. They currently hang in a gallery on a wall at my university, with a selection, on the opposite wall, of photographs presenting the place where the *Cap Rouge* once moored. It is the absence in both sets of images "that is the blessing and burden of being alive." This exhibit is a celebration of the spirit of that place, for those who carry the memories, the "keepers of the absent and the dead." It is also a celebration of those who are touched for the first time by sitting on sacred ground.

References:

Gibb, C. (2006). *Sweetness in the Belly.* Anchor Canada.

Shields, C. (2001). *Dropped Threads: Holes in the Discourse.* Eds. Carol Shields and Marjorie Anderson. Toronto: Random House.

THE TAO OF TOFINO: IN BETWEEN ARTIST AND COMMUNITY

DAVID FLOODY

Is this an esoteric essay on the metaphysics of ancient Chinese philosophy? No, nothing so abstract, so formal or so grandiose. This reflection is more like *Winnie the Pooh*, appropriately enough for Vancouver Island I suppose, in which a bear like me might be influenced by his surroundings if he sat down under a salmonberry bush, heavy with summer fruit, and attempted to write a novel. No artist, no matter the medium, exists without context. The writer, the painter, the carver, the composer, the performer, any artist, even purposely standing apart as the most trenchant critic of his or her time and society, still has reference to the places that shape them, to their particular *Tao*.

Living and creating in the midst of Clayoquot Sound with its mutable moods and myriad expressions of rock, sea, greenery and sky is my writer's oxygen. To breathe this place is to be deeply invigorated, and as a writer of narrative, it's the Tofino content of characters and their stories-in-the-making that energize and renew my consciousness of the community.

My wife and I are relatively recent arrivals to Tofino, moving here in late 2006, although we'd been planning to build on our lot on First Street for fourteen years. I had recently retired from teaching in a city high school in southern Ontario, itself a vibrant and diverse community. I looked forward to writing novels full-time, a long-held dream finally about to be realized on the west coast. But why here?

My thirty seasons as a teacher were ending. The open landscapes of southern Ontario, the excitement and intensity of life in Toronto, the variety of artistic and cultural amenities always had been pleasing to us. We'd had good careers and satisfying friendships, but it was largely a place and time for work. When I turned to writing novels, I turned west. I wanted Tofino and 'Tofino Time.' So did my wife. After three decades of effort, this place and time became our home.

The social context of the extreme west – this village of 1600 full-time residents, made complex by the influx of thousands of tourists in high season, and a million visitors annually – was certainly a new way of living for us. We had no particular preconceptions. Upon reflection, the writer in me did worry and wonder. What do we mean by community? How far does a neighbourhood extend? Is the paradox of Yogi Berra's observation, "no one goes there anymore … it's too crowded," inevitable for Tofino?

The night of January 30, 2007 was a turning point for this artist in his community. I attended my first Tofino council meeting as a 'Tofitian.' A group of South Chesterman Beach residents had brought forward a controversial bid to rezone the area from full-time residential to allow for short-term vacation rentals. The issue was divisive and passions ran high. It was at once a singular and plural experience, each of us together in that moment.

Before Mayor Fraser called the meeting to order, a young girl of two or three was darting back and forth, giggling, visiting, talking and asking questions of the man attentively following her, whom I assumed to be her father. No-one paid them much attention. However, when the meeting began, the man took his seat, as a councillor at the front of the room. I'd made presentations to councils back in Ontario when children were in the audience, but none where a child listened quietly, in her councillor-father's lap, the whole time presentations were made. I was surprised at first, but after a while I too no longer paid her much attention.

One of the most senior members of the South Chesterman Beach community, Mary, rose to share her memories of that place. She reminded me of my grandmother telling stories. We listeners witnessed a living, oral history of South Chesterman, filtered through the lens of her experience – the people and events, the particular tenor of the neighbourhood and how it had evolved during her years there. She went well over the five minutes allotted for each speaker, but no one in the audience became impatient; not even the mayor interrupted her story. The community members accorded her the respect her experience deserved. We were keeping Tofino Time. "Half The Speed – Twice The Pleasure!" as a local magazine by the same name puts it.

We were all taking time, like the child sitting down with her father; we were sitting down with the council, sitting down with the grandmother, sitting down with the community. Tofino and the nearby village of Ucluelet are under the same development pressures as many other wildly beautiful places in Canada and the world, yet sometimes I wonder if the most precious resource we are running out of is in fact time. Tofino time, part of this place's *Tao*, is an essential element I am given as a novelist residing and writing in the community.

⸰ But what's really at stake here? What *is* community?

I believe it's all of us together in the Community Hall. The values represented by the grandmother and the child and all of the rest of us, with our factions, our emotions, our competing interests and the values in between. I recognize there's a risk of fragmenting community through vacation rentals by eroding more traditional notions of belonging to a place.

My guts were churning for most of the meeting. But I was alive in that setting, a character in Tofino's evolving narrative, a vital participant plotting consensus in the midst of division. I surprised myself by voicing my opinion. With that act, I realized my consciousness of community, and touched its *Tao*.

Vacation rentals are transient by definition – socially ephemeral, yet with a significant cumulative impact, not the least of which is psychological. Are such rentals an opposite of community? Maybe. But my personal experience with vacation rentals is somewhat ironic given my concerns for fragmentation. While my wife and I waited for our permanent housing to be built, we stayed in a vacation rental. The owner, Brenda, made possible our plan to spend three days over Christmas with a good friend in Vancouver by offering to tend our two cats. We'd only met her once, a month-and-a-half before. To me, that's community. And she wouldn't take a cent. That's generosity.

The meeting continued into the night. Councillors listened, looked to the Official Community Plan and the majority voted to refuse the bid, that time. Perhaps most importantly, the dissenting residents had their say before us all. We are still part of the same community, still in its flow.

As a writer, I now find my inspiration in such moments which compose the everyday life of Tofino. The portrait of the starving artist in the lonely garret struggling to birth his or her masterwork is not a picture of me. My novels are my 'children,' and it takes the whole village of Tofino to nourish them to maturity. The desk where I write overlooks a gravel path that is an informal extension of Gibson Street. It was created and maintained over the years by local members of the community who use it, and there I see much transpire. I experience this path as an active, literal manifestation of the *Tao* of Tofino, the village's particular 'pathway of life.' How inspiring that I live and write beside it, infused with the boisterous laughter of children playing; reluctant students, trudging with heads down and shrugging their book-bags from one shoulder to the other; conservation officers in khaki uniforms brandishing their bear spray; young mothers pushing their strollers with one hand and tugging their two-year-olds forward with the other; 'Tonquin Beach Tom' with his bare feet impervious to the granite shards and a green garbage bag of returnable bottles on his shoulder like a sort of environmental Santa Claus; a young black bear the conservation officers were seeking walks in the opposite direction, causing me to phone the daycare centre to alert them; and dogs – lots and lots of dogs – my favourite, the intrepid wire-haired terrier who lost his right front leg when he came between croquet mallet and wooden ball as a pup.

Could a writer invent more original and engaging moments than these? And they are there for all to see, ready to become part of the lore of this community, shaped in the pages of my novels. I have only to wait, watch, listen, and every conscious moment embrace this flow of life. There is always another story waiting to be written.

FORMATIVE YEARS
SHARON MCINNES

Of all the animals that migrate, we are surely among the most restless. But humans retain the influence of the geophysical habitat in which they pass their formative years. And often, it seems, we are drawn back to our childhood homes – if not physically, then mentally; if not out of love, then out of curiosity; if not by necessity, then by desire. Through such ramblings we find out who we are.
John Janovy Jr.

I've never been much of a rambler, at least geographically. For most of my adult life I lived happily in Vancouver, rambling only to Mexico on holiday each winter. But in 2007 my husband and I retired to a gulf island off the coast of British Columbia. Neither of us knew what living on an island would be like, and although I had vacationed on Gabriola for twenty years, "holidaying is not living," as one dubious city friend stated. Still, we were optimistic enough to sell our seventeenth floor apartment on a busy intersection and make the leap across the Salish Sea.

We spent much of our first year getting a grip on the expansive garden we'd acquired. Oh, and having company. You get a lot of company when you live here, especially in the summer. One morning my visiting younger sister began snapping pictures of me in the back garden, commenting on how odd it was to see me there, so clearly enjoying myself. Apparently, I had always given her the impression that gardening would be a burden. Really?

But her comments got me thinking. It was true that when I was poking around in the garden I experienced a contentment I hadn't felt for a long time. And sitting on our deck in the evenings, admiring the big leaf maples, giant cedars, and Douglas firs surrounding me, a kind of comfort I barely recognized often snuck up and surprised me. Then, one day, it dawned on me: to my childhood self – still alive and well, apparently, though long-neglected – this little piece of land we'd adopted brought back vivid memories of my first home on Lulu Island, a rural paradise long since swallowed up by the city of Richmond. Way back then, home was a blueberry farm where ring-necked pheasants bathed in dusty fields and great blue herons dotted wide ditches.

My Granny raised chickens next door. On weekend mornings I helped her feed them and gather the eggs; then I watched as she candled them, still warm, in the darkness of the kitchen pantry. Today, when I crack open the orange-yolked farm eggs we purchase down the road, I remember the mystery and fragrance of that pantry. And when I sink my hands deep into a forty pound bag of birdseed, filling my palm with black oil sunflower seeds and millet and cracked corn for dark-eyed juncos and fox sparrows and spotted towhees, my fingers remember the scratchy bags of Buckerfield's Feed that the eight-year-old-me scattered on the ground for Granny's hens.

Every spring Granny's yard, connected to ours by a well-worn path, teemed with long-stemmed flowers that Dad sold to a grocery store in Chinatown. He took me with him Saturday mornings, the back seat of the car bursting with daffodils. Mr. Wong arranged the flowers in tall silver cans lined up on wooden shelves in front of his store. I always thought they looked beautiful. Today the Shasta daisies and black-eyed Susans that line the fence of our property on Gabriola take me back to those glorious mornings. And now, as I dig up a gorgeous yellow Oriental poppy and move it to the front of the garden to create a more pleasing palette, and as I select and position smooth beach stones around the roots of my clematis, I remember Mr. Wong's big hands arranging Granny's daffodils with such care.

I had, somehow, somewhere, lost so many of these memories. Not that I didn't remember where I'd lived as a child but I had forgotten the *feeling* of living in the country. I had forgotten the solace of being sheltered by towering evergreens. I had forgotten the thrill of the incessant hum of bumblebees at lilac bushes. Now it makes sense. When I sit on the back deck in the mornings, I am mesmerized not just by the beauty of the trees around me, their dappled greens illuminated by the morning sun, but by nascent memories of traipsing through the forest near my friend's house as we looked for the perfect spot to build a tree fort. And now, when I stop whatever I'm doing to listen to the melodious song of the purple finch on the pergola, some part of me, I'm sure, recalls the non-stop backdrop of birdsong my friends and I barely noticed as we played in the woods.

I remember, too, lying on my back in the middle of our blueberry patch watching the clouds waft by, the scent of peat in the air, bushes double my height heavy with dark blue berries. In those years there was time to indulge such sensuous pleasures, just like there is now. Surrounded by nature and blessed with more free time than I've had since childhood, I am rediscovering those parts of myself that got lost during my life in the city. Now I have time to watch a snail emerge from its shell. Time to watch violet-green swallows build a nest under the eaves of our garden shed. Time to stretch out on the lawn and watch the night sky. Time to remember who I am. And it turns out that who I am, in part at least, is a writer.

It's not that I haven't written before. In my twenties I was writing, albeit sporadically, usually as a means of working out life's traumas and dramas, of trying to discover who I was beyond a daughter, a student, then a wife, and finally a mother. Somehow, the process of translating my experience into language, of selecting the right word, tossing out a clumsy phrase, discovering a metaphor that joined and deepened my disparate worlds consoled and grounded me. But all of that writing was meant for me alone, and I certainly never included "writer" in my list of identity attributes. Until last year, that is, on our annual trip to Mexico, when I filled in the "occupation" blank of the Tourist Visa with a new word: writer.

For a while after that daring proclamation had been made (to myself, most importantly) I wore my new identity tentatively, like red stiletto pumps. But the more of my articles I saw in print, the more stories I submitted, even the more handwritten rejection notes I received, the more comfortable those shoes became. Soon, when a stranger asked, "What do you do?" I answered without much hesitation, "I'm a writer." But too often an annoying inner voice still commented, "Really?" Then last spring, after reading a poem at an outdoor poetry event, surrounded by sandstone and sea, I felt it in my bones: I *am* a writer. Those awkward pumps were becoming well-worn favourite sandals.

Now the practice of writing shapes my days. Four days a week, several hours a day, I close my office door and write, accompanied only by the red-headed house finches, chestnut-backed chickadees, and downy woodpeckers that visit the Japanese cherry tree outside my window. Then, twice a week for three hours at a stretch, I write in the company of two or three others. We meet solely to write – no critiquing, not much chat, just working on our individual projects, separate but together. This regular gathering reinforces my identity as a writer. But more than anything else, it is this place, this lush west coast island where bald eagles soar and deer munch grass along the roadside that continually breathes life into the writer in me. Here, surrounded and nurtured by wild beauty and a vibrant artistic community, I still write for me, but also for others, as an offering: essays, articles, and poetry, often about the natural world that inspires me, and stories whose characters emerge like self-sown flowers in my garden, taking my hand, leading me further and deeper into my own unfolding life. Such a blessing.

Reference:

Janovy, J. (1992). *Vermilion Sea: A Naturalist's Journey in Baja California*. New York: Houghton Mifflin.

MY VICTORIA

ROBERT AMOS

Author's note: This chapter is based on an interview conducted by Lia Tarle, March 3, 2009.

Victoria Food and Florist, acrylic (See page 137 Colour Insert)

I remember coming over the hill at Royal Oak and seeing the city of Victoria spread out before me, sun sparkling off the Straits. I thought, "This place looks fantastic! For a landscape painter it's made-to-order. Look at the mountains, the ocean, and those big trees: this is a beautiful city! Toronto doesn't have any of these things." And before long, I noticed the cultural diversity here, especially the Asian and First Nations cultures. It all seemed so different on the island.

I worked at the Art Gallery of Greater Victoria for the first five years. During that time I surveyed the Gallery's collection, and I noticed that among the 10,000 works of art they had collected and stored I found only one that represented the city of Victoria. This seemed like a serious oversight. When I later set out on my career as an artist, I thought it would be a good idea to fill that gap.

In Toronto, the artists always seemed to be preparing to make it big in New York, London, Paris, or Berlin. Toronto apparently was a place on the way to somewhere else. But here in Victoria, it seems to me, nobody is striving to make it elsewhere. We're on an island, we're isolated and we deal with it. This is it. Yet it's not lonely here. I've noticed that this place is like a magnet for creative people. There is something about the environment that is very conducive to creative endeavour.

What is it that makes it so attractive? I would say that this place is very feminine in its aspect. I know that's not a very scientific thing to say, but it seems to me that many places in this country, most of them in fact, could be typified as masculine. Let's choose Calgary for example. In Calgary the land is very flat; the climate is extreme, from cold to hot; the buildings are vertical. There are towers that go up and up and up. Calgary's economy is boom-and-bust, based on resource extraction and taming the wilderness. To me, those are masculine characteristics.

Here on the island, we're surrounded by water, which moderates both temperature and climate. It's not too cold and it's not too hot. The kind of male ambition that results in high-rise buildings and boom-and-bust economy doesn't really work here. We don't have an industrial base, and we're not building superhighways on the way to anywhere else. One has to be content to live here, and that kind of contentment is visible. I have noticed that a great number of the people who are important to me in this community are women. We've had women mayors and directors of the art galleries, commercial and institutional. There are many well-respected women in this community who are authors, dramatists, and artists. It's a place where the most appropriate way of life is what I would describe as 'nurturing.' That's what we really do well here. We nurture plants, we nurture children, and we nurture our own creative impulses.

I like being here. I don't want to travel to try to sell my ideas elsewhere. This place is not a 'farm team' for somebody else's big idea. The characteristics of the art culture are unique, and different aspects come into play which are not readily understood in other places. For instance, this is a place where there is a great deal of spirituality in evidence, whether in aboriginal culture or the influence of Asian art, or even the residual attitudes of the hippies. A lot of very intelligent and creative people moved to this island from New York and Los Angeles in the late '60s and the '70s. Those 'dropouts,' with their tie-dyed t-shirts and LSD, as they are often portrayed in popular culture, also brought openness to spirituality which I believe is a worthwhile theme to explore in art. As I recall, the attitude was different in Toronto. The idea of mixing religion with art in the '70s . . . for heaven's sake, don't even mention it!

I see the stay-at-home quality of island life as a positive thing. A prominent artist of the previous generation, E.J. Hughes, lived and died in the Duncan area. A very conservative artist, he worked close to home. He never wanted to go anywhere. His course as an artist was set in the early 1930s, and he pursued it in a single-minded way until his death in 2007. Hughes had the good fortune to be discovered by an art dealer from Montreal named Dr. Max Stern. Dr. Stern sold Hughes' work to the famous art collections all over this country: the National Gallery, the Art Gallery of Ontario and all the wealthiest collectors. And those people realized that Hughes, with his very focused west coast vision, was creating art that was magical and beautiful. Because of that focus, his work has been recognized and greatly honoured all over this country. I learned from his example that it is possible to make isolation a very positive thing. Hughes helped me to realize that you *can* see the big world in your own grain of sand.

I have always thought that the proper activity for an artist is to take a look at the environment and then report back. Today most people don't look, and almost nobody ever reports back. I try to create art that takes note of a sense of community and locality, which seems a rare thing in the larger homogenized world. Subject matter is always part of my artwork. And when a subject I paint or write about becomes outdated, old-fashioned or obsolete, my artwork can take on the quality of an antique. Instead of trying to be generic, I make things which are very specific to my community.

All of my artworks have a location and a story: I was there. The situation moved me in the first place and that's why I painted it. I'm not creating for an unknown audience. I'm holding up a mirror to Victoria, and showing what it looks like to me. People can buy my originals or inexpensive prints, or just watch me at work in the street. Beyond painting I am also a professional writer, writing about art not in an art journal or novel, but in the daily newspaper. My approach is to make art accessible to everyone, and I believe in promoting a more democratic perspective on the arts in general. I believe that my activities add up to a project bigger than simply my painting and writing. It is all a performance piece, inscribed on the body politic of where I live. It is about building an artistic and cultural vision rooted in my community.

...AND TOPOGRAPHY

WANDA HURREN

(See page 137 Colour Insert)

As I write this, it is my third "winter" living on the west coast of Canada. For most of the other forty-nine years of my life I lived on the prairies. My new friends here on the coast sometimes refer to me (and not without a slight touch of exoticism) as a "prairie girl."

My move to Vancouver Island was not only for the warmer winters but also because of the particular aesthetics this place evokes, which I had noted on previous visits. Given that Victoria is more often equated with rain than sunshine, and given that I grew up close to Estevan, Saskatchewan, a place purported by the television weather channel to be the "Sunshine Capital of Canada," this quest for sunlight might seem odd. But as a photographer, the light on Vancouver Island was what caught me.

In the summer of 2003, I was a visiting scholar teaching at the University of Victoria. In my off hours, I rarely stepped outside without my camera and extra rolls of film. I rose early many mornings to capture the light in its variations coming across the back garden. Taking notes and photographs, I recorded the light at various hours, like the images of lemons in a bowl in early morning light, late afternoon light, early evening light as proof. An afternoon trip to a laundromat turned into a study of sunlight (present even in the brand of laundry detergent), yielding up silver gelatine images of puffy terry towels stacked on washing machines, with the afternoon sun through southwest windows providing the most exquisite back lighting.

As a disciple of the Miksang[1] tradition of photography, I often engage in the practice of using my camera as a tool for the contemplative and meditative practice of paying attention to here and now, and to what is stopping me. During my first few weeks living here, I ventured out with my camera, but I returned home having not once raised it to my eye. After several months in Victoria, with some dismay I had to acknowledge that I had not taken even one photograph. There was just too much to see. Too much of everything. Too many trees, leaves, grasses, blossoms, ocean views, mountain views, city views, streetlights, hanging baskets, misty evenings, brilliant sunny mornings. I just couldn't see anything. Nothing was stopping me.

And that was true on several levels. Perhaps it would be more accurate to say nothing/something was stopping me. A particular set of thoughts was stopping me from raising my camera to my eye – in fact, stopping me from seeing or noticing my present surroundings. In fact I couldn't stop thinking about what I was not seeing: prairie swarms of mosquito blizzards under July schoolyard lights; September sun sparkles through chain-link fence surrounding the community pool (*Closed for the Season*); blue snow shadows in the footprints along the back lane.

Living on the west coast, it seems that I am caught in a perceptual space that I can only describe as liminal. It's that space of noticing where I am but recognizing that part of my acute awareness of here and now is related to what is *not* here and what is *not* now. It seems to me that I am only able to appreciate my aesthetic surroundings in relation to where I am not.

During my first summer here on the coast, I flew out to Saskatchewan for a wedding. It was the long weekend in August, and the prairie was so dry that wild fires were burning. Gazing out at the fires along Highway #18, I was already categorizing what I was seeing as "not west coast." And on my return to Victoria I was registering what I was seeing as "not prairie." What to do about this? I do not believe it is a diminishing of the aesthetic qualities of either geographical location, but it is a recognition, for me at least, that any geographical location

---

[1]*Miksang* is a Tibetan word meaning "good eye" and 'the associated tradition of contemplative photography was developed by Michael Wood who bases his photographic practice on the teachings of Chogyam Trungpa Rinpoche.

can only be what it is because of what it is not. Not very profound, but for me, as a photographer, it is an understanding that is both intellectual and visceral. I believe I do not raise my camera to my eye until I notice what is stopping me, and so far, what is stopping me is a curious mix of here/not here, because of the curious mix of where I am/not and who I am/not.

The series of triptychs that follow, titled *and topography*[2], grew out of a conversation I had with a friend about places we had lived. Knowing that while I now live on the west coast of Canada, I had lived most of my life on the prairies, my friend commented, "Oh, well then I can see how you would appreciate weather ... and topography" (as if there is no topography on the prairies). Through this series of triptychs I am expressing the idea that geography and identity are cumulative events and never mutually exclusive. I can only make sense of the west coast in relation to what it is not, and much of my sense-making about who I am in this place is closely related to who I used to be, but am no longer, in another place. All these layers of being work together linking places and identities.

Topographical and highway maps comprise the first layer of the triptych pieces, vellum paper with text composes the second layer, and colour positive Polaroid transfers of geographical locations make up the top layer. The text running along the lower edge of the vellum layer for the first two pieces of each triptych reads: "prairie prairie prairie prairie," and the images and topographical maps are of prairie spaces. The third piece in each triptych reads simply "not" and the topographical maps and images are of west coast spaces.

* * *

One day, to pass the time while waiting through a "one-sail wait" for the Tsawwassen Ferry, a west coast friend wanted to show me a short cut through the forest to a pub at a nearby marina. Somehow we ended up following the wrong desire lines[3], and it took us much longer than estimated to reach the pub. When we came out of the trees across from the pub, my friend had a scrape on his elbow from a fall, and the heels of my tall boots were caked with pine needles and a foresty type of mud. Smiling over our beers, we agreed that, concerning (prairie) topography, we had just had a "not" experience.

---

[2]Hurren, W. (2008). *...and topography* (photography and mixed media). *postcartographia* joint exhibition, May, 2008, Xchanges Gallery, Victoria, BC.

[3]The landscape architects' term for trails formed by people to get where they want to go, the way they want to go, in spite of roads and formal pathways.

prairie prairie prairie prairie prairie prairie prairie prairie prairie

(See page 138 Colour Insert)

prairie prairie prairie prairie prairie prairie prairie prairie prairie

(See page 139 Colour Insert)

(See page 140 Colour Insert)

WIND

WEATHERGRAMS
KIM GOLDBERG

Author's Note:

> My "mission" as an artist (if I have one) is to prompt people to do their own
> creative processing. Much of what I write is deliberately disjointed, fragmen-
> tary and non-narrative (or at least non-discursive) for that reason. I want
> readers to fabricate their own meanings. Living in downtown Nanaimo, I
> spend my days wandering the graffiti galleries and homeless campgrounds
> where I find the kind of inspiration that has led to my latest book: RED
> ZONE, poems of urban decay.

Weathergrams (See page 140 Colour Insert)

Monday: slugs only appear slow

Edges are always the first to go. The sandy cliff sliding into the sea. The mind breaching its picket fence. The curling margins of these paper-bag weathergrams I have been hanging in the riverside park at the end of my street, where homeless people sleep every night on vague beds of bracken and salal. Who are these drowsy piles of bone and Salvation Army clothing cat-curled in that shadowy space between slumber and death (for indeed some of them never wake)? Between fresh water and salt (for this is the Millstone River estuary washing into the Georgia Strait). Between foreground and background (for the police do not roust them here, hidden from public display).

Tuesday: stones tell the best jokes

I have lived on the tattered edge, the bastard cusp, the half-wet lip of a meniscus my entire life. Spitting distance from that ever-shifting stew pot of potentialities we call the Pacific. Knowing only the edge, how can I answer the question of what influence this geography of extremity has on my art? It is like asking me what influence breathing has on my art. A good one, I think. Perhaps even profound. But I have yet to experience non-breathing. At least not in a sustained way where I could really get to know it, work its static energies, weave a wizard's robe from dormant air to perform my magic. (For that is art, isn't it? Magic.) So am I qualified to submit an answer?

Wednesday: earthworms perform secret alchemy

Start with a used paper bag, a ball of jute, and a few wooden beads. (Your weathergram must be entirely plant-based to decompose properly, for that is the point—the inescapable unravelling of all things, including language, message, perception.) Cut the bag into strips that are three inches wide and eleven inches long. Fold down the top inch-and-a-half. Punch a hole near the top. Thread some jute through (about a two-foot piece) and knot it with a bead. Write your message in magic marker or calligraphy pen down the length of the weathergram. (You may want to do this *in situ*—let the circumstance of your geography guide your hand). Tie it to a branch or bush. Walk away.

Thursday: every feather has a story

"Art" is not a thing I do at a keyboard or an easel or behind a lens or under a stage light. It is not about doing at all. I am not a human doing. Not really, not when all the shaling crags of social convention have slid off this narrowing body, and the loose rubble washed to sea. What is left at the end, however small, is me. A human being. And art is a way of being human.

I wanted to read my poetry in the Pearson Bridge underpass, downstream from my weathergram park. Homeless people roost here too, in their hibernaculum behind the wall, while the Island Highway mutters them to sleep. When my friend Leonard slept alone and out in the open one night, he awoke to three men beating him. He spent the next month on life support. Nanaimo is like that. Other towns too, I suppose. Safety comes in clusters, barricades, invisibility, which can be scarce out here on the world's final reach. I wanted to feel the sound of my words echoing in the cathedral of the underpass, bouncing off its pigeon-struck vault. I wanted to learn if words uttered could change the thing being spoken about. Would these mastodon columns release their hallowed souls upon hearing themselves described? Would Leonard's mashed-in nose become a cactus-dotted box canyon with no escape? One never knows these things if poetry won't leave the haven of the coffeehouse, won't stand on the precipice, wind-smacked, tongue-kissing the infinite.

Friday: cloud-popped she began to rain

Is my inability to answer the fundamental question a failing of my knowledge, or my language? Has my grammar done this to me? Do I lack the appropriate tools for self-expression? Why am I writing with a keyboard and not a sea pen? Why do I not use the keyhole limpet for the letter "o," a purple sea star for my "A," a periwinkle apostrophe? The entire alphabet is percolating beneath my feet, gurgling answers to questions not even dreamt. How could I be so dense, so herd-minded, so school-taught out here on the ragged edge? Pay attention, Kim! The quantum matrix of sub-linguistic particles is slam-dancing at my ankles. I almost feel them now, popping sockets, needling up my legs, aiming for my head I guess, or just trying to get my attention so I can assemble them into words and string theories and geodesic fishnets. They are waiting for me to wake up and design a syntax befitting bivalves and echinoderms and all the intertidal alcoves of a mud-sluiced mind . . . *Marat, we don't want to wait anymore! We want our rights and we don't care how. We want a revolution now!* Was that them? What kind of an essay is this?

Saturday: her tree-frog heart sprang off

Crashed
as wave, as borderless boundarygone
toptorn wave   Cast
out

from shorn
sea, from wonderless stupefied
uniform sea   Left to
wander

the beach
the forsaken legless genreless
beach   The
unstoppered

wave, taking
not shape not precision not scissors
to cloth   The naked
wave

when fundamentals
fall away, when spent thought lies
splayed   In tall
grass

vacant as
shotguns, vanished as brainstems
writ   In wet sand
blasphemous

banished, clamped
as bass jaw, upswept as gulls, shunned
staked   Unflocked
expatriated

becoming
the rolling wave, the locating wave, the unshapable
wave   The
unbroken wave

Sunday: pond holds sky & stones equally

I apologize for my poetic outburst, for leaping the paddock fence, for toppling off the wrong side of that steel rail I have been teeter-totter-walking all week. If you let me stay, I will try to do better. However, in my defence I would call Patrick Lane to the witness stand since he has been heard to say: the only difference between poetry and prose is the length of the line. And who am I to disagree?

Where does the poem end and ordinary discourse (or life) begin? Where does the land end and the sandy sea-bottom begin? This is not a trick question so much as a summons to mindfulness. These boundaries we think we see. Are they worthy of our trust?

If I had grown up in the desert or on the prairies or in Paraguay, that is to say a landscape of continuity with regard to the three elemental states of solid-liquid-gas, would I be able to more clearly discern the end of poetry, the commencement of prose? Does life at the furthest edge, here on the lip of vastness, detune us to compartmentalization? Does it blur the cobbled boundary between art and a bottle-picker's knapsack? Does it hand us a stick and leave us poking at all boundaries until a gust lifts each away like a garter snake's cast-off husk? How long is the British Columbia coastline as the heron flies? As the tide scours it? As the bull kelp darns it? Is it longer than a question mark? Will it fit inside a stray shopping cart?

FINDING HOME, FINDING ART
PETER CRESSEY

When I was sixteen in the early eighties, I started an apprenticeship doing work that I expected to be similar to what I had learned from my
father, a Triumph motorcycle mechanic. But my experience over five
years was more industrial, not a craft, not intimate; instead I worked in a large
garage where I felt like a cog in a machine. Everything was prescribed – fit this
to that in this many hours and clock in and clock out. I felt used and limited and
finally, when I quit, rebellious towards work in general. The notion of creative
labour hadn't occurred to me yet.

When I left England in the summer of 1991 to arrive on Canada's west coast,
I was instantly hooked. Nature and the wilderness here fitted some childhood
ideal of misty mountains and gnarled forests. I spent the long days of that first
summer hiking, camping, making friends, and as it happened, becoming involved in logging blockades in the Walbran valley. It was an exhilarating time,
and a time that sealed my new connection with this land. Then summer slowly
faded into fall. With some friends who were also from elsewhere, I rented a small
cabin beside the ocean, west of Sooke. After having only experienced the giddy
days of summer, I found myself totally unprepared for the winter.

It wasn't long after we moved in that the sun motored downhill and the light
in the cabin started to go with it. Nights grew long while mornings and late afternoons were dim. The cabin was nestled in a thick growth of skinny Spruce
trees. There was no direct light, only what reflected in through the low, narrow
gap that was our ocean view.

Summer had been all about the rainforest. The moss, huge trees, epiphyte
ferns and more moss were all indicators of plentiful precipitation, clues along
with the name *rain*forest to what other seasons might be like. We were young
and naïve. It was a rude realization when the north Pacific lows started moving
in, hunching the shoulders of the spruces and pushing heavy waves onto the
shore. I found it hard to get up in the morning, and my city friends were busy
in Victoria. It was like wearing a lead hat.

Soon after our arrival, my health-conscious roommate got sick and stayed
that way for months. It was a local, Rusty Sage, who told us toxic moulds can

grow anywhere, and are especially bad when the west coast winter can make everything damp to the touch. Sure enough, we discovered a thick black layer of mould under my roommate's mattress. Rusty was a homeopath, dowser, and furniture-maker. Our frequent visits to his home due to my roommate's illness became a turning point in my notions of purposeful work, and my discovery of an artist's life.

On yet another rain-washed afternoon, we noticed a crow hopping awkwardly on Rusty's driveway, one wing jutting at an uncomfortable angle. It might have been hit by a car, or attacked by some predator. The wing was probably broken. I thought of leaving it. I'd never had luck trying to intervene in the lives of injured wild animals. But I happen to love crows. This one was easy to catch, and while my roommate pushed our bikes up the driveway I carefully carried it to the house.

Turning up with the injured crow was the key that opened a door to mutual interests in the natural world and became a reference point for the beginning of my long-time friendship and eventual apprenticeship with Rusty. The house had many examples of his partner Anne's watercolour paintings and Rusty's own furniture. There was something about these well-crafted pieces, an element that was different and new to me. My eyes sharpened to the warmth of wood and thoughtful lines, the individual expression that was craft. As the rain fell steadily outside I sat comfortably in a double rocking chair. The house gave off a subtle glow that was an antidote to the washed-out drabness of this west coast winter. I realized there was something gained and not lost from the surroundings.

In contrast, when Rusty first showed me his workshop I thought it very cluttered, sawdust everywhere, even in the cobwebs hanging from the ceiling. A badly tuned radio added noise, and all the surfaces in the place were coated with a fine dust. In a different setting so much dust would be a sign of inaction or neglect, but beneath these layers, the cast iron of the tools were polished from use. There was a sense of strength, focus, and production that told of self-motivation and direction. From this clutter and sawdust such beautiful objects came.

I share with Rusty an English working-class background. One of the things he acknowledges as a major influence that helped him break from the narrowness of class-based work and culture – a culture he saw as being centred on distraction – was the experience of visiting the Museum of Anthropology at the University of British Columbia in Vancouver, a place full of First Nations art and artefacts. He felt inspired by a culture in which life and art were not separated. The most ordinary of objects were beautifully decorated with designs that reflected a way of life directly connected to place. This contrasted with his own background, in which art was for the upper classes, divided and separated from life. Maybe art was something we had both lost. With form and function combined, thought Rusty, a person could make a utilitarian box or basic furniture beautiful. And that was how he wanted to live, with beautiful things around him at home, not having to go to a museum to visit them. He made me think about art in new ways, and like Rusty, I came to re-evaluate my life.

Where he lives and works is also an influence. How could it not be? The ocean winds bring eagles, hawks, ravens, storms, and sunsets. The respect Rusty feels for place is reflected in his home and garden. He and Anne let their yard grow wild in places, providing shelter for birds and animals, like families of quails displaced by the spread of housing developments recently impacting nearby ecosystems. In choosing to live in this location Rusty used intuition as a guide. In fact, while initially touring the house and garden to determine whether or not to make a home here he used a pendulum as an aid to his decision.

I felt Rusty's intuitiveness during my apprenticeship with him as I learned to appreciate the formation of *edge* in furniture. The line draws one's eye into the design and beauty of the wood. In shaping curved and straight edges, I was taught to use touch as an aid to sight. Fingertips are more sensitive than the eyes to the free flow of line. The end result brings subtle irregularities of the 'hand-made' and invites touch in return. There was always more than what I could see. Working with wood wasn't just techniques and math, but an attitude of thoughtful awareness of differing qualities of illumination in natural light; closing my eyes and letting touch lead; being aware of the changing weather and humidity; picking a sunny day to move wood into the workshop from one of the drying sheds. Even so, we'd still get caught off-guard by sudden squalls coming off the ocean, sending us running for half-finished pieces that were outside for sanding.

Most of all, Rusty taught me how to be absorbed. He would point out how forcefully, even frantically I worked, digging with the hand tools, fighting against flow instead of letting the tools work for me. The tense movements reminded me of my previous life as an industrial mechanic. Then I began to change how I used my body. In understanding wood, there is rhythm and glide, restrained effort, and patience to not finish something until it is ready. This practice not only raised my level of craft, it brought me to a new plane of bodily awareness, including knowing how previous jobs had impacted me physically and mentally.

Relaxing my muscles and experiencing work that was meaningful to me helped free the grip of the English class system's negative voices, and those ideas of what I could and couldn't do. The pessimistic outlook of work as a meaningless wage packet, your inescapable lot in life, not only divorces art from life, it also removes any creativity from work. I feel lucky in what I'm doing and realize that it is a privilege to work in craft.

While I still labour occasionally with Rusty, I have my own workshop now. Although my skills are always progressing, it still takes me a long time to finish a project. My accountant looked at my yearly income and quipped, "This is more of a lifestyle for you, isn't it!" Quite justified … but maybe not a *style*. I am drawn to work to the best of my abilities, exploring potentials in design and construction. This is not a process that comes fully formed out of a book or from plans.

Intuition and instinct are involved. A piece will often look quite different from its original design, and now I recognize that finished creations emerge from and reflect my entire life's experiences.

Most of the wood I work with is old growth lumber salvaged by a local miller. It is beautiful, tightly grained and stable, its rings like rice paper pages from some weighty volume full of memory. My appreciation and admiration are tinged with sadness for the reckless loss of the ancient forests which produce wood of this quality. Most of Vancouver Island's forests have been clearcut and shipped away as raw logs. We still see the barges in Juan du Fuca Strait from Rusty's workshop window, laden with trees never fully appreciated or valued.

I spent some months in the Walbran Valley that first Canadian year, living in the old growth rainforest under massive trees, amid anarchic wildness. We used blockades and tree-sits to slow and stop the road building and logging. Yet I would only come to fully see the significance of it all while driving back to civilization through the barren clearcuts and tree farms. To understand that something so precious is only a fragment of what has been lost and is still being lost deeply influences my work. It is a reality that is sharp like a blade. All parts of the creative process are crucial to me: the forest, the wood, the meaning of my labour. I don't mean some rhetoric of "honouring the tree," but letting both forest and tree influence me, to being more present with the material, its significance, and how I want to live my life differently from a culture that has devalued it.

WHO I AM, HERE
MARY ANN MOORE

I was raised in a valley in eastern Canada and now I overlook one in the west. Perched on the side of a stony hill in Nanaimo, the third-floor suite I share with my partner Sarah is a sort of tree house at the top of a terraced garden. Sitting at my writing table in front of the window, I can see the giant Douglas Firs behind the house. Three of them, along with an arbutus, become my daily spirit guides. I name them: *Arbutus, Constant, Stillness,* and *Serendipity.* They are the elders to my apprenticeship here on the east coast of Vancouver Island.

The arbutus, an evergreen without needles, is a wonder to this Ontario-born poet. It twists and turns to adapt to its habitat, even on a cliff at the ocean's edge where there is very little soil. The arbutus cleverly creates burls to store water so she can survive a drought. Cut a branch off and she will sprout a new limb. Wherever she grows, *Arbutus* is on the edge, reaching out, risking everything. *Constant,* one of many Douglas Firs, is bare on one side, and Arbutus leans toward her with small arms of protection. *Stillness* is partially hidden to me by other trees as I sit at the table but I can see she is very full with branches heavy with cones. The only tree that is swaying, *Stillness* is a memory prompt that invites me to contemplate her subtle movements, and she does it with whimsy, her curved top now waving to me in the breeze. *Serendipity* defines her own shape. Each of her branches takes its own skyward or earthward path. Her trunk is divided into two slender sections. While parts of her appear to be uniform, other details are completely unexpected, such as the base of her trunk – how it is thickly entwined with ivy.

This window is where I reflect. Write a poem. Even dream of sheep, in part because I believe my Irish ancestors may have been shepherds and because I think of Alberto Caeiro (one of Fernando Pessoa's heteronyms), who wrote "The Keeper of Sheep," and his words serve as a motto:

> I've no ambitions or desires
> My being a poet isn't an ambition
> It's my way of being alone.

My partner and I both work at home in close proximity to one another. I don't think that's why I also need a bedroom of my own, or maybe it is. Every morning when I wake up and look at the mercurial sky, I give thanks for my own room. This is where I write down my dreams, think about my writing projects, sit at the writing table in front of my window, and burn some sage. At night, I write in my journal, and read in bed as late as I want.

Is how I got here as important as what I am here? Will I change the names of things as my forebears did? At the end of May 2005, we moved across this country from Ontario, where I had lived all my life. Sarah had been thinking about the idea of land that knows you, where you feel alive and at home, as prompted by a book I had given her to read, *The Dance: Moving to the Rhythms of Your True Self* by Oriah Mountain Dreamer. We realized Guelph wasn't that place, and the writing circles I facilitated, ironically called *Flying Mermaids Writing Circles & Retreats,* took on a new direction. A mermaid, after all, can't be landlocked.

We imagined a moderate summer, a milder winter, a climate of new possibilities. We didn't retire from creativity; rather we became re-inspired with the help of a brand new muse. That muse is Vancouver Island surrounded by the Pacific. I had moved quite frequently in the past but always within a 200-mile radius of the family homestead near Eganville where my ancestors from Germany and Ireland had settled. Moving across the country meant a lot of letting go of my past.

Short story writer Alice Munro spends half the year on Vancouver Island and still returns for half the year to Clinton, Ontario. She apparently has said she feels an intimacy with the land there. While I feel heaviness and sentimentality about my Ontario roots, here I'm open to new possibilities beyond my imaginings. I feel excited, new, an apprentice, as if I have no history at all. Letting go of stuff, familiar routines, has created new space.

During the early months of settling in Nanaimo, it was as if I had downloaded everything I knew and remembered. There was nothing left to go into a poem. Could it be I had exhausted my subject matter, my life, and there was nothing more to say? "I" was only a possibility. I was like the fallow field, and this place was the farmer allowing the soil to rest for a season. That fallow field was a potent space. As I reflect back on it now, my state was one of acute awareness, the awareness that is a poet's condition. While the poet's state is about remembering, it is also about seeing up close, and listening to the heartbeat of who I am here. It's shining a light on each thing, each situation, so as to see it anew, to create an honouring ceremony out of an ordinary event.

The poems I wrote during the months following my move seemed to lack depth. I was empty, having let go of so much to clear the way for a new life. Even the book I had been writing, a memoir to encourage others to tell their stories, had been an outpouring that left me blank and depleted. I attempted to describe that blank state in a poem called "Arriving":

> I listen to the song emerging
> so new that fingers
> mouth the words, so new
> I don't know who I am.

Now I wonder if we ever really leave the traces of who we are behind. As I walk through the rainforest out to the rocky shore with its moss-covered cliffs at Neck Point in Nanaimo, I imagine this is what my great grandfather's homeland looked like, and in that moment I feel as though his Irish coast is part of me, as is this southeast coast of Vancouver Island. But the land on which I stand belonged to the Snuneymuxw, who have been here for 5000 years. Their winter village was Departure Bay, where ferries come and go. The Snuneymuxw still know their village as *Stlilup*. Further south are sites of other ancient villages, now the location of the demolished foundry and arena, as well as a hotel along the banks of the Millstone River. All serve as examples of more recent occupation that layers the land. The Snuneymuxw territory stretched from Departure Bay to Mount Benson, and from Cranberry Hill (the area we know as Cedar) to Neck Point Park, including Gabriola Island. Many people have learned First Nations traditions and adopted them as part of their spiritual practice. I have always been uncomfortable with that, as I know my ancestors have done enough appropriating of First Nations culture, or rather the annihilation of it. I walk cautiously, trying to remember my ancestors' ways.

For some time I have considered writing to be my spiritual practice. I had an evangelical upbringing while living with my grandparents during my early years, yet today my church is Cathedral Grove or Pirates Park on Protection Island where great blue herons sit on their nests of eggs high up in the trees along the shore. And right here at home, sitting at my writing table looking out to the garden and Mount Benson, above which eagles circle and soar, I am sustained by the solitude and the silence, the opportunity to listen to what's next. I acknowledge the tree guides outside my window, especially *Arbutus* who is so adaptable. Sometimes I feel I've become too comfortable and wonder how it is I will reach out, risking all. Sometimes I share my own writing practice with others by teaching writing courses and offering writing circles. I am kept buoyant by meeting writers at readings, retreats, and festivals. The writers drawn to Vancouver Island make up a startling array of talent. Some are not known, others are very well known, and all of them have been welcoming. I have found this to be especially gratifying and nourishing to my creative life. I'm also inspired by their daring example.

Poet and memoirist Wendy Morton organizes several poetry events across Canada, in Victoria and Sooke where master poet retreats take place. I've attended four times, working with Patrick Lane. I met poet and spoken-word artist Sheri-D Wilson at the Poetry Gabriola Festival and had the opportunity to participate in her workshop when she came to Nanaimo. She encouraged attendees to write about an epiphany each day and had us make a list of the things we planned to write about. One item on my list was "Why I won't get married even though lesbians are legal." When Richard Van Camp, a nationally acclaimed storyteller and a proud member of the Dogrib (Tlicho) Nation, asks, "What were you born knowing the world needs to remember?" the question resonates with me as I consider what service I have to offer the world through my writing. On my list is the importance of voice and community.

For example, Ivan E. Coyote's storytelling abilities come from the heart and are full of poignancy and humour. She tells stories of the everyday, her encounters with people, her family, her work in the world, and the challenges she faces as a person who doesn't fit into any gender box. I felt more acknowledged as a lesbian because of her stories about her lover or about identifying her life as queer in a primarily heterosexual world. When I say "acknowledged," it doesn't mean I hide myself and my relationship with my partner. We're very much part of the community in whatever we do. But it's rare to hear stories that reflect us and are inclusive of lesbian, gay and transgendered people. Take Tracy Myers of *Tongue & Groove*, a quartet that fuses jazz, funk, country, and Cuban rhythms with personal political texts. Tracy has been an inspiration to me. Her opinions are expressed with a lively beat, whether they are about Canadian politics, or issues affecting women. When I write, and when these artists write and perform, we are saying, "I want you to know *this* about me, and what is important to me." Together we shine a light on what would otherwise be left undercover. I wrote a poem some years ago, "I Want You To Know This About Me." It was written for readers and listeners with a future lover in mind:

I left a husband and children
for a life
I wanted to be better.
Please help me see that it is.
And please forgive me
for the times I miss the safety
of doing what is more common
and what is expected.

I gave up a lot of "safety" to be more like the off-the-beaten-path arbutus tree; a tree I didn't even know existed in 1983, the same year I left my marriage. The arbutus is symbolic to me on many levels. Nowadays, I choose to be part of a community that speaks out for those who have been silenced. Just the fact that the rainbow flag was raised above City Hall in Nanaimo for the very first time in 2009 is a sign that there is a gay community to be acknowledged and celebrated here.

All of the poets, writers and spoken-word artists I've mentioned are examples of those who deny silence in the world, all sorts of silences that matter to them. They are as inspiring to me as the ground full of ancient treasures, from the mossy rainforest to the arbutus reaching towards the untapped potential of the ocean. Christina Baldwin writes, "Personal writing is a private process that serves as the source of significant change in our journey. We proceed from the story into action." What could that action be for me?

* * * *

These days, the parts have caught up with me – the south-eastern Ontario story, my ancestors, the ancestors of the land on which I now stand, and the land itself. It all comes down to a great listening; me to the earth, the earth to me. I ask myself, what is my relationship to this sacred earth on this central portion of Vancouver Island? What can we create together? It's a sort of surrender and like the arbutus, the layers peeling to expose a brilliant skin underneath.

Releasing my hold to what was and what was never to be leaves me free, non-grasping, open to a vision of *here*. There is some residual disappointment about the work that didn't get published and work that was completed but nobody got to read, at least not yet. Still, I continue to write. Plants make their way into poems like the delicate fawn lily that blooms for only a few months in spring. One day I describe my lover as a fawn lily: . . . smelling of mystery, raw, fresh like the fawn lilies, soft, so soft, and open, awake and alive to wonder and touch, lips plush, tongue tentative and daring like the hummingbird, quick and small, quivering and red.

Here there are many messengers. The great heron becomes a teacher of presence and awareness. Names of sea slugs become characters in an imagined comic strip – Red Flabellina and Pearly Nudibranch. A tiny periwinkle snail that lives in the same square metre of beach for up to twenty-five years becomes my penultimate mindfulness teacher. Imagine how well it knows its square of land.

At my table, in my own room, I thank my guides: *Arbutus, Constant, Stillness,* and *Serendipity*; the sheep of my ancestors; and the poet Pessoa. Sappho, the poet of Lesvos, is beckoning again. As is the turkey vulture that sees the big picture, and the periwinkle snail that helps me see things up close, together bringing harmony with my earthly and spirit relations.

My roots are not here and that feels good to my mermaid, mercurial ways. I am exploring the tenuousness of living on the edge. I find projects need to be over soon enough to have the pleasure of sharing them. I could think of my long-term relationship with Ontario as a marriage I have now left. My new relationship is still with writing, and each project a sort of love affair. When I sit down to find out what's next, the story unfolds for me. It's about newcomers to the west coast and what they learn about themselves and how they become part of the landscape. When I enter silence to hear their stories, the characters are loud and bold, revealing themselves, because they have been silent for too long.

Notes and Acknowledgements:

Baldwin, Christina. *Lifelines: How Personal Writing Can Save Your Life.* Sounds True, 2004.

Oriah Mountain Dreamer. *The Dance: Moving to the Rhythms of Your True Self.* HarperCollins, 2001.

Pessoa. *Poems of Fernando Pessoa* Trans. Edwin Honig and Susan M. Brown. City Lights Books, 1998

"Arriving" was included in *Witch in White*, a chapbook of poems by the Glenairley poets edited by Patrick Lane (Leaf Press 2003).

"I Want You To Know This About Me" is included on *When My Heart is Open*, a CD of poems by Mary Ann Moore (self-produced 1999).

Information about the Snuneymuxw First Nation is from various articles in the *Nanaimo News Bulletin;* Curator David Hill-Turner at the Nanaimo District Museum; and Snuneymuxw Elder, Dr. Ellen Rice White.

THINGS THE CITY NEVER GAVE ME
BERNICE LEVER

This partial list of things the city never gave me includes raindrop rhythms on my wooden roof, muted music of wind dancing with lacy arms of cedar interrupted by chirping chickadees, dramatic cawing crows or honking geese over slap-splashing waves, and mysterious ferry horns booming through foggy evening light. Every day has artistic moments, from a ballet of small island deer stepping down rocky slopes to the silent wonders of humming-birds sucking up blossom nectar, and eagles gliding and circling against the mountain horizon before their lightning dives for prey. Everywhere the natural world astounds me. I would never have taken up such writing from my city home, yet on this island, the pace allows me to absorb my natural world. Simple moments like feuding grey and black squirrels make me smile as I study a gigan-tic web swaying in the breeze between trees.

Part of this appreciation is rooted in my walking. I walk everywhere here. Walking seems to be the first choice on Bowen, so opposite to the metaphors and symbols of my past city life: elevators clanking, TV (horror) news, subway screeching rails, taxi horns and ambulance sirens, all endless ear-grating noises. Instead I absorb sunrays, both morn and eve, that form golden ribbons a kilo-metre wide across Howe Sound; full moon nights that engulf the darkness with light; and the canopy of stars when the moon is away, constellations so clearly twinkling their shapes.

The growing smoggy haze over distant Vancouver reminds me to appreciate pure sea air. No more asthma from city fumes and particulates of many sources. I am snug in my wooden chalet. I know visitors find us "quaint" in jean shorts and fleece or jogging suits with hiking boots, but in fact many Bowen Islanders are artists with international fame who enjoy different lives here. We get our share of art, dance, music, video, and literary readings with our neighbours be-fore they begin their continental tours. Over the decades, a long Bowen list notes many famous permanent and summer residents, but it is the personal interac-tions that matter. A "Hello!" at the post office shared with a well-known writer, a returned smile in the general store from an international singer, a wave by the gallery from a great painter. This makes Bowen special.

My Bowen Island is a place of healing and inspiration, of learning and friendship. It is where I chose to retire. It happened by chance, as such moments in life can, when I was invited to rent a place while the owner was away. Little did I know when Jan handed me a key and a scrawled map to Bowen Bay, adding, "Just a handshake, and pay me when I return in August," that I would stay on. After a few months, I was hooked on Bowen life.

Jan, who writes verse tributes for all special occasions for those involved in his many activities, was feted for his ninety-fifth birthday with a community celebration that overflowed our local Legion Hall. Many tributes from Norway to Bowen were given, including a special stick slapping song by our Black Sheep Morris Dancers, a solo performance by a local singer and writer, and the gift of a ceremonial First Nations robe. A sturdy, fun loving Norseman and chronicler of sagas, Jan is a Bowen Island inspiration to *all* for living fully. His motto is a Danish saying, "Live while you have love, and love while you have life."

And it is these friendships with all sorts of Bowen's creative folk that have sustained me through literary rejections (which are always more plentiful than editorial acceptances) as well as family turmoil and more. I couldn't have written *Fat Rain* anywhere but here.

FAT RAIN
Sometimes the winter rain
slips straight down creating
plump orbs that cling
to bare bark until
our apple orchard
has diamonds adorning
every stiff branch.

Tiny nuthatches hide under
thick cedar hedges avoiding
these silent water bombs
that so delight us, ever
keeping dry inside, amused
by these gentle syllables on
our wooden eaves from fat rain.

Bowen continues to feed me poetic food from all directions and on all levels. Living in this community will sustain me in grace as I continue to write more poems from my days of peaceful reflection and caring Bowen interactions in a marvellous blend of people and nature.

THE BOOGEYMAN, FIRST COMPOSITION, THE SPELLING QUIZ, AND THE PLAGIARIST

KEITH HARRISON

An open letter to readers:

To connect up and flesh out what I can recall about being three or four years old up the far west coast might be easier on the reader but harder on the truth. To fill in, amplify, and link up these fragments of my remembered self might offer a more pleasing shape of telling but would feel too neat.

I was struck by how the TV footage the first few days after 9/11 was in difficult-to-follow bits and pieces. Coming mostly from street-level videotaping, these finite accounts by dazed, nameless amateurs conveyed how multiple lives were disrupted beyond understanding. These personal and incomplete versions of what happened – was still happening – overlapped, conflicted, and faltered. This media presentation of unfiltered, nearly random interviews of people, who lacked well-modulated voices and telegenic faces while relating private moments and obscure incidents, created something so chaotic it felt truthful. Then a network began to run a printed message on-screen: "Attack on America." Immediately, all the un-varnished, unfinished individual stories of loss and hope and disbelief and half-comprehending anguish were resolved by the self-assured anchorman, bending the diverse material into one simple meta-narrative. That overarching political statement encapsulated or discarded the many different truths people had experienced, and signalled that regular programming (and advertising) would soon resume.

That earlier reporting via fragments is vaguely similar to what is attempted here: to try to catch the disorganized and shocked aliveness of childhood. With this piece about Port McNeill, I wanted to give presence to the felt newness of the past, its startling disconnections–along with a sense of what can't be retrieved, of what has been lost even to memory.

Through making this life sketch, I've learned something. It seems that my novels have been an unconscious search for how to combine the two languages I heard as a kid: the "literary," educated, proper one that my parents spoke and the "bad," direct, sometimes brutal one that the loggers mostly used. The words of my fiction form a hybrid of these two opposed kinds of English, both of which are needed, I feel, to shape fully the imaginative truths about being human. Style, for me, hasn't been chosen but imposed, by the lottery of autobiography and geography.

Cheers,
Keith

* * *

Alurch of sudden air. On the float-plane from Vancouver, coming down to Alert Bay. A kid of two or three telling Mom I'm going to be sick. The pilot slides open a panel in the floor. That's how I remember this. The water: clear as glass, and getting closer and closer. My mom holds my arm very tight while I lean out over the square hole of ocean. I am too scared to puke, too terrified I'm going to fall right into that deep shine.

The plane hits the hard wetness and zips through the spray. Cormorant Island just ahead. At the dock we get out and stand on a fat pontoon that is rocking. "Do you want to be sick?" Not really. But a thin trickle from inside thrown out into the air floats slowly through the clean water.

* * *

On northern Vancouver Island, near the logging camp at Port McNeill, a kid of three or four, riding in the back seat on a road that keeps curving. Out of no-where – except boulders and trees and a sky that isn't raining – I announce, "There's a boogeyman around the next corner."

As we come around the bend, there in a clearing is a black bear. Down on all fours, not huge, but big, with real fangs and claws. It turns its head to look at us as our car slows. Laughter from my Dad and Mom, and we drive on. My brother and kid sister silent, stunned even more than me. I'm stuck to the seat but float-ing. Bathed in a weird heat.

Three or four more twists in the road that could have been dirt or gravel or a primitive pavement before I test out my new power: "There's a boogeyman around the next corner." The whole car goes very quiet. My chest tight while everyone leans forward. Twisting their heads to see … bushes, grasses, grey rocks, the dark forest, and and and … only things that don't move. My brother laughs. I feel naked and shrively, like someone drained the tub.

Wanting that sudden chill off my skin, a few minutes later, my voice pale and skinny, I try again. No one hunches forward to see what's waiting. Nothing. My brother Doug razzes me. Then he starts to give me advice, about which kind of cor-ner is best for boogeyman predictions. I'm grateful my parents don't call me a phoney.

At the next bend, Joan screeches, "There's a boogeyman around ..." Like I invented some kind of game she could play too. (Was secretly happy when no bear answers her voice.) Why didn't I quit while I was ahead?

* * *

Drawing on slidey paper with waxy colours down on the wooden floor, inside of a rainy day. Copying the shapes of letters. Not even trying to write out words. Somehow I know how to spell my brother's name, making the letters I saw in books and from sounds heard in my head that came from loggers.

It is late afternoon when Dad comes in from work, just as I finish. His heavy white-grey coat above me. Something bad. I feel trapped by the page in front of me.

Will he spank me? He leans down, picks up the piece of paper which reads: DOUG IS A SHIT.

Dad turns away, his mouth open strangely, hiding a grin.

* * *

There is a chopped-down wilderness right outside the two rows of shacks. Bears in the early morning show up in the backyard gardens. A bit scary even to cross alone over the one road to visit a friend (Brian?). Maybe he's six years old. He loads brown sugar – five, six, seven spoonfuls – onto his bowl of cereal. Doesn't he care if his teeth fall out? After breakfast, he goes out of the kitchen, smiling, and returns with his Dad's gun.

The two of us walk out the back door. I stand right beside him as he fires the rifle at a tin can on a stump. The noise fills and empties my ears (and comes again). Never heard that loudness before. I pretend I have to go home right now. I don't show I am scared to death.

* * *

Running and running with Doug everywhere. The fields, the planked pier, down on the crunchy beach, up at the playground. The only time I'm hurt I'm up in the air. On a teeter-totter, when a bigger kid jumps off. My jaw-bone bangs on the iron handle. My face slippery with blood. The Doc sticks the split skin back together with thick adhesive tape. Mom worries it will scar. (It does.) I'm distracted by the strong smell of disinfectant, that's like and not like the sea.

Mom was horrified for days after they accidentally shut a large rat inside my sister's bedroom. Joan, only two, slept through the night, unhurt.

* * *

A float-plane takes us down the coast, out of the wilderness, away from bears, noisy heavy machines, and the ocean's edge. Kindergarten in westside Vancouver, then grade one at Trafalgar School. Concrete pathways, neatly mown grass, and high walls out of shaped stone.

Miss Swanson hands back our spelling test. Pausing by my desk, she says, "Don't try to be funny." What does she mean? I glance down at the list of twenty-five words printed in pencil, each on its own line. I notice she has circled an answer. I misspelled "ship" as "shit." I would never have the nerve to do this on purpose. I knew nothing of Freud back then. I am confused about how this bad word popped into this proper place, out of nowhere. Shame (or child-like cunning) keeps me from speaking. But I notice I have been given a perfect score. She thought I was joking. I was rewarded for a mistake, so humour is a kind of success.

I hand my grade one report card over to my parents. They study its letters: 'O' and 'N' and 'U.' For that whole year, in almost every subject I receive 'N' for normal. But in all three behaviour categories, I always get a 'U,' unsatisfactory. The only 'O' is for art: outstanding. By grade two, I have learned to be dull (or was I just pretending?). In both behaviour and art, my designation is now 'normal.'

But this is the year I write my first book. Four pages long. Sitting at the oval kitchen table banded in half-shiny metal, its hard surface flecked with dusty stars. My story tells of a panda, who is a cowboy called Curly, who wears a red bandana, who catches rustlers. Pictorially, there is no evidence of curliness. His solid, straight-furred form comes from a weighty chunk of panda-shaped metal painted black and white that sits up and looks me in the eye. This kind of bear doesn't live up the coast on Vancouver Island. This bear eats bamboo shoots, not flesh, like mine. The plot line of his story copied from a cowboy comic book. The panda's speeches lifted out of the dialogue balloons. The picture boxes that I form and fill float together and apart. Like the waves of the Pacific. Mom says it should be published. But I didn't make it up (I almost say) except for changing a cowboy into a gentle bear with a six-gun.

* * *

This telling over again now in fragments is like that small comic book. How else to piece together the early life of a novelist finding usable bits of language? It would be untrue to smooth everything out into a continuous, well-creased narrative unfolding.

At Port McNeill, I felt a raw emptiness beyond the reach of culture. Dead trees in the constant logging trucks, keeping everyone there. Yet along with the stench of a beached whale, dead and rolling on pebbles in the tide, there were words. And two parents who cared about them (and us). Doug now a law partner; Joan, a nurse heading up a mental health team.

Outside, alive in that salt sea air back then, there was another language that hid itself in curses and jokes and bare naming and loud laughter. Breaking again and again, slapping like the waves against the wooden pilings of the wharf, telling of distant truths.

THESE WORDS, THIS FARM, MY HEART: A JOURNEY OF LOVING INQUIRY

AHAVA SHIRA

Life Work

I write these words under the shade of an umbrella, while the gardener, my friend and mentor, wields a chainsaw to clean up the remains of a downed tree. He has been nurturing and sustaining this land for over eight years, longer than any of us who live here now. He is teaching us how to care for the land. Gardening is the work of his life. Writing is the work of mine. I have been writing longer than I have been living on this farm.

Here on Butterstone Farm on Salt Spring Island, I live within a silence that is also full of call(ing)s and responses, and move inside a stillness punctuated by seasons of storms and feasts and lazy summer afternoons. Settled amongst family and community, I work amidst myriad other living beings: robins with their rituals of forage and maple buds' slow but steady unfolding, interconnecting through an intimacy of geography, biology and (auto)biography.

On Butterstone Farm I express feelings of love and connection through listening, watching, walking, even drinking water from our well that's fed by Lake Maxwell. Here I live with intention toward kindness, softness, healing, peace. Here I marvel at the diverse melodies of the Cranberry Valley: birdsong, windsong, frogsong, chainsaw song, passing truck song.

Here I catch light from words as from the sun, and a sky full of clouds, like a page of poems, emits its own brightness. Here I revel in the innumerable shades of green, new growth and old growth, seed growth and weed growth, your growth and my growth. Here as I attend to each moment, become familiar with the cycles of the land and its inhabitants, I come to understand the Buddha's teaching on impermanence, how everything is on its way to becoming something else.

Weaving of my Being

In the grated mud and ice, between banks of trees emptying of snow, I poke in on the house going up in the lot at the end of our big field. So many days at home writing, sitting on various chairs and couches, peering at the screen, with only in between peeks at the trees through the loft's south, east, or west windows, I need to venture out and remember myself to the landscape.

As I walk I ask myself questions about publishing. Why I feel so divorced from it, and why for most of twenty years I chose to "just write" rather than deal with the rigmarole of sending poems and essays out for publishing. Just now I get the idea to write a novel about a girl who does the same. I can explore why, and take up this position wholeheartedly without thinking I have been doing something wrong.

In the fall of 1998, I self-published my first book of poetry, *Womb: Weaving of My Being*, with my own Butterfly Press. Having moved out to the west coast six years earlier, I experienced the ocean and mountains and vast sky and rich green forest like a womb surrounding me. Within this inspiring landscape, I began to write the poems that fill my first book with stories of childhood wounds and their post-traumatic effects, as well as stories of the empowerment I found in nature and feminine spirituality. I wrote poems that lifted me out of the role of victim, acknowledging how my personal experiences of violence were not isolated incidents but part of the social issue of women's oppression and its roots in male-dominated society. I loved having my own book of poems. It opened many doors for me to perform and to teach. However, I never felt legitimate and would often criticize myself for not having been published by a "real" publisher. Still I mostly ignored the tasks involved in having my poems published by others. I chose performance as my way of sharing, preferring the immediate connection with an audience, the intimacy and sensual pleasure of reciting poems, and being able to embody a poem's emotions through facial expressions and physical gestures.

As I have been working on my doctorate over the past two years I have been encouraged to publish, and several poetic essays and poems of mine now appear in academic journals. Although I cherish reading others' poems, as well as articles, novels, and non-fiction essays, I somehow still feel uncomfortable considering my own work in print. But as I like staying at home on the farm, I must publish in order to share my work.

Here my words curve through mystery and mastery, toward story and poetry. Here I listen to how they all sound together, the way some words whisper beside each other while others scream into each other's ears.

Story Sisters

I am beginning a new writerly journey with two women. We come together to tell stories and play in the body with movement and voice. I was inspired by *Performing the World*, a conference I attended in New York City, which focused on the connection between the performing arts and social change. There I encountered many people from around the world whose work bridged the disciplines of performance, education, politics, creativity, and therapy. I returned to Salt Spring with a desire to keep alive the joy that I had experienced at the conference. When I put a call out to the community by email, two women responded. We still don't have an official name, but the other day I called us *Story Sisters*. Initially we thought we'd write our stories on our own, come together once a month, and read them to each other, but instead, we decided to improvise. I had done it before, performing improvised stories on stage for an audience, but never for such an intimate group.

Since then we have all taken to improvising. The results can be deeply moving. We learn so much about stories and how they can be told, and how the story doesn't exist in that particular form until we tell it that way. We are the weavers. We pull details from our lives. We put them together to tell a story that feels whole and meaningful. The process is about listening, trusting, and going with the flow.

The feedback we offer each other helps us to reflect on pace, especially appealing details, most intriguing events, or characters. These are our life stories, yet the stories move from personal anecdotes into collective visions and meanings. The themes deepen and resonate as we move around the circle from one story to the next. We are continually astounded by the intimacy the group offers, and by what we learn about each other and about ourselves. I feel excited about what we bring to the group, ideas we have gathered from our spontaneous explorations and from our understandings of the creative process as women who write with an awareness of the cycles of island life.

And this is where it all begins, the hands dance across the keyboard, mind disappears, love enters through the cracks in conscious doing. All is quiet and sharp and present. I come here to retreat, release, revisit old stories, glory in the telling of new ones, diving into words, language and lessons on the stony path of journeys between these words, this farm, my heart.

FROM TORONTO TO BULL HARBOUR
LIBBIE MORIN

Many years ago, at the grown-up age of nineteen, I got married. Three years later my husband announced that we were being "transferred," baby, two cats, and all to his first job posting as a Marine-Air Operator at Bull Harbour, Hope Island, a tiny dot of untamed land that lay like a comma off the north tip of Vancouver Island.

"You'll LOVE it sweetie. No noise, no traffic! Nature in all of its glory!" he continued, sensing a chink in my city armour. I gave him my by now infamous 'chicken eye,' the slight narrowing of one lid with accompanying opposite eyebrow lift.

"I'll be getting isolation pay and they fly us outta there once a year . . . FREE!" His confidence proved infectious.

The deep drone of the De Havilland engine prevented any conversation throughout our maiden flight from Vancouver. It was during this interlude that my imagination took the helm. As we flew towards Hope Island that first day, I conjured visions of a brave and hardy pioneer settlement: a tiny village infused with camaraderie; maybe even a community garden to offset the canned staples. As we unloaded our few and precious things onto the government wharf, I shared this vision of a new life with my dear husband.

"Oh, didn't I tell you?" he mumbled, head bent, as we walked from the dock towards our home for the next two years, "there are only eight other adults on the station."

My head jerked hard.

It was mid-afternoon by the time I stopped the hustle of unpacking and gave myself the comfort of a coffee. The grey Arborite table seemed to snuggle under the large window and it was here that I sat and gazed out over the harbour. It was a view that most of us only see in high-end travel magazines. The building itself was a shiplap constructed, two-storey, pine, cedar, teak, and brass beauty of a home. It sat on a naturally built-up sandbar that connected the two sections of the island. Hope Island boasted an intimate harbour deep enough to welcome freighter boats and grey whales alike. The rainforest that ringed this refuge was ancient and undisturbed. The channel outside the mouth of the inlet held promise only, for it was far too wide and the currents too powerful to allow any exploration by the station's one and only small boat. On the opposite side of the house, looking out through our bedroom's multi-paned wooden windows, and just over a berm of fallen cedars and dense salal, ranged an unlimited expanse of Pacific Ocean, and the next stop, Japan.

But while we weren't totally alone, we were isolated. The meaning of isolated was beginning to subtly make its presence felt in a brand new way. It took me a couple of months to stop looking both ways before I crossed the one and only gravel road, which supported the one and only ol' beater on the island. I learned that you have to gut a salmon before you freeze it, whole, and not in a bag of water. I learned how to spike white bread with vodka in order to get the crows to shut-up. I learned to burn my garbage using gasoline as starter fluid without singeing off all of my eyebrows. I came to know when, during a soft dewy morning, the colony of resident eagles would be at the water processing plant and how to walk quietly next to them on newly found silent feet. Soon after, those same soles learned to walk bare on pebbles and to almost levitate on top of limpet-encrusted rocks, to test for slick bladder wrack and semi-sink through mucky tidal shorelines without care or worry. In fact, those first few months slipped away in these newfound experiences. It felt as if I had just unpacked the last of the moving boxes when summer surprised me with autumn. I survived my first season in this alien land.

My old cares began to fall by the wayside. My fear-driven survival skills born of the city went through a metamorphosis. Courage was seduced by curiosity. I found myself seeking out movement in the bushes, for now I hoped to be re-warded with a glimpse of feather or fur, busy with purpose. Animals alive, not frozen or abstract like on the pages from Reader's Digest or Canadian National Geographic. My vision began to offer shape shifters, like the tip of the deadhead in the water that revealed a seal, whiskers and all. The air became a signal to me that the tides were moving in and out, the trail of salt, sweet grass, mud, and decay lingering. All that my new instincts had been waiting for was trust. I lived outside more than in, no longer at the mercy of that downtown city blueprint. The fears fell away, that is, until my first genuine west coast storm.

I remember how that November day crept up on us. Somehow, the soft grey daylight made the wind less troublesome. It was at nightfall that the storm really started to make its presence felt. Our child was long asleep, safe in that place where newborns go, the house was swept and cleaned, dimmed and tucked in for the night, and my husband had gone to work for the evening shift. At first the night enveloped the island with a deeper black-grey. Then the knocking at my refuge with fists full of wind, rain on the sky's breath, a one-two punch to the walls: one to the window, another to the porch and one-two-three to the windows again; a couple of punches down the chimney for good measure. The tempest had not only arrived, it was trying to move in. I did not know which way to turn my llama-like ears. This was a new experience. How dare it just sock in, unannounced, like an uncouth uncle?

I must have had my 'city-glasses' on that day, because I never saw it coming. I didn't know that wind could increase its velocity from thirty-nine to sixty-four miles per hour, change direction from vertical to horizontal, and pick up a 300% increase in water volume all at the same time. This trick allowed my uninvited guest to crawl under the kitchen windowsill, where it gurgled and babbled along the sash, crying to get in while the wind whined and sang along in crescendo. On top of the sounds and sensations was the added layer of the storm's colour, or more precisely, the lack of it. I needed to understand this new type of black. The weeping windowpanes denied me any view so I ventured to the back door and gripped the brass knob with both hands. I wedged my toe gently against the bottom of the door for additional insurance, and proceeded to open Pandora's Box.

The door did not open as one would normally think of 'open'. It was more of a convulsive billowing synchronized to some crazy Whirling Dervish dance. And the sky was blacker than I can describe. The wind exhaled a tremendous symphony of rumble-and-whine. The very ether of the storm seemed to whisper, "*This is what the end of the world looks like!*" I did not need or want to see more. I shouldered the all-too-thin door shut and threw the latch. I thought of my husband's safety and was reassured in remembering that his office was housed in a no-nonsense bunker from the last war. He would be okay as long as he stayed inside.

Yeah, I've heard it before, "pansy city pants". But I knew something about the original radio station on Triangle Island, the one off of the western tip of Vancouver Island, the one *before* Bull Harbour. Both the station and the operator's residence were guy-wired down in many places. They both blew down, twice. So, short of having a few hundred metres of heavy gauge metal rope and some serious cement anchors, there was sweet bugger-all I could do except daydream about subways and basement diners and tall brick and mortar buildings that would serve as windbreakers if only I were among them now.

It was a long night. I just kept breathing and bracing. I was still awake when my husband eventually 'blew' home in the wee hours of the morning, grinning and none the worse for wear. And, you know what, those storms, well, they invited themselves back again, still unannounced, but at least I knew what to expect. I repeated the breathing exercises until I could fall asleep and stay there without worrying about our home turning into a pile of toothpicks.

The season moved forward and I added the category of 'winter' to my lesson roster. I learned that my large yellow umbrella would not stay right-side-in, no matter how many expletives I threw at its underbelly. I learned that my husband really didn't need hot food taken up to him in the dark, in the rain, and he loved me still. I learned that one should be careful and respectful of the unknown,without fear.

The moment finally came when I was sitting on the beach during a storm. No thoughts, no fear, just being alone. And I let go. Truthfully, it was more like being pulled out of my skin. I allowed it. I got it. I was safe, no matter what. It was hard to look Beauty full in the face, yet somewhere, between the rigid definitions of the city and the testing squall and the love of my husband and the beauty of Earth and solitude, somehow within those sixty seconds, I got it.

Soon after that my hubby became my confidant to the stories that had been hiding inside. Words no longer apologized to me for their inadequacy, but demanded their birthright. I came to appreciate the fact that our move to this place was a precious gift and I learned what was important: to thank him. As it turned out, he had trusted in my courage, even when I did not. On the other side of fear was the gift. I had come home to be myself, and it is not often that someone hands you the key to paradise.

THE FINE ART OF TAKING ONE'S TIME
JOHANNA VANDERPOL

It is January 19th and I am sitting outside in the sun, wrapped in my house-coat. As I write in my journal, Cowichan Bay is a stone's throw away. The sky is a perfect hue of blue. Now a heron circles and lands on a rock nearby. I anticipate the smell of salt in the air as the tide shifts. The water is calm and the sun creates a dazzling sheen on the surface. I feel its intense heat on my right cheek and forehead as honking swans glide into the cove. Ravens are croaking in the distance, somewhere up the mountain. A breeze passes and reminds me of my son. His name is Naseem, "gentle breeze" in Arabic. And he has grown into his name nicely, a gentle soul on the cusp of becoming an adult.

Where else in Canada can I sit outdoors in my housecoat, in the middle of January? Yes, I am grateful.

On the other side of the cove lies sleepy Cowichan Bay village, gently held by a light mist. It is Monday and the bakery, cheese shop, and fish store are closed. The quiet is soothing to me. Even though I have lived in this area for more than three years now, my body still remembers living in Peterborough, Ontario, and the hectic pace of an accountant's life. In leaving that life, my purpose was to find what I perceived to be a creative culture, where I could develop the artist I felt deep down inside. We sold everything we owned. I ended my thirty-year career in accounting, said goodbye to the city in which I was raised, and travelled 4,600 kilometres west.

My first time in the village of Cowichan Bay, I saw a sign on a door of the local cafe that read: "Mellowside Café: The Fine Art of Taking One's Time." I will never forget the feeling I had upon entering there. Time stood still and creativity took over. This was a departure from the mainstream where taking time is not the norm. I remember thinking: *I have arrived*. It was the door sign, in fact, that allowed me to manifest my intention to live a more bohemian lifestyle, honour-ing my pace while still being productive. I have since developed my creativity as a writer, author, and speaker, and deepened my practice and teachings on how to live a flourishing life of authentic happiness. This is now my favourite spot to have a coffee and work on a writing project by day and enjoy many a fine jazz musician by night.

I came to Vancouver Island to meet my soul, to write, to publish my first book, and to find my 'tribe' in a community of like-minded individuals. For the first two years, I kept saying to myself, hardly able to absorb the truth: "I live here? I live here!" Now I was part of a place where I saw beauty every day, outside my window, on the way to the grocery store, or on one of many hikes within just twenty minutes of my home. Whether I need clarity, a break, exercise, or "just because," I wander to viewpoints where I can see the Gulf Islands, Sidney, even Mount Baker. This walking affords an altered state of mind that is conducive to creative projects percolating in me.

But the view is not the only way the west coast has helped me successfully move through my challenges. From the moment of my arrival, I felt supported by people at every turn, to be as I am, to relax, and to settle into the deeper well of my writer-self waiting to be born. Little by little, I had the time, encouragement, and permission to see what was there to be mined and brought to the surface through expression. In my training as a life coach, I have learned that the environment always wins. The coast has offered a winning environment, where I can be more of who I am.

On the other hand, Vancouver Island has challenged me with months and months of rain, weeks of grey skies, and cold marine air. It has challenged me, while hiking the Juan de Fuca Trail, with a shattered elbow. It has confronted me through intimate relationships, and has shown me that I carry my old internal patterns wherever I go. Place could not change that. The first time the word 'sin' had any kind of real meaning for me was the day I saw beauty here without feeling it. I was disconnected and removed. This felt like a sin, to be seeing what is sacred while somehow being unable to absorb it. When my inner landscape is at odds with this place, I turn to the special energy here that allows me to sink into the core of my being, with sensations of groundedness and inner strength. When I climb Mount Tzouhalem, I receive comfort and clarity in the bigger picture. And, along with the support of others and the love of my son, I am able to choose different, perhaps higher thoughts. The island nourishes my soul in many ways that I believe allow me to contribute my greatest good to other people. What could be better?

MOUNTAIN, SKY AND SEA: THE ART OF GAZING AND IMAGINING

BILL ZUK

There are many places of great natural beauty on British Columbia's west coast which offer peace, quiet, and solitude, where you can gaze, reflect, and imagine away from the maddening crowd and the fast pace of life. You do not have to travel long distances along the coast to be captivated by the majesty of towering mountains, the timeless quality of ocean waters, or the exotic magic of stars and galaxies – readily accessible even in urban areas. As an artist, this is what makes Vancouver Island, and Victoria in particular, special for me. I am drawn to the ring of vistas offered by the mountains where I live. Their ancient origins, massive stature, and spiritual presence are profound and form an integral part of my artwork. The story of their connection to 'gazing'– which involves scanning in a meditative state of awe and wonder – and 'imagining' – that includes fanciful thinking – begins in my own back yard.

Mountains in Our Midst

My wife and I live on a lower slope of Mount Tolmie where geological history indicates periods of glaciation 15,000 years ago, and a subsequent period 8,000 years ago when glacial sediments were transformed into a hospitable environment for plants, animals, and people (Mount Tolmie Conservancy Association, 1996). The Salish peoples called this mountain Pkaals. They harvested the oak meadow plants for medicine and food, like the tuberous Camus lily bulb, a favourite vegetable dish.

Now this mass of craggy, moss-covered substratum fills our front yard, spreading into a corner of our basement. Young children who visit are always amazed when we tell them we have a mountain living in our basement. They love clambering and perching on the outcropping, which runs from floor to near-ceiling height. Over the years, we have become accustomed to sharing our home with Mount Tolmie, and Tolmie has become the subject of a series of my sketchbooks (Zuk, 2009), as many other Vancouver Island mountains have become subjects of my art.

Peak Beauty

The most spectacular features of Mount Tolmie are its summit and views. Some might say Tolmie is really an overgrown hill, at a height of 120 metres above sea level. Though its height is more modest than some, a short hike to the top along any one of several winding paths takes me to another world, as I noted in my sketchbook:

> At the top, I find myself sitting on a bumpy, glaciated ridge with deep scratches and crevices. I can imagine the torrential slurry of ice, boulders, and gravel that scoured and abraded the rock mass during the glacial epoch. In the distance, the Sooke Hills are covered in mist while Mount Olympus, home of the gods, is shrouded in cloud and barely visible on the Washington Peninsula. To the southeast, Mount Baker pushes its white cap into a porous powder of baby blue.

This is the first step of a gazing experience. It begins by attuning yourself to nature, by entering into a state of calm and tranquillity, and by developing an intimate connection with the natural surroundings (Dalton, 2009).

Malahat Mist, digital print (See page 141 Colour Insert)

Malahat Mist is a digital print that records a scene of gentle light filtering through mountains, hills and trees. The impact of the scene stirred my imagination and led to a short alliterative poem entitled *Malahat Mountain Mist:*

Mountains rise and fall
Like gentle beings
In soft silk mist.
Valleys dip
And melt
And merge
In far-off fog.
Only a
Slender
Silvery
Spar
Rises
From the
Milky mist

This photograph reminds me of an essay by Rudolf Steiner who suggests that we are "equipped with two sets of sensory perception – one physical and capable of perceiving objects in the material world, the other spiritual and capable of sensing the spirit" (Regier, 1987, p.58). Perceiving and sensing the physical and spiritual stirs my imagination and inspires my art making. I continue to be drawn by the allure of the physical character and charm of Mount Tolmie with its gentle slopes, small open meadows, and tangled Garry Oaks. I also sense its life force and celestial presence as it rises to touch the sky.

Life Force aims to encapsulate the intrinsic beauty of Tolmie by reducing and distilling it to pure, geometrical forms with triangles featured prominently in this shifting, faceted composition. I created *Life Force* with the idea of working towards the essence of artistic simplicity in an effort to move closer to a purification of thinking processes (Pohribny, 1979). Because triangles call to mind images of pyramids, one of the most enduring architectural wonders of the world, the comparison to mountains is, in some ways, ideal. In ancient Egypt, pyramids were thought to embody the Sun God Re who rose from the primeval mound to create life. The pyramid epitomizes glory, energy, and might. Mount Tolmie has those enduring qualities for me, and like a pyramid, Tolmie remains solid, withstanding tremors and quakes caused by shifting movements of subduction plates far below the earth's surface in Georgia Strait.

Life Force, print, artist proof (See page 141 Colour Insert)

Cosmic Splendor

I turn to another of my sketchbook accounts of Tolmie:

> I rise slowly to my feet on the highest point of rock to experience the
> fullness of the landscape. It forms a series of concentric circles with hills

and mountains looming in the outermost ring and a moat of dark blue water lying within. Closer, a scattering of city dwellings form a dotted mosaic that blends into the forest growth. Finally, the skirt of Tolmie spreads like a protective shield with rocky bluffs, sprawling trees, and open meadows.

This great expanse harkens to the words of Black Elk, a revered Medicine Man of the Lakota people:

> *Everything the Power of the World does is done in a circle. The Sky is round and I have heard that the Earth is round like a ball and so are all the Stars. The Wind, in its greatest power whirls. Birds make their nests in circles, for theirs is the same religion as ours. The Sun comes forth and goes down again in a circle. The Moon does the same and both are round. Even the seasons form a great circle in their changing and always come again to where they were. The life of a person is a circle from childhood and so it is with everything where power moves.*
>
> From *Black Elk Speaks*

Ursa Spirit draws upon multiple levels of meaning associated with cosmic consciousness and explores hidden meanings in art (Tuchman, 1986). *Ursa Spirit* is a tribute to mountains: the chevron shape with its purple-green magma pushing up from the base; the stars and galaxies whirling in concentric circles; spirit bears travelling in a circular path among the stars. The spirit bear, or Kermode, has special significance in the far west coast. Aboriginal nations honour and respect the white bear, especially the Kwakiutl and Tsimshian. Its Tsimshian name, Mosqm'ol, is found in numerous stories. One of the stories speaks of Raven who travelled among the black bears, promising every tenth bear cub would be born white to remind us of a time when the world was clean, pure, and covered with snow and ice blue glaciers (Tessier, 2000).

Biologists tell us that the spirit bear is a species of black bear indigenous to the rainforest areas of British Columbia from Princess Royal Island to Prince Rupert and inland to Hazelton. This bear has a genetic anomaly that results in a white or creamy coloured coat, a characteristic found in only ten percent of the black bear population. The provincial government has declared the spirit bear the official animal of the province. My artwork celebrates the unique qualities of this bear in relation to the 2009 United Nations Year of Astronomy, a global effort to inspire a sense of awe and wonder in the universe.

Ursa Spirit, print (See page 142 Colour Insert)

Sky to Sea

Contemplating the sky and sea reminds me of two modalities of visualization (Gawain, 2002). One is a receptive mode which involves relaxing and allowing impressions or images to enter our consciousness without choosing details. I prefer to call this mode 'gazing'. The other is a more active mode where we consciously choose and create what we wish to see or imagine. A sketchbook account looking down to the sea from the heights of Mount Tolmie is reminiscent of the two modalities:

> Cargo ships come and go down the stormy straits of Juan de Fuca and the Gulf of Georgia. I gaze at the silvery waters and through my binoculars spot a container ship with a long, black, sleek hull and burnt orange

top deck outlined in the dim light of the late afternoon sun. It cruises slowly past a small red-capped lighthouse on one of the scattered islands and then reappears to pursue its tedious journey through whitecaps and choppy seas.

Sky to Sea Sketches

Sky to Sea records some of my impressions of Mount Tolmie in several thumbnail sketches from tiny close-up rock and tree scenes with boulders, treelines, and rhythmic rock patterns, to imagined connections between landscapes and ocean vessels. A ship teeming with scenery appears in the lowermost sketch. Every space from bow to stern is filled with the landscape of Mount Tolmie, even the aerial pole, which contains an angled tree. The notion of Canada as an exporter of raw material does not escape me, nor does the slogan "Super, Natural British Columbia," which has appeared in countless tourist information guides. Rather than tourists coming to see the beauty of the province, they will see this ship exporting it out of the province, and out of the country.

Mountain in a Glass

I recall a recent exhibition catalogue dealing with the ethos of humour, and the Greek scholar, Ahnokatos, who lived in the time of the great thinkers

Aristotle, Socrates and Plato (Roukes, 2008). Ahnokatos was noted as a brilliant ironist of great wit who thought that, to be truly creative, you must look at everything in reverse, turn the world topsy-turvy, symbolically speaking. He promoted the use of surprise, contradiction and the unexpected because these have the potential to tickle the funny bone. My final tribute to mountains involves a tongue-in-cheek exploration that began on a car trip to Sooke, a community thirty kilometres northwest of Victoria. In my sketchbook, I recorded some highlights:

> We are on an afternoon trip to Sooke, once a prosperous fishing and logging community. Mountains are on my mind as we stop at the Sooke Fine Arts Show and then at Mom's Café, a 1950s-style diner. Baby blue upholstery and a large floor model Wurlitzer jukebox grace the interior, reviving the nostalgia of a bygone era. Our meal is generous and flavourful, down to the fresh blackberry pie with ice cream and a lavish swirl of whipped cream topping. As we depart, I look more closely at the jukebox with its large curved plastic face bathed in luminous neon light. Without really thinking, I insert a quarter and press a selection button pointing to "Blueberry Hill". The machine comes to life with a heave of whirling gears and the strains of Louis Armstrong's music filling the air. The waitress who served us calls out, "That's my favourite piece of music!" I respond with a smile, "Next time we'll be back for blueberry pie."

This episode fueled my determination to continue a series of imaginative artworks depicting mountains as ice cream desserts from a previous exhibition (Zuk, 2004). *Ice Cream Mountain* is based on a celebration of the 2002 United Nations International Year of Mountains devoted to the conservation and sustainable development of the world's most rugged and inspiring places. It uses a neon cybre colour palette reminiscent of a Wurlitzer jukebox and revives the soda fountain ice cream parlour era too, allowing imagination and fantasy to roam between exotic sights and elusive mouth-watering extravaganzas. *Ice Cream Mountain* brings me back once again to Mount Tolmie.

Living in Mount Tolmie's midst is like being in the protection and nurturing care of a worldly matriarch. Tolmie has opened my eyes to the richness of her geological and cultural history and the diversity of her flora and fauna. She has allowed me to roam freely over her pathways and provided a place of refuge and solitude to develop my artistic ideas. She has opened up opportunities for gazing and reflecting on the mysteries of the universe, especially when constellations shift their positions and comets flash through the heavens. More importantly, she has stirred my passion for nature which resonates with the thinking of Claus Oldenberg: "I am for an art . . . that makes flowers weep and the heavens tremble and the stars to forget their places" (in Gates, 2007, p.36).

Ice Cream Mountain, print (See page 143 Colour Insert)

References:

Dalton, R. (2009). Drawing from nature and experiencing wonder. *British Columbia Art Teachers'Journal, 5(11)*, 16-26.
Gawain, S. (2002). *Creative visualization*. Novato, CA: Publishers Group West.

Mount Tolmie Park and Guide Map. (1996). Victoria, BC: Mount Tolmie Conservancy Association.

Neihardt, J. (1979). *Black Elk speaks*. Lincoln, NB: University of Nebraska Press.

Oldenberg, C. in J. Gates. (2007). What is my concept of art? *British Columbia Art Teachers' Journal, 49(1)*, p.36.

Pohribny, K. (1987). *Abstract painting*. Oxford: Phaidon Press.

Regier, K. (1987). *The spiritual image in modern art*. Wheaton, Ill: The Theosophical Publishing House.

Roukes, N. (2008). Westward ha! Visual art in the wild west. Exhibition catalogue. Calgary, AB: Triangle Gallery of Visual Art.

Tessier, T. (2000). *White spirit bear*. Surrey, BC: Hancock House Publishers.

Tuchman, M. (1996). *The spiritual in art: Abstract painting 1890-1985*. New York: Abbeville Press.

Zuk, B. (2004). *Directions 1999-2004*. Victoria, BC: Sterling Press

Zuk, B. (2009). *Mount Tolmie sketchbooks*. Victoria, British Columbia.

ISLAND RHYTHMS

SANDRA GWYNNE MARTIN

For most of my life I was a city girl dreaming of a country life. My work in the city combined my two interests of commerce and the visual arts. I worked with a fine group of Canadian artisans, representing their work nationally and internationally. I loved my work. But always, there was the writing and the reading, the poetry tucked into small bits of time found in moments during the week. An annual retreat kept me connected to other writers and gave me an entire week of writing and communing with colleagues. And, always, while running my gallery and visiting studios, there was this small island in the Pacific gulf, waiting. I fell in love with Galiano Island as a young adult and its song called to me for twenty-five years. The goal to move here and write directed my non-writing career: work hard, and then move to the island. I sometimes look back and liken my arrival to Julie Andrews in *The Sound of Music* when she sings and twirls in the alpine meadows, her joy absolute. I am like her, only off key and slightly motion sick with the twirling. But nonetheless, here I am.

A move to a new life marks a moment of being alone on the planet: a stranger in a strange place. But then life happens. Neighbours come over for coffee; pot-luck dinners entice; someone shares the dog-walking path every morning. Conversations begin and once again the land of dialogue and social connection unfolds. Community beckons and so again comes the balancing of the writing and life outside the writing. Unconnected to the larger mainstream centres, this island locale houses a much smaller infrastructure. There is no movie theatre or fast food diner. No bank or pharmacy or shopping centre. The local amenities exist within a three mile hum of country road. Beyond this stretches forest and rock and field, and at almost every turn, the ocean. Most homes are hidden from view. There is a remoteness, a sense of being away. But this is home now, not a holiday stay, and knowing my time here is more fully my own feels both exhilarating and alarming.

This island is a generous lover, giving and demanding. It says, *"Look at the quiet here, the space; look at the time you have to devote to your craft. Use it all. It is a gift."* And I suffer some anxiety over this gift. I write, grateful for the time. I don't write and consider myself an ungrateful wretch. With this gift before me, how can I do anything but write? And then, slowly, the island reminds me about boundaries. From my studio I look out over fields and forest and with windows open I hear the creek at the south end of the valley. Two donkeys, brothers, share the land with us. I watch them roam the fields. They move through their day with such care, such slow deliberation. They browse through the grasses, making careful choices. They have taught me much about patience and adaptation and gratitude. Their movements, their languid days mark my writing. I am convinced that their presence lowers my blood pressure and deepens my breath. My day begins with feeding these two brothers and cleaning the barn. Daily chores shape the structure of my days. I feed the three dogs and the cat, towelling them dry if rain or puddles or snow dampen their morning excursion. Then house chores demand attention; outside maintenance chores linger and phone calls or social duties tap impatiently. Soon, all that's left is the afternoon and the night for writing, unless, as is often the case, there is an event in the evening.

This island breathes differently. Long, slow breaths. A new rhythm. There is grace here, as if permission has been given to honour the quiet, the slowness. When I write, I have a sign on our front door that reads: *"If no one answers, I am in my studio writing. I know you are there because the dogs are barking your presence. I am pretending you are not there. Knock if this is something that I would qualify as a life-altering emergency. Don't go home and call because I don't answer the phone when I'm in the studio. Other than that, I'll be happy to pour you a drink after 7:00 p.m."* Offence is never taken, and boundaries are not construed as reclusive or unsociable. There seems to be a mutual realization that solitude is one of the requirements for living on this small, relatively unpopulated island. We all value the peaceable alone time that allows us to do our work, whatever that may be. But this staking of territory, my writing territory, has been a slow process; one that keeps showing me that the non-writing time is continually informing the writing time. I only have to remember to listen, and to be observant, to feel the island's pulse in the soles of my feet.

This island is a conversation. I can attest to many compatible conversations, full of discovery and story. There are times when we argue and even times when we do not speak. I have thrown things at this island in a rage, shouted at its intractability, at its small universe. I have cursed its fine trees, railed against the ease with which they topple telephone lines and power lines and leave me in utter darkness. I have learned that darkness is not romantic as I walk to the woodshed in torrential rains and push wheelbarrow loads of wood to the porch door. That darkness is not romantic when the firewood supply is low and the cold is settling into the very bed sheets and blankets. I kick the island ground when I remember our decision not to buy a generator. I have shouted, *"I'm bloody cold and everything, everything is wet! Give me the city!"* But then, when the rains stop and the island is quiet from its beating, I think about forgiveness. So we begin speaking again. I have to ask myself if I am a fair-weather islander, if I am even worthy of claiming this place as my muse.

This island textures and colours my writing. It shows me the seasons, the burnish of the grasses in early spring and the red hues of sandstone at low tide. And seaweed. Every ocean walk I find yet another radiant seaweed — purples and teals and blues and burgundies, shades I thought reserved only for opals. I have learned the shedding of the arbutus bark and the sharp bite of stinging nettle tea. I have felt the velvet moss hidden along the undersides of branches and know that when the wind blows from the northeast, my neighbour's dogs will howl a haunting wildness. This island has become my teacher. I have learned to listen in its classroom, to be silent and attend. There is a dance that we do, the island and I; a push-pull, a give and take. When the quiet and the stillness roar, the city calls my name. But off-island, I quickly tire of the hurried rush, and crave the island's voice. Riding the ferry back, I call this island home.

The city offers an inherent anonymity, one that is fluid with mood or need. We experiment, moving in and out of its social groups, looking for a comfortable fit. Here on this small island, there is either personal space or there is community space. There is no anonymity, at least not for long. Though I may not know every name, I know every face. An islander knows who parents which child, who is partnered with whom (or not), who will be performing at the local café on Saturday night and whose car has resided in the ditch for the past four days. I know that an unfamiliar face is likely a weekender or a visitor. And that most of us were, at one time, that unfamiliar face. This communal closeness informs my writing in two ways: it allows me an intimate picture of the human condition and it reminds me that this small circle is indeed representative of the larger circle. It shows me, up close, the wider world. It is rich fuel for the writing engine.

Ultimately, the island shows me beauty every day. It shows me quiet and space and allows me to ponder in solitude without complaint. It infuses all five senses with abundant generosity. It says *"Look over there! Did you notice that lavender yesterday in the field at the end of the road? Have you ever seen a purple that deep? Did you see the moon last night, how it lit up the deer feeding in your orchard like a movie crime scene? Did you smell the wisteria this morning and beg for its bloom to last forever?"* The island takes me by the hand and walks with me through my day. It is my companion, my wise and honest writing partner. And sometimes, when the fog rolls across the gulf, I watch the mist swallow the entire island, leaving me mute in its thick cotton. Galiano vanishes and I wonder at its absence, its grey cloaking, its time alone. And then I understand that it, too, needs solitude. It needs time away from our need, from our constant searching and naming and claiming. And when the fog disappears and the island reappears, we carry on, knowing that we will always, both of us, return.

FIRE

ART OF THE SOAPBOX
GREG BLANCHETTE

Where? Up here? My goodness, is this an actual, real soapbox? Oh yes, "Sea Wench," I see it now: authentic! And the microphone's on? Can everybody hear me? Lovely!

Ahem. Thank you all, for allowing me to speak at today's Tofino Soapbox. This venue is a godsend for our town, the unacknowledged Bitching Capital of B.C. (Ha-ha, joke – maybe). I know Soapbox speakers are supposed to tread lightly, so as not to upset the many visitors to our fine town. But it's January, Tofino, and the only tourists left here are the storm-watching masochists, so let's dispense with the tourist-town whitewash and just get down to it, okay?

I'm talking art, darlings. A-a-art.

I mean west coast art, that stuff chipped out right here in our drafty garages and slopped onto canvas in our damp back room studios and tapped out at our cold, gloomy desks. The stuff that sparks from our wrinkled fingertips and oozes from our mouldy brains.

Okay, I can see you already rolling your eyes and thinking, *Here we go, another boring Canadian praise-the-arts lecture.* But that's where you're wrong, precious, for (to bend an artistic phrase) I am not here to praise west coast art but to bury it.

Don't we just love to pat ourselves on the backs and tell ourselves how thrilling and diverse our local art scene is? But I beg to differ. Tofino, I *grovel* to differ! Take our local music scene. Look at the living rooms and bonfires and stages around town and what do you see? Guitars! Electric gee-tars, acoustic gee-tars, red gee-tars and blue gee-tars. Nothing but gee-tars. Add the requisite drum kit and bass and you have . . . why, an exact clone of every rock band that ever existed since the 1950s.

Spank me if I'm wrong but there are hundreds, maybe *thousands*, of different musical instruments out there. And the best we can come up with is another three-piece rock band? *Please!* It's gotten so bad I practically faint from delirium when I see any instrument *but* a gee-tar on a local stage. Like Ronnie at the Mermaid's Ball, with his lips wrapped round a big, bright trumpet. Gorgeous!

Oh, 'tain't hopeless, I know, I know. Thérèse bangs a mean djembe; I've seen Ava plinking a ukulele; Sandi actually sings a capella, the nerve. But eight of ten

Tofino musicians lugging around gee-tars? Sacrilege! It's like every painter in town using only *blue* in their paintings.

And speaking of painting (such a clever segue) . . . if you examined the entire visual arts output of Tofino for the last ten years, you'd pretty much conclude that Clayoquot Sound is one gigantic, flaming *billboard* for SuperNatural BC: breathtaking sunsets, dramatic beachscapes, and noble members of the animal kingdom romping in the wild as they've done since creation. I mean really, urchins! If all you had to go on was local art, would you ever guess there was a single clearcut or barren salmon stream or social problem anywhere in Clayoquot Sound. Not even a solitary, pining, dark hour of the soul, come those long winter nights! I ask you: How representative is *that* of this delicious sound we all know and love to hate?

And more to the point, my feathered friends: Who dares say so out loud? You practically have to sign a Sacred Code of Rah-Rah to even enter the town limits when it comes to the arts. But where in west coast photography or painting does a human face appear, or a human story? It's rare, apart (of course) from the grinning hordes in rented wedding duds and dutifully joyous wedding faces. I hate to say it, but maybe there are already a few too many elaborate, high-end *postcard* images for the tourist market out there.

Ouch! What the hell was that . . . a brussels sprout? That hurt! Who carries brussels sprouts around with them? Oh, angry artists do? Yes, well . . . could we possibly channel that passion into something a bit more *productive?* No, no, you foaming-at-the-mouth watercolourists, I'm not attacking you. Oh, very well, I suppose I am attacking you, but I much prefer the word "challenge." I'm *challenging* you. We're all such big fans of reality TV these days, well, this here, as the cowboy says, is a dose of reality.

Yes, of *course* I'm generalizing shamelessly, as arts maven and soapbox ranter that's practically my job description. I have "shameless" tattooed on . . . well, you don't need to know. And yes, of course our arts scene has much to recommend it: its tenacity; its celebration of the land; its grassroots enthusiasm. Bravo! But let me also remind you burning heretics of something playwright Arthur Miller wrote in his 1987 memoirs: "*The whole country seemed to be devolving into a mania for the distraction it called entertainment, a day-and-night mimicry of art that menaced nothing, redeemed nothing, and meant nothing but forgetfulness.*"

Is that what artists are now: Mimics? Entertainers? Jesters? Purveyors of pleasant-looking knick-knacks to mount over the mantelpiece, or bits of doggerel to fill some idle beach hours? Tell me it isn't so!

Okay, calm down, calm down. Although I must admit, it *is* warming to see people riled up over something these days – over *anything*, never mind art. We're all so bent on being cool about everything that we end up freezing our own hearts solid. Ooh, I like it, that was good.

But speaking of doggerel, there was another wise old man – yes those existed once, before we debased the entire culture – maybe it was Wallace Stevens, I don't remember the details, who gave much thought to a sense of place and what it means to the folks who live there. People, the old fart said, do not live in places but in the description of places.

And who provides those descriptions for us? The Canada Council? The Premier of BC? I can hear you all groaning inwardly, you heathens, convinced I'm about to say *Artistes!* and lecture you about going to more boring Canadian movies. But I'm not. I surely am not. Because we *all* describe this place, every one of us, in a massive, ongoing, collective act of imaginary creation. We describe it to ourselves and each other every time we sit down in Tuff Beans or knock elbows in Beaches or shoot the breeze on Main Street. "Did you see the mist against the mountain this morning?" "The house sold, I'm being evicted." "Sunset beach-walk on Chesterman's, you coming?" "Those boneheads on council did it again!" And from that ceaseless gale of self-description settles out the dynamic, ever-shifting place that we live in.

We all describe. But you artists in the crowd, you painters, writers, photographers, even you potters and, what, wind-chime makers, all you foaming, gifted tossers have a sacred place in this process, because *your* descriptions are the ones meant to *circulate*. They travel out into the world and affect (or maybe infect) other people. You send our descriptions out to the spheres, and they're reflected back to us from there.

Oh-ho, you laugh, do you? *What does description matter?* You ask: *Can I take it to the bank? Will it pay my mortgage?* Let me remind you of the 1990s: a collective act of description in Tofino that caught fire beyond anyone's expectations and *burned* this little town into the imagination of the world. And gave us the description whose echoes we still live in today, for better or worse.

Description, cellmates? Hah! At the last Green Breakfast I talked to a guy from Ontario. He's an environmental consultant, a hard-nosed greenie, and he sheepishly told me he'd been nervous about coming to Tofino, in case he accidentally did something non-green like idling his car or tossing a recyclable into a trash can. Can you imagine, he thought we might lynch him. Little old harmless, beach-littering us! But such is the power of description, and apparently, out there across the mountains, Tofino's a rabid national beacon for . . . something.

And all this has consequences, doesn't it? Ever huger consequences, the way the world is going. Wade Davis, the famous Canadian anthropologist (and ooh, such a dreamboat), nailed it beautifully in his recent Massey Lectures when he said it hardly matters whether our descriptions are true or false: "*What matters is the potency of the belief and the manner in which the conviction plays itself out in the day-to-day lives of a people. For this in a very real sense determines the ecological footprint that any particular culture will have on the earth and its environment. A child raised to believe that a mountain is the abode of a protective spirit will be a profoundly different human from a youth brought up to believe that a mountain is simply a pile of inert ore ready to be mined.*"

That airy-fairy notion takes on a sudden, dramatic heft right there in your own guts, the moment you learn your local mountain, the one you can see from almost anywhere in town, is in the sights of an international mining conglomerate. Our collective description of innocent little Clayoquot Sound has up till now not included an open-pit mine, and the new picture comes as a shock, especially since those seeing the "pile of inert ore" are not you or me or our friends and neighbours, but men we've never met, shooting the cuffs of their expensive suits in a Vancouver office. And if the dynamite comes and the noise and dust fill the air and blast rock obliterates the Catface Mountain slopes, we'll find the descriptions of this place we live in hugely altered.

Yes, description is always coming home to roost, for good or ill. It's there for Ahousat and its people, and Ucluelet down the road, and for everyone else around the world caught in the octopus grip of opposing forces and desires.

Now, I'm not saying *yea* and I'm not saying *nay* to anything. That's not up to me – it's up to *us*. I'm just saying that as townsfolk, we are *all* artists, and as artists we have a sacred trust to make our description authentic. We are voodoo. We are witch doctors. We don't just live in Clayoquot Sound, we *create* it.

My goodness, is it hot out here? I'm sweating. Oh dear, I've been blathering again, haven't I, and you're getting restless. I'll be quick. Shout all you want, but please, no more brussels sprouts!

I'm just saying that we're out there as a creative town: an *arts* town. And that's the nub, isn't it? Art at its root is not about purple paint or pleasing harmony or brave words. It's about creativity, of all sorts, busting out of us in every way. In a proper arts town, that creativity spills over into breakfast, into buses, into every blessed corner of our lives.

Just look at our business model. The way it goes now, if someone opens up a … a barber shop and it does halfway well, next season three more barber shops open and everybody starves. You see it over and over. If anything ever needed some hard-headed artistic thinking, pigeons, it's west coast business.

And I say make it so. This goulash of a world needs to see all the fresh ideas it can muster, in art, in government, in enterprise, all hitting the canvas or the town hall or the bottom line. Mercy in a tree, if the Tofino brain trust who pulled the storm-watching craze out of their butts could pick up the greenie ball and run with it, we'd be up to our hot pants in gawkers year round!

Tofino, your artists have bigger fish to fry than postcards. (Ha, there's a mixed metaphor for you!) So for the gods' sake, sabotage the same-old. Hijack the habits that cruise you blindly through your day, and make it so easy to *not* see what's going on. Do an almighty *El Kabong* with your metaphorical gee-tar on your way to the music store to pick up your didgeridoo and your zither. Write a song a month that *isn't* about love or surfing. Paint a picture a month that's *not* scenery. Take a photograph that *doesn't* have a beach or an eagle in it. Write something that's going to make somebody's jaw drop.

Whew! That's it for me, Tofino. Thank you so much for this time on Tofino Soapbox. I did run on, didn't I? I must say, I don't like the look of this crowd. I don't like it one bit.

References:

Timebends: a Life, Arthur Miller. Penguin, 1987. New York. p. 477.

Wade Davis quote from Sacred Geography, fourth of his 2009 Massey Lectures, originally broadcast November 5, 2009, on CBC Radio. (It can be heard in streaming audio at www.cbc.ca/ideas/massey/massey2009.html). Also published in *The Wayfinders: Why Ancient Wisdom Matters in the Modern World*, Wade Davis. House of Anansi Press, 2009. Toronto.

A TREMOR AT MY FEET
JANINE WOOD

The west coast of Vancouver Island is an area known for regular tremors and minor earthquakes. It is a place where residents live with the awareness that "the big one," a major earthquake, could arrive at any time. It is appropriate then that my life here began in the spring of '92 with a tremor that entered my feet from the ground, travelled up my body, and exited out through the top of my head. To this day I don't even know if it was an earthquake at all. I can never be certain, as I was the only one who felt it.

I had come up island from Victoria with a small group of friends on a camping holiday. Soon I had caught my first wave surfing and well, that pretty much sealed the deal. I decided to settle in Tofino. My artistic initiation began at my home on Chesterman Beach, now known as Solwood. Here my living room hosted an African Drum Workshop. I was elated to be surrounded by this new and exciting group of people. That event became the first of many such workshops and classes to follow: astrology, yoga, didgeridoo, painting, magic classes, talking circles, natural medicine, pottery, tai chi, massage, meditation, reiki, dance, and more.

My initiation was complete when I met Henry Nolla. He offered to help me carve a drum, and this marked the beginning of a deep friendship. Henry became both my dear friend and carving master. Our connection elicited so many things over the next decade, but the most important was the ability to live in peace as an artist. Henry was living art. He lived in acceptance of all that life brought to his door. The lessons he taught are still present as I attempt to apply his wisdom to my own unfolding life. Though Henry has passed on, his life influenced and touched so many, and we honour his memory by living artfully. For me, that means pursuing my first love: dance.

My art making began in childhood. I studied classical ballet from age three, with tap, jazz, and modern to follow. Like so many little girls, I wanted to be a dancer when I grew up, but my turning point came and went when I was fourteen. My family and teachers were ready to send me off to ballet school in a neighbouring city. With the reality of imminent departure and change, suddenly the life of a ballet dancer, though remarkably beautiful, seemed very difficult, lonely and harsh. I decided to let go of that dream and stay at home. Still, I continued to dance seriously through the rest of my time in my home town and stayed involved in a dance community after moving to Victoria in 1986.

I thought that leaving for Tofino would mean having to let go of that life once again, but fate intervened when I met Sahra. Soon we were moving furniture around my house to accommodate dance sessions, and over the next few years we choreographed several performances. I felt like a dancer again. It was so fulfilling to open that channel once more. Life was good, but the best was yet to come.

It happened during one of my trips back down island. I was kicking up a salsa storm at a Victoria cafe when I bumped into my friend Monique. Also a dancer, she encouraged me to check out the flamenco studio she had discovered. Once again, life as I had known it changed. The music, the movement, the passion! I felt as though I had finally found an art form that would satisfy my desire to express all that I feel and all that I am.

Flamenco classes, flamenco music, flamenco performance. The next few years had me driving down island once a month to study dance. It was worth every moment on the road. The classes helped me to build the foundation on which this new and very demanding art form was to find expression.

Within a short time I had recruited a few exceptionally talented friends and began teaching them in Tofino what I had learned in Victoria. All have since incorporated flamenco into their own dance careers. We eventually formed a small troupe, "Flamenco de la Costa," and performed in a variety of venues, including local plays.

My own enthusiasm slowly extended itself into the community. I was encouraged to offer classes and it was in this way that I became an instructor of flamenco. Many students have passed through my classes over the years. Some take only a few sessions for interest's sake; some have continued their pursuit of flamenco in other places in the world. And happily, some have remained faithful to both Tofino and flamenco, becoming my "Familla Flamenca," my sisters, my students, my teachers, my friends. Flamenco is the one thing that has remained a regular feature over the years, and something I am told occasionally rattles the dishes in the neighbour's kitchen.

After five years of travelling to Victoria, I finally decided it was time to go to the source, the Mecca of all flamenco students: Andalucía, Spain. With the recommendation of my Professora in Victoria, I travelled to Jerez de la Fronterra, armed with only the address of a lady who rented small apartments and the name of a teacher with whom I was to study.

Spain welcomed me with open arms, for which I am eternally grateful. Within one hour of arriving I had rented a small apartment off Plaza Angustia, home of the *Palomas Blancas* (White Doves), and was in a class with one of the foremost *Maestras de Flamenco*. I was in heaven. Later that night I attended my first flamenco performance. There, my chaperone introduced me to the young woman who would become my personal instructor and dear friend. It was with her that I experienced my first authentic *Juerga* (flamenco jam / party). Over the decade that followed I studied seven major pieces or *Palos* with her. In the world of flamenco, each major dance solo usually runs from five to fifteen minutes and has a specific design or order, adding another layer in the intricacy of this tradition. I was completely immersed into this world that I so deeply wanted to understand.

I returned to my home in Tofino with a deepened yet still very primary understanding of this form of dance. Something I discovered by dancing and performing with Sahra, Jade, Joanna and others, was that Tofino provided an exceptionally supportive and even eager audience with whom to share our art. Tofino audiences have a reputation for warmth and excitement and I have witnessed this on several occasions from both sides of the stage. It became the perfect environment for all of us to break into ourselves as flamenco artists, a humble but priceless beginning. Here we enjoy such freedom. Our audience simply liked what we were doing and encouraged us to do more.

Living out on the far reaches of Vancouver Island has required a deeper determination and dedication to the development of my artist self. I remain on a mission to understand flamenco, not just to dance it, but also to become the dance and allow it to become part of me. There is something in the flamenco world known as *duende*. To achieve *duende* one must embody the very spirit of flamenco. I see it as a form of channelling and have witnessed it only on rare occasions. It is something that you can spend an entire life seeking to achieve. For this to happen in any art form, a certain level of dedication is required, and dedication without passion is a sterile and limited thing. As for myself, I have no choice but to embark upon this quest, for flamenco has taken me by force – my body, heart, and soul.

Through flamenco I have found a voice for my spirit, grounding me with its deeply complex, exotic rhythms, while lifting me up through its sensual femininity. It has become my own dance of life, where my warrior nature reveals itself. I know now that I will never stop dancing. Since that first journey to Spain, I have returned to the source seven times. With each visit another veil falls away to reveal another facet, another face in the spirit of this powerful art form. I believe that I have now entered my master studies, which require focus, dedication and discipline. Like yoga, meditation, and prayer, flamenco has become part of my spiritual practice. It gives me strength and helps guide me in my journey towards uniting my Self with the Divine.

Growing as an artist in this small community has had an effect no other experience could have provided. Out here, away from the trappings of contemporary life, each one of us has the chance to become whatever we desire. There is nothing to hold us back except our own limited vision or level of courage. Out here, on the edge of this magnificent and powerful part of Earth, I have learned to follow my heart. And when its compass is pointed in the direction of my creative spiritual path, I know I will find my way to the source of all things. With each class, rehearsal, and performance, I bring that tremor back, and I'm no longer the only one feeling it.

Thank-you Tofino. Thank you Henry. Namaste.

LETTERS TO DAD: YOU SET THE BAR HIGH, DON'T BE DISAPPOINTED

KEVEN DREWS

Dad:

We knew something was wrong with you, seriously wrong with you, May 8, 2009.

I was sitting at the computer in the back cabin on your Tofino property, the cabin you built by hand, cutting beams out of fallen cedar, spruce, and hemlock logs in the 1990s.

As I was pounding away on some story for the *Westcoaster.ca*, the online news service I launched in October 2005, Yvette and I heard you and Mom pull into the driveway.

"They're here," said Yvette.

I didn't get up from the computer. I kept on task, figuring you'd walk into the front of the house with your black suitcases and unpack in the master bedroom, just as you had done so many times before.

Suddenly Mom appeared at the cabin door.

"Your Dad needs your help," she said. Worry creased her face.

I shrugged, rose from my chair, put on some shoes, opened the door and sauntered across the lawn, over the deck and onto the driveway. There you stood, next to your Toyota, rigid as a board, motionless.

You looked stunned.

I can't remember what I said. Whatever it was, it must have sounded inane. Perhaps it was something dumb, like "Do you need help?"

I guess it doesn't matter now.

Mom grabbed your right arm, and I grabbed your left. For the next twenty minutes we shuffled you down the sidewalk, up the cedar stairs, into the house, and onto the couch.

Baby steps, that's what you were taking. At one point, as we climbed the second set of stairs into the house, I feared you were going to topple backwards.

Once inside, I turned on the TV. You just sat on the couch and watched, saying nothing. How odd, a retired teacher with nothing to say. You always had something to say.

* * *

Dad:

You'll be disappointed, but I'm writing to tell you I need to take a break from the *Westcoaster.ca* and reporting. I may even shut down the site. Just writing this letter feels like a chore.

I know. I know. It's a shame, especially when you consider how far I've come in my own battle against cancer. I know you were there the entire way, visiting me in the hospital and driving me to appointments, but I need to place my decision into a larger context – my health, which isn't very good.

Six years have passed since that horrible day in April, 2003, when doctors at New Westminster's Royal Columbian Hospital diagnosed me with multiple myeloma, an incurable cancer of the plasma cells. I'd lost vertebrates. My kidneys were close to shutdown. I was close to death. Yet somehow, things worked out. Call it divine intervention. As you know, I survived a stem-cell transplant in June 2003 and two relapses: the first in the fall of 2005, when I lost a chunk of my skull, and the second in the spring of 2008, when I lost half my right pelvis. I'm still on Revlimid, that new drug, a derivative of thalidomide, costing $9,000 per month. Revlimid, a new drug, a derivative of thalidomide, costing $9,000 per month. Unfortunately, it saps me of energy. I get tired so easily now.

* * *

Dad:

You did a good job of hiding your illness from us for months, but the charade ended at the supper table May 8, just a few hours after you arrived in Tofino. What gave it away? You barely ate and you barely spoke.

On the table was a variety of Chinese take-out, including sweet and sour pork, your favourite. Instead of serving yourself, Mom served you, ladling a little of each dish onto your plate. The only thing she didn't do was cut your meat the way your own mother used to.

You picked at your food. Fried rice and sweet and sour pork remained on your plate. You, a child of Second World War Germany, a child who was forced to eat dirt because there was not enough food, allowed us to throw it away.

Second clue: we tried to converse, but you couldn't maintain a clear thought. You stopped mid-sentence, your face clouded with confusion. You actually began to grin, in a silly sort of way.

"You gapped," I said.

"You just lost it," Mom offered.

"I'll get it back," you answered, but you didn't.

We shuffled you back to the couch, and for the rest of the evening you watched TV. We all thought you had suffered a stroke. If only.

We'd forgotten entirely about the skin cancer you'd battled a year earlier. We'd forgotten about your recent doctor appointments, the results of which you hid from us.

How could we have forgotten about any of that?

* * *

Dad:

As tough as life has been, I'm proud to say I've built a pretty damn good publication. I did it with the emotional support of you and Mom, Yvette, and of course a few friends, including Mike, Susan and Lloyd, the webmaster. I did it even though I promised myself and others I'd never work so hard again. Looking back now, I know why I broke my promise.

Sure, I had told everyone I'd come to accept my new position in life, after my first battle against cancer. I told everyone I realized I was no longer in control. But I still held a lot of anger. I was angry cancer had stolen my career from me and crushed my dreams in 2003. I was angry I never realized my full potential — not like you had done. Few people see the social progression that you saw in your lifetime. You went from peasant Prussian farmer, displaced person, refugee of war, to vice-principal with a master's degree in education.

That work ethic rubbed off on me too.

* * *

Dad:

No creative muse stood behind the *Westcoaster.ca*. There was only a strong work ethic, a desire to succeed, and of course anger and passion.

Oh, yeah, having faced the possibility of death, I wanted to leave something behind too.

When Yvette and I returned to Tofino in September 2004, I saw so many stories going unreported or underreported. For some reason, news just happens in Clayoquot Sound. Perhaps it has something to do with the motley crowds of people living in or visiting the place: environmentalists, fish farmers, conservatives, surfers and even a few loggers and their supporters. It's also a beautiful place that can steal your soul. I guess that's why up to a million people visit the place every year.

I grew aggravated, and by the following summer I developed plans to launch a print newspaper. When that proved to be too costly, I launched an online publication. You supported me the whole way.

"Don't give up," you told me that December, two months after the launch and just days after I overcame my first relapse. You sat with me and encouraged me to keep going. I listened. Imagine that, I actually listened.

Soon we broke our first major story. In August 2006, the District of Tofino announced it was shutting down the town due to the first-ever water shortage. We led the news coverage, filing stories to *The Canadian Press* and appearing on *CBC* and *CKNW* radio and *Global News*. The rainforest was facing drought. Tofino never really ran out of water, and with the *Westcoaster,* we made our mark.

Soon media outlets from the rest of Vancouver Island and across our province were regularly checking our website for story ideas.

Breaking big stories became an adrenaline rush. Before I knew it, I was working sixteen-hour days, trying to get the scoop. Some weeks, I even worked seven days straight, much to Yvette's chagrin.

Over the next few years the *Westcoaster.ca* continued to break some big stories, including the heartbreaking disappearance of a little boy from Bellingham, Washington in February 2008; and on the other end of the news spectrum, the filming on Long Beach of the Twilight series' *New Moon* in March 2009.

You kept on encouraging me, and I just kept going. My pace was insane.

I confronted you Saturday May 9, after I'd returned from covering and writing a story, of course. It was a bright, sunny morning. The sky was blue. From what I can remember, there was a slight breeze on the beach, and the tide was rising. Joe, a Tla-o-qui-aht carver, was steaming a canoe on North Chesterman Beach just down the road, in front of the late Henry Nolla's carving shack. Dozens of people had gathered to watch Joe prepare the canoe for presentation to a former hereditary chief. It was a good-news story.

Around noon, I returned home. Mom and Yvette told me they were heading into town. They were worried about you and asked me to try to convince you to go to the hospital. I told you I'd be back in a few minutes, but I wasn't.

Energized by my news fix, I entered the back cabin, plugged in my digital camera, downloaded my photos and began to write the canoe story. About an hour later, I returned to the house and caught you shuffling to the master bedroom. As you lowered yourself down onto the queen-sized bed, I sank onto the brown chaise lounge nearby. The room was dark, lit only by a small amount of daylight entering the window.

"Something's really wrong," I said. "Cancer pain doesn't make you gap in your conversations."

You knew I was speaking from experience.

I told you we were worried you had suffered a stroke. I asked when you had first noticed your thoughts becoming foggy, and you admitted it had been several months.

"Maybe we should go into the hospital," I said.

Finally you agreed.

When Mom and Yvette got home, they prepared to drive you to Tofino General. I stayed at home to work. I was still working an hour later when Yvette called.

"Where *are* you?" she demanded.

I jumped in the Jeep and drove to the hospital, where the on-call doctor said you hadn't suffered a stroke. You likely had a brain tumour and you needed to return to New Westminster.

I wouldn't be sending in any new stories for Monday, imagine that.

As we departed Clayoquot Sound, I wondered if you'd ever see Tofino again.

We arrived at your condo in New Westminster sometime around 2 am, Sunday, May 10. Mom and Yvette carried your luggage upstairs as I helped you from the Toyota, into the elevator, up to the apartment and into bed.

Then we all crashed.

Just a few hours later, I think you ate a little bit of toast and returned to bed. Still groggy from the lack of sleep, Yvette, Mom and I walked out for a little Mother's Day breakfast. Later, Yvette and I bid you goodbye and headed back to Tofino.

I didn't work once we got back. I was just too tired. Making a return trip to Vancouver from Tofino in less than a day would be too much for a healthy person. Making such a trip as an unhealthy person and then trying to keep a business running . . . well, I guess I'm insane because I tried. I worked Monday and Tuesday. I just kept going.

What happened over the next two and a half weeks remains a blur, a bad dream, just a series of unending, exhausting events. Doctors found a tumour on your right-front temporal lobe and wanted to operate. The skin cancer, a malignant melanoma doctors had removed a year earlier from the back of your neck had returned with a vengeance.

Mom wanted us to be there for the surgery. I remember arriving in the Emergency Room of Royal Columbian Hospital and finding you in a bed just down the hall from where I was first admitted at the end of March 2003. I remember later that afternoon buying you an anti-stress toy and a Rubik's Cube-type game from the hospital gift shop and then later that night a large-print Bible from a nearby bookstore.

I remember returning to the hospital every day.

I remember arriving one day to find you in a new bed on the fourth floor.

I remember the surgeon asking for Mom to consent to the procedure.

I remember writing in my journal, trying to put it away and you saying, "Uh-uh, don't." You were still encouraging me.

I remember the visits from your older sister, Herta, your niece, Margaret, and her partner, Roy, all from Black Creek.

I remember going to a Vancouver Whitecaps game with Yvette, just like we used to when I was a kid.

I remember our family doctor sitting down with us in a hall near a window overlooking the Pattullo Bridge and the Fraser River on a Sunday afternoon.

"How much time does he have?" I asked.

"Between two weeks and a few months."

The cancer had spread to your brain and several internal organs. Removing the tumour would improve the quality of your life.

Yvette had to return to Tofino that day.

Go, go, go, go, go. That's all we did for the entire week. There was no time to process anything. I stayed in New Westminster and kept up a similar pace for another five days. Mom's brother, Bill, and his wife, Sharon, arrived from Kelowna. Mom's sister, Zoanne, arrived from the interior, and her brother, August, and his wife, Marla, arrived from Gold River. Your niece, Irene, and her husband, Chuck, arrived from Vancouver Island. We visited you daily.

Somewhere in this crowd of arrivals, doctors conducted the surgery and removed the tumour. When we all visited you afterwards, you had a bandage on your head and were in a bad mood. When I called you Mr. Grumpy, you got really mad.

Friday afternoon, I headed back to the island. After I left, your eldest son Steve, his wife, Tara, and their two children arrived.

It's weird. I don't remember writing a single story for the *Westcoaster* the entire time I was in New Westminster. But as soon as I got back to Tofino, I resumed. I really should have taken some time off. I really should have just slowed down. Why was the *Westcoaster* so important that it drew me back to Tofino while you were on your deathbed?

Yvette and I returned to New Westminster. The phone rang just before 7 a.m. Saturday, May 30. The nurse said you were going downhill fast. We flew out of bed, dressed and jumped in the Jeep with Mom. The sun was shining.

On our way to the hospital, the cell phone rang again. The doctor asked Mom about the resuscitation order. Mom's answer? No resuscitation.

We prayed you wouldn't die until we made it to the hospital.

We parked the vehicle and walked up to the fourth floor.

Your breathing was shallow.

Your face was grey.

You looked so thin.

Mom began reading you the 23rd Psalm.

"It's too early," I said. "It's not the right time."

Over the next few hours, we called as many family and friends as we could, even those still in Germany. We wanted to give them a chance to say goodbye.

By noon, you were still with us, so Yvette and I headed off to lunch.

During the afternoon, friends visited to say their final farewells. By 6 p.m. the doctor told us to take a break and have some supper. You may have been waiting for us to leave before you'd die, she said.

We had supper at an Italian restaurant down the road.

After returning to the hospital, Yvette and I stayed with you for another hour. I told you I was proud of you. I said you were a great father.

"You can go," I added.

By the time I got back to the condo, I was drained. I tried to go to sleep, but the sky was still light. It wasn't even 9 p.m.

I'd never heard crows outside your condo in New Westminster, but I heard them during the early morning hours of May 31, just before the phone rang. I hadn't slept well. It must have been 4:50 a.m.

A nurse told Mom you'd passed away a few minutes earlier. Just like the day before, we dressed, jumped into the Jeep and headed for the hospital. As we drove, we could see the sun rising in the east, over the mountains and the Fraser River. I'd rarely seen those oranges and reds before. I'm just not a morning person.

On the fourth floor, we found you in a private room. Your hair was dishevelled and your face looked thin and drawn. You looked ninety, not your sixty-six years.

Your left hand was already cold to the touch, but your right was still warm.

Nurses soon delivered tea, coffee and cookies.

We called your best friend Ken. Dressed in a dark suit, he arrived at the hospital by 5:30 a.m. We said a few prayers, read a little scripture and then said our final goodbyes.

I barely cried. I wanted to, but I couldn't. I was just so worn out.

We returned to the condo.

Mom said she needed to go to church. I should have said no. I should have said I needed to sleep. Instead, I caught a quick nap before Yvette and I took Mom to church and then lunch.

At last, completely worn out, I lay in bed and slept for much of the afternoon.

Perhaps if I'd taken some time off after your death I would have recovered my strength, but I didn't. I continued to wear myself down. We planned your burial, which took place in Tofino Saturday, June 6. Then we planned your memorial, which took place in Surrey one week later.

Two weeks after that we were getting ready for the Calgary Stampede, where you and Mom had planned to sell reusable bags. I stayed in Tofino to work but followed shortly after. Once the Stampede ended, we drove back to Tofino, but I didn't take any time off.

As I write this, I must confess that the pace has never let up.

To top it all, an ophthalmologist has diagnosed me with cataracts in both eyes, a direct result of my own cancer treatment.

* * *

Dad:

Just last week somebody told me I'd been through a lot of shit in the last eighteen months. I guess they were right. Some of it was forced on me. Some of it I created by myself. Cancer was forced on me. Beating it once would be too much for most people. Most people would have counted their lucky stars, slowed down and enjoyed life.

But I didn't. I actually began working harder than I ever have and I kept it up while battling through two relapses. Yeah, I was motivated, by anger and passion. And yeah, I wanted to leave a legacy. But my crazy pace caught up with me, and your death proved to be the breaking point.

I wore myself out commuting between Tofino and New Westminster while you were on your deathbed.

I wore myself out trying to continue running a news website.

I wore myself out helping with the funeral and memorial arrangements.

I wore myself out working the Calgary Stampede.

Dad, I've got nothing left. I'm spent. If I continue with this pace, I'll work myself to death. I hope you'll understand why I just can't do it anymore. I tried. I gave it my best. Don't be disappointed if I shut down the *Westcoaster.ca* and if I quit.

Postscript:

Keven Drews shut down the *Westcoaster.ca* in early 2011. He says he didn't receive the support needed to make the publication profitable – a must considering he is now the father of twins. In the late spring of 2011, he moved back to Vancouver and started a six-month contract with a national news wire service. Just what happens after the sixth months remains a mystery to him. Keven says he still has not come to terms with his Dad's death, and wonders, like most sons, how he could have had a better relationship with his father.

THE AWAKENING OF THE ARTIST IN A YOUNG MAN

ADRIAN DORST

If a career can be defined as a line of work that one returns to again and again and which earns you a living, at least some of the time, then I have had four or five careers during my lifetime, one of them as an artist.

My artistic career began inauspiciously in 1971 when I picked up a piece of driftwood on a beach near Masset, on Haida Gwaii. I had hitchhiked from Vancouver to Prince George with my girlfriend, Susan, enroute to the Charlottes to begin a new life. At Prince George we had managed to hop a freight train to Prince Rupert and from there hitch a ride on a seiner to Haida Gwaii. In Rupert I spent my last hundred bucks to buy a rifle in order to hunt the gazillion deer, which everyone said infested the islands, but which in reality you could never find. I later learned why. The only hunting being done there was in the dead of night by pit-lamping, and with a military base at Masset, there was lots of competition.

We lived on North Beach in a pup tent just big enough for two until it was inundated with rain three inches deep from a night-time deluge. That was the end of our camping because my girlfriend insisted, not unreasonably, on better accommodations. We subsequently lived on a salmon troller in Masset Harbour, with barely enough room for two people to stand up at the same time, but it was dry and an improvement over the tent.

A few weeks later we moved into one of the semi-derelict houses on the south side of the harbour just over the causeway where my neighbour was a soft-spoken young Haida man of nineteen. He was learning to carve faces on discarded Styrofoam fishing floats from an old poet called Hibby, nearly as derelict as the houses. After a few deft strokes with a sharp knife to create eyes, nose, and mouth, Hibby added a length of frayed rope for hair and, voila, he had his basic head and all the cash he needed.

Since I had no job to go to, and having developed a philosophy that time is far too precious to spend it working, I instead passed my days hiking the beaches and looking at birds, a passion of mine since I was a kid. I think it was late November by this time and with the weather cooler and wetter, my girlfriend had abandoned me for a trip to Vancouver. In any event, on one of my solo walks, a piece of driftwood caught my eye. It was very close in shape to that of a human hand. I took it home with me and accentuated its appearance by whittling away at it with a pocket-knife. Thus were awakened my first instincts as a carver, albeit with a helping hand from Mother Nature.

Four years passed before inspiration struck again. It happened while hiking up a steep logging road on Cortes Island's Green Mountain, where circumstance had led me after a few more of life's zigs and zags. Beneath a grove of ancient Douglas Firs that had escaped decapitation due to some defect in their trunks, I picked up a chunk of wood with a peculiar shape. With a little imagination I could see a hooded warrior holding a large shield in one hand and a dagger in the other. I tucked it in my pocket and took it home for some minor alterations, but mostly just to clean the dirt off and polish it up. This carving remains one of the best pieces I ever did, or more accurately, never did, because the alterations needed were so minimal. Mother Nature had done most of the work. A year or two later I gave it to my friend Clara for her birthday.

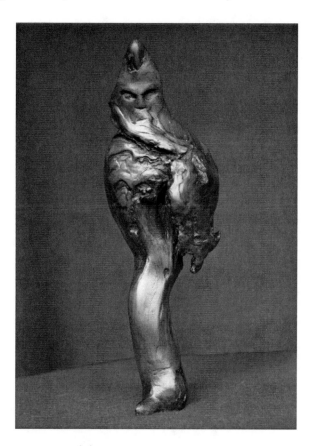

Hooded Warrior (See page 144 Colour Insert)

Ah, but a gift from God is not so easily discarded. You see, subsequently, whenever I dropped in on Clara to drink tea and chat, I immediately gravitated towards this piece. I would pick it up and run my fingers over its smooth finish, admire its mysterious demeanour, and generally be captivated by it all over again. Common sense prevailed when Clara realized who it really belonged to and gave it back to me on my birthday. I accepted, of course, and it lives with me still, proudly displayed on my bookshelf.

Not long after finding *Hooded Warrior*, I acquired a large chunk of yellow cedar cut from a beach log and began to chip away at it to create a hawk. This was my first attempt to create form out of nothing. For some reason I took two years to finish it, probably because I was by now busy tending to a little boy conceived in the pup tent. But after carving the individual feathers and tinting the whole thing brown using shoe-polish, I sold it to a young waitress working in the Maquinna Hotel restaurant in Tofino for minimum wage. She had scrimped and saved, she told me, so she could give it to her Dad as a birthday present. I was moved.

Tofino during this period had a community art centre known as the *Gust of Wind*, with workshops, a display area, and a coffee shop. One day, a picture hanging behind the counter caught my eye. It depicted Jesus having a hearty laugh. This was such a refreshing change from usual Jesus depictions that I decided to carve it as a portrait in red cedar. This proved not nearly as easy as I had thought, because the result ended up looking more like an overweight and balding, middle-aged tourist than the Saviour of Men. I had heard a story that local artist extraordinaire Godfrey, or Goof, as he was affectionately known, once had an artwork develop a crack and break in half. Nonplussed, he had simply banged the pieces together and continued on in a different vein, saying it looked better than before. True or not, it was an inspirational story and I decided to continue with mine despite the setback. I added a false tooth made out of lead, dark glasses, and a cigar for his grinning mouth. It didn't matter that he was no longer Jesus.

Just as I was bringing him to completion, two women from the mainland showed up at the *Gust*. One of them had fled from home after a fight with her husband. She and her friend were hanging out in Tofino to let the old man seriously worry for a while. On seeing my latest carving, she offered to get me a laugh box to tuck inside the hollowed-out mask. I had never heard of a laugh box before but it seemed like a good idea. True to her word, she sent me one two weeks later, complete with batteries, and I fastened it to the inside of the mask with the trigger button protruding from the back. The now comic mask henceforth hung on a wall in the display area of the *Gust of Wind*. Beside it I pinned a small sign that read, "Please do not push the nose." If you pushed the nose in violation of the order, the pressure triggered the switch at the back and loud and raucous laughter issued from the grinning mouth. Typically, a visitor would study the mask and sign, consider for a moment, then cautiously push the nose. As laughter echoed through the *Gust*, they were of course caught with their hand in the cookie jar, so to speak.

When the *Gust* was shut down in 1980, I presented the mask to Maureen Fraser, who had a small bakery nearby and who had been forced to suffer through the brunt of the obnoxious laughter ringing through the building. Today, the *Laughing Tourist* can be seen hanging in Maureen's *Common Loaf Bake Shop* among her other masks collected from around the world. The cigar is gone, as are the dark glasses, and not surprisingly, so is the laugh box.

So, what was this? Performance art? If so, it was conceived out of a mistake, with the help of a chance encounter due to a domestic dispute, and with a helping hand of kindness. 'Serendipity' in other words. Let no one deny that there are mysterious forces at work in the universe.

And the Jesus portrait? I started a second one, which turned out quite nicely in the end, though without a laugh box. However, when I brought a born-again Christian friend in to see it, he was visibly disturbed. Jesus having a hearty laugh was apparently too radical for him. The piece was eventually purchased by an Alberta-based art collector visiting the *Gust*, who had also fled from home after a fight with his spouse. He also bought a carving from another Tofino artist depicting two cats fighting. He told us it reminded him of his relationship with his wife. I can only hope that *Laughing Jesus* brought joy and laughter to them both.

I continued carving a variety of works during that period, mostly in western red cedar. Some were of birds, a theme that came naturally considering my passion for them, but one was a portrait of a pretty young woman with wind-blown hair swept across her face. At the time I was not consciously aware of whom I was carving. Later, however, I realized that it was a likeness of Isobel, a young, red-haired woman who had come knocking on my bedroom door a year or two earlier to read me a poem by Shel Silverstein called *Hug o' War*.

Minutes after the poem was read, we were wrapped in each other's arms as comfortably as if we had known each other our whole lives. We were birds of a feather, united in love. Our birthdays, it turned out, were only three days apart, so there may have been an astrological basis for this close connection. I no longer remember just how long we lived together in our "wee house," as she called it, but too soon, circumstance and necessity intervened to push us in separate directions.

We remained in touch for years until fate intervened again. During the chaos of the Meares Island environmental battles in the mid-1980s I lost her mailing address, my only link to her. The connection was broken and through no amount of effort on my part could I find her again. And she, of course, had no way of knowing that it was not by choice that I stopped writing. Today I realize that this carving was shaped by my longing for her. But it may also represent the conflict between longing and freedom, for I was only too aware that many an artist's fire has been doused, and many a free-spirit's wings clipped by the demands of family.

Isobel's portrait was bought by a man named Gordon. Together, Gordon and his wife Patty worked as caretakers at Clayoquot Resort on Stubbs Island. His large boat, which was being converted to a live-aboard at the 4th Street Dock, was taking on water after a severe storm. I phoned to alert him and he rushed over from Stubbs Island in his speedboat. Enroute to town, he passed my handcrafted seventeen-foot cedar-strip canoe, *sans* crew, rapidly travelling in the opposite direction,having been blown off the dock. Gord managed to save his boat. Mine I found a day or two later, smashed to pieces on the rocks at Vargas Island. Perhaps Gord felt badly about my canoe because he bought the carving a week later.

Selling my work was important because it kept me fed while allowing me freedom. But the sale of a work was also important as a measure of its worth and a validation of my efforts. If others found my carvings appealing enough to buy, I reasoned, then the carvings passed the 'test'. Despite occasional sales, money was often scarce and I had to rely on providence to see me through.

A year earlier, Gord had asked me to caretake the resort while he and Patty departed for a week or two. I was delighted. I no longer remember much about my time there, but I do remember the day I ran out of food and had to paddle into town for groceries. This is where providence came in. Having exactly two dollars to my name, I bought potatoes and carrots, but could afford nothing more. Without fish or meat to complete a balanced meal, I headed back with what I had. A hundred yards out from the First Street dock, coming my way fast on the outflowing tide was a dead Mallard duck, freshly shot by a local hunter. Meat! The current was so swift that the duck actually hit the side of the canoe with a thump. I leaned forward, grabbed the bird by the neck, placed it in the bottom of the boat and thanked the universe. I had been provided for once again.

Unexpected gifts and miraculous events, I find, happen only when you don't plan them out of existence. The message in the story is this: if you're an artist or a would-be-artist, don't sweat the small stuff like food and shelter. Faith will find a way.

There is a limit, however. I once knew a musician so devoted to his music that he lived with only the barest essentials, which were reduced to the clothes he wore on his back and a fiddle. An overcoat served as his sleeping bag and tent. He told me in all seriousness that he had at one point come to the conclusion that eating was unnecessary and had subsequently attempted to abandon the practice. Reality has a way of clashing with unsustainable theories and he was forced to re-evaluate his belief.

I learned early on that the sale of my works bought me the freedom to continue doing what I liked as opposed to a nine-to-five job, which would have meant doing something I didn't like and no time for art. Selling a work, to point out the obvious, requires a meeting between the art piece and a person who covets the piece and has money in his pocket. Even here, serendipity often comes into play.

In the winter of 1980-81, I lived on Chesterman Beach. With lots of time on my hands during the long rainy season, I worked at carving a Mallard Duck in flight out of red cedar. (Mallards, it seems, figure large in my life). It was painstaking work to fit the wings on flawlessly but in the end I succeeded. With a rich, reddish brown hue to the wood, it was a beautiful piece that was designed to hang on a wall.

That winter I had bought an old, thirty-foot long International school bus from a group of rock musicians playing at the Maquinna Hotel. They were happy to get rid of the beast as it was burning oil, and I picked it up for a reasonable price. I mean, how many people buy their home free and clear for twelve hundred bucks? So when summer rolled around, I began to prepare to travel to the Okanagan Valley, as I had done on several previous summers in my old Ford pickup truck and camper. My son, now eight years old, had come to live with me and the bus would be our home.

To fund our trip I would first have to sell the duck. If I failed in this I would be forced to abort the journey and return to Tofino. Arriving in Victoria, I decided to begin with the Royal British Columbia Museum gift shop. No sooner had I entered the store than a familiar face greeted me. It was Clayoquot artist Joe David, originally from Tofino and a big name in the galleries of New York. After exchanging a few pleasantries he asked to see the bird tucked under my arm and asked me what I wanted for it. I named a figure that would easily see us to our destination and back and he reached for his wallet, counted out the money, and placed it in my palm. It was that easy.

Living in Tofino in those days one was never far from other artists, but a million miles removed from the art world. Indeed, it was not a concept we encountered or thought of very often. I finally came face to face with it, however, when I found myself on the streets of Vancouver with my young son Quinn. We were near downtown, waiting for the National Film Board theatre to open. Since we had some time on our hands, and because the Vancouver Art Gallery was nearby, I decided to find out what great works Vancouver had on display. It didn't quite work out that way. A chap who fancied himself an artist had gone through the phone book and invited people with names like Cook and Baker to a party, where he photographed them. These photos were then displayed on the walls of the gallery and a tape recording played, calling out the surnames of said people. If there was some deep message here, it went right over my head.

The adjoining room wasn't much better. On the wall hung black and white photos of people with egg on their faces. I was not unmoved, however, and turned to an elderly gentleman nearby and muttered, "What a bunch of crap." "You're not kidding," he whispered. Then I was struck by a thought: Is an art gallery not a place for freedom of expression? And shouldn't the response of the public be welcomed? Perhaps the purpose of this form of art was to provoke a response. And why was everyone shuffling silently through the gallery? Well by

God, I would respond. "What a bunch of crap!" I bellowed in a loud voice. Everyone in the place turned to look, but no one said a word. Feeling much better, I headed for the exit.

I learned later that this is called conceptual art. Near as I've been able to figure it out, this practice is the result of the intellectual mind wanting to get in on the game. But it seems to me that, without heart, passion, and intuition there can be no art, and that mere cleverness is a poor substitute.

A far more agreeable experience occurred on a visit to the Royal BC Museum. There was a single room devoted entirely to carvings in argillite by Haida artists. I was fascinated by how the Haida of the 19th and early 20th centuries would copy a European item such as a flute, and make it their own by adding small frogs that wrapped their arms around the holes. It happened that during the hour or so I spent viewing these treasures, no other visitor entered the room to disturb me or break the spell. What I remember these many years later, more than the individual works of art, was a strange kinship I felt with those who had shaped these works. I could almost hear the artists joking and laughing, see their strong hands gripping the tools, and smell the woodsmoke of a nearby fire. This experience was somewhat akin to when one is alone in the wilderness and the presence of the "other" manifests itself. Try to express it in words though and it collapses into a slag heap.

This experience left a lasting impression and my respect for the skill of these artists grew exponentially. My own first venture into stone happened about eight years ago when my friend Paul, who sculpts in soapstone, gave me a large chunk to experiment with. Paul is a minimalist. "The less you do, the more you get paid," he once told me. His style is not without merit however, and the French writer Antoine de Saint Exupéry would have approved. In *Wind, Sand and Stars,* Saint Exupéry wrote, "Perfection is finally attained not when there is no longer anything to add but when there is no longer anything to take away . . ." (p. 42).

In sculpture, that would work in reverse, but you get the idea: simplify. Before beginning a carving or sculpture, the artist studies the wood or stone and visualizes what's inside, then takes away everything else. Simple. I studied the rock for a while and decided I could see an orca. Yes, an orca and something on its back. Oh yes, a naked lady riding an orca. Go figure. I set to work.

I began the piece with the woman astride the toothed beast, clinging to the dorsal fin, then continued with the whale below. While I had made the human figure fairly small, the orca was so much bigger that I ran out of room for the tail. Overall, the sculpture looked reasonably good, but, no matter what I did, I could not overcome the chopped-off look. I stuck the piece on the mantle where it stayed until the day I had a visitor from Washington who, as it turned out, was immersed with everything about orcas and who headed an organization that worked to protect them. Perfect! As she was about to leave, I grabbed the orca and naked rider off the mantle and placed it on her lap to give to her as a present. She blushed and protested; she was a Catholic girl, but she accepted and took it home. I don't expect to see the sculpture on any of her organization's brochures, but you never know.

Selling art is unpredictable. Unlike Paul, who sculpts them two at a time and sells them three at a time, I am not blessed with the Midas touch, but I do get lucky now and then. A number of years ago my wood carvings and soapstone sculptures had built up to the point where I was in possession of five pieces simultaneously – two goose bowls in alder, a large hawk in red cedar, and two raptors in soapstone. This collection represented many months of work. There was a Christmas craft fair coming up, but I had doubts about the venue and was still undecided about participating as late as the night before the event. On the morning of the fair I chose to give it a try and proceeded to set up my table. The doors opened to the public at 11 o'clock in the morning and by 12:30 I was completely sold out.

Have you ever been present at a department store sale where they keep the doors locked until the exact time of the sale, then limit the items to one per customer? They do that for a reason, to affect a mass psychological feeding frenzy. I think that's what took place around my table that day, triggered by a fortuitous moment that brought a small group of people to my table just as one couple was buying not one, but two pieces. After that, potential buyers were nearly body-checking each other out of the way to get to my table first. In no time at all, I was clasping a roll of cash in my clenched fist and making plans for Mexico. Now it is undoubtedly true that keeping prices reasonable also helps a sale. There's no point, after all, in pricing yourself out of the competition. One artist I know never sells a thing because the prices he asks are too out of reach.

Is money an important part of art? You bet. Master carver Henry Nolla, who once worked in a uranium mine but escaped that fate to live a simple life on Chesterman Beach, once told me the story of an unproductive, would-be artist who had come to watch him work and who continually asked him where he got his inspiration. Henry, who with his stately physique and long hair and beard looked rather like a druid priest and had the wisdom of one, answered, "I go to the kitchen cupboard, I open the door and look to see if it is bare." Henry didn't tell me what the man's reaction was, but his girlfriend who worked as a cocktail waitress to support the two of them suddenly snapped to attention and said, "Say that again." Henry understood that an empty stomach is a great motivator.

And what have I learned from my years of dabbling in creative endeavours? That life is both unpredictable and well-ordered; that there are universal laws which permeate and govern everything; that there is still great mystery in the universe, even at the day-to-day level. And that art ultimately is not separate from life, but thoroughly interwoven with it and part of the mystery. I believe that for the artist, art should not be an end in itself, but a means to a more enlightened life. Treat art as the end and you miss the point.

To the aspiring artist I say never doubt yourself, and don't stray from your path, keeping in mind that you can never see your path ahead, but only on looking back. Make sure you honour yourself by being true to who you are and never think that your small efforts are inconsequential or unworthy. There is simply no way of telling where they will lead.

Remember the young Haida man I told you about who was learning to carve faces on Styrofoam floats? He became a very accomplished artist and carver, working alongside the renowned Bill Reid for several years, and later assumed leadership of the Haida nation.

So love life. Love art. Love your neighbour (but not your neighbour's wife). Be happy and celebrate your joy though art.

References:

Antoine de Saint Exupéry, 1967, *Wind, Sand and Stars, Harcourt.* See http:// books.google.ca/

Silverstein, Shel. (1974). *"Hug O' War"; Where the Sidewalk Ends: The Poems & Drawings of Shel Silverstein*, Harper & Row Junior Books, 10 East 53rd Street, New York, N.Y. 10022 . Copyright © 1974 by Evil Eye Music, Inc.

COLOURS

MARLA THIRSK

I was never going to tell this story. It was my dark secret place; my shame, my hidden part. But it is also my story of rebirth, my finding of place, my discovering of colour.

The first colour was Grey. The endless rainy skies, the cloud-filled landscape of this remote place, Ucluelet, on the west coast of Vancouver Island. Grey was the colour of the loneliness I felt, stuck in the expected lifestyle of marriage with the two young children and the hard working husband. The husband who was never home.

It was the colour of my dead heart.

The second colour was Red. The leaving of the marriage, the abandoning of those two young children, the running far away into Adventure with whomever crossed my path and allowed me to cling to them.

It was the colour of my shame.

The third colour was Blue. The wrenching of my heart when I thought of my children, the longing for the ocean and for this place.

It was the colour of my tears.

The fourth colour was Black. The darkness of addiction, the bleakness of toxic relationships, the living without hope.

It was the colour of the end.

The fifth colour was Yellow. The opening of friends' arms to me, the healing of my heart with the realization of my dream to be an Artist, and the reconnecting with my sons.

It was the colour of coming home to Ucluelet.

Now I have all the colours in the smiles and love of my grown children; the sunrises and sunsets; the wildness of the landscape; the respect and acknowledgement of my peers for the Artist I am.

And they are all colours of peace and place.

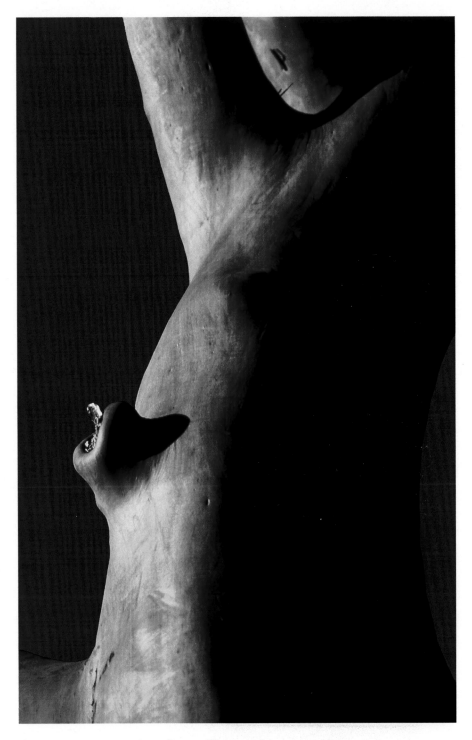

Anita Sinner– *Woman in Repose* (see page 7)

Robert Dalton– *Garry Oak on Mount Douglas, photo montage* (see page 14)

Robert Dalton– *Emerald Stone, pastel drawing* (see page 15)

Robert Dalton– *Germination, Coloured pencil drawing* (see page 16)

Robert Dalton– *Blushing Rose, watercolour painting* (see page 17)

Robert Dalton– *Ekklesia, acrylic painting* (see page 18)

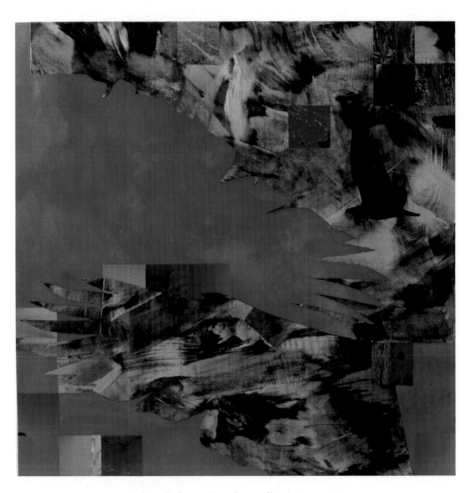

Robert Dalton– *Coastline, collage* (see page 19)

Robert Dalton– *Approach, mixed media* (see page 21)

Robert Amos– *Victoria Food and Florist, acrylic* (see page 46)

Wanda Hurren– (see page 49)

Wanda Hurren– (see page 52)

prairie prairie prairie prairie prairie prairie prairie prairie prairie

Wanda Hurren– (see page 53)

Wanda Hurren– (see page 54)

Kim Goldberg– *Weathergrams* (see page 57)

Bill Zuk– *Malahat Mist, digital print* (see page 88)

Bill Zuk– *Life Force, print, artist proof* (see page 90)

Bill Zuk– *Ursa Spirit, print* (see page 92)

Bill Zuk– *Ice Cream Mountain, print* (see page 95)

Adrian Dorst– *Hooded Warrior* (see page 121)

Mark Hobson– *Keeping Watch, acrylic on canvas* (see page 170)

Celeste Snowber– *Photo: Jacqueline Dingman* (see page 177)

Avis Rasmussen– *Off Meares Island, oil on canvas* (see page 207)

ROOFING

MICHAEL ELCOCK

Living on BC's wild coast can be a bit like being in a small boat at sea. You can't call the electrician or the plumber – or the roofer – when you're miles from town. When something breaks you just have to figure out a way to fix it.

Back in his hippie days my brother-in-law, Dave, built a cabin on Kumdis Island in Masset Inlet in the Queen Charlotte Islands, or Haida Gwaii as the islands are now known. He's a respectable physician these days, but he still spends time there in the summers. Last year he asked me to come up and help him put a new roof on the cabin.

"There's not much to it," he said. "We'll get it done in three or four days, then we can go fishing, and play some golf."

I'd seen photographs of Dave's cabin. The roof was steep. It had a couple of difficult dormers, and a nasty pitch to it.

"No shingles or shakes," he went on. "We'll do it with roofing felt. Simple stuff. You just roll it on and tack it down."

I had worked with roofing felt. It's heavy, awkward stuff. I didn't think it would be as simple as he'd said. I said yes anyway because I like my brother-in-law, and anyway I needed a break.

Haida Gwaii lies about sixty miles off the coast of northern British Columbia, five hundred miles northwest of Vancouver. The islands are the home of the Haida, a strong and spiritual people, and as I was to discover, a beautiful place of mists and strange light.

Dave met me at the small airport at Sandspit and took me down the road for a quick round of golf. It was a rough little course that hadn't seen a mower in weeks. The greens were impossible to distinguish from the fairways, but the nearby woods were filled with enormous ravens, and bald eagles that were even bigger. Eagles are territorial birds, and it was unnerving to line up a putt as a great dark shape slid down the sky in my peripheral vision.

Those nine holes turned out to be the extent of the recreation that Dave had promised. As soon as we finished the game we took the ferry over to Graham Island. The back of Dave's big Cummins truck was filled with tarpaper, roofer's goop, nails, and roofing felt.

It rained most of the way up to Port Clements, a fishing village on Masset Inlet. Some of the houses there were rundown and looked as if they could do with Dave's roofing skills. But others were cheerful with fresh paint, geraniums in pots, and little decks facing the sea. And out by the wharf sat a wood-floored pub that Dave said had hardly changed in years.

His skiff was moored at the wharf and we filled it with the supplies from the back of the truck. The rain had changed to a persistent drizzle.

"It'll take us about half an hour to get to the landing on Kumdis," said Dave, handing me a rain jacket.

The outboard fired at the first pull and we took off across open, bumpy water towards the slough that separates Kumdis from Graham Island. Half way across Dave said, "There's a good fishing spot up here," and turned the skiff towards the forest. We raced up a shallow inlet, the bottom clearly visible under the skiff's hull and advancing towards the surface. Dave guided the boat onto the bank, dragged on a pair of waders and hopped out.

"For Christ's sake, Dave, we're not going to sit out here and fish, are we? It's pissing rain and getting dark. We need to get this stuff to your cabin." The drizzle had stopped. Instead rain was lashing the surface of the inlet like machine gun fire. I was soaked.

"I thought we could catch some supper first," said Dave. "You might be right, though. They don't seem to be rising just now."

He pointed the skiff back towards the slough. The forest closed in on both sides of us as the slough narrowed, and then Dave hauled on the helm and turned us sharply to shore. The skiff grounded on a shallow, muddy beach. We were immediately attacked by swarms of horseflies and no-see-ums.

A slippery path took us deep into a forest filled with magnificent, high-canopied trees – lithe and thick-trunked cedars and sturdy Douglas Firs – an old, old forest.

We came to a boggy clearing, and there sat Dave's cabin, no electricity, and a rickety outdoor biffy at the edge of the woods. The roof was even steeper than it looked in the photographs, and a lot farther from the ground.

The conditions inside the cabin were grim. The roof was leaking badly. Dave had set out an array of buckets, pans, and jam jars to catch the drops. It didn't take long to see that most of the drips liked to move around, and that others were changing rapidly into cascades. The receptacles had to be emptied and re-positioned every few minutes.

Dave was used to this. He had lived here for a dozen years and raised three children in this cabin. He dipped into his backpack and produced a bottle of Dalwhinnie malt.

"This'll warm you up," he said. He went over to the sink and picked up a dirty glass and sloshed it out with brown water from the hand pump. He dug some crackers out of a box of supplies.

We'd picked up a home-smoked Alaska Black Cod in Port Clements, so we prepared that for supper and lit the fire against the damp. Soon the fire was a working crematorium, incinerating the mice that had been caught in the traps Dave had set out earlier.

The baked cod and boiled potatoes went down well with a bottle of Chardonnay. A dram of the Dalwhinnie set us up for sleep, and lessened my inhibitions about the mould flourishing in the foam mattress on my bunk.

The deadly crack of the traps woke me up several times during the night. Dave had bought some expensive Feta cheese that he said these particular mice seemed to like. In the morning we could see that some of them had died messily, leaving blood splattered across the wooden floor.

"They prefer peanut butter," I advised Dave. "We'd be better off eating the feta. It's too good for mice."

Now it was morning, and nature was calling, but the outhouse leaned at such an angle that I was afraid to enter in case my weight made it topple into the waterlogged ditch below. The ditch was green with standing water, alive with a rich variety of bugs. An examination of the toilet's rotting seat suggested that it might not even support my weight. Dave was making tea when I returned to the cabin.

"That toilet of yours is appalling," I told him. "The thing's been built without any idea of the mechanics that are involved in using it."

"I didn't build that one," said Dave smoothly. "The one I built was burned down by a careless smoker."

"Well, I can't use it. It's totally unhealthy, not to mention dangerous. And you a physician! It very nearly threw me into that filthy creek out there."

"There's another one in the forest, down near the landing. Gerry built it a few years back. We can go there later. Gerry won't mind if you use it."

Breakfast was fried eggs and onions, and bread toasted in the frying pan. Dave made up a pot of 'kickass' coffee to get us through the day.

Finally we were up on the roof, removing the old cedar shakes Dave had nailed on nearly thirty years before. He had felled and milled several trees on his property back then, and split the shakes himself. The shakes must have been thick when he nailed them onto the roof. I could tell by looking at the pieces that had been protected from the weather. But the rains had worked away at the exposed surfaces, tearing them up over the years and wearing them down so that some were little more than dust, held together by failing remnants of cedar resin.

The roof had two pitches, both of them amazingly steep, and we had to work about thirty feet off the ground. The land around the cabin was irregular and uneven, strewn with old stumps and branches Dave had never bothered to clear away.

"Where's the scaffolding?" I asked during a break. "There is no scaffolding," said Dave, "I banged together a bit of a platform over here, though." He took me round a corner and pointed at a rickety construction tacked onto one wall of the cabin. It was about six feet long with a thin plank to stand on.

"It would take us a couple of days to build that all round the house so we can work from it," I said. "Have you got enough wood to do that?" I hadn't seen any two by sixes or two by eights anywhere.

"No," said Dave. "No wood. I figured we could just move this around as we need it."

If the scaffolding had to be dismantled and put back together again every time we'd need to move it, and again later, when we had to put the roll-roofing on, it would take us months to do the roof. Besides, the little structure wouldn't be long enough for the two of us to handle the roll-roofing in the first place.

"What about a ladder?"

"Over there." Dave pointed to a wooden ladder he'd put together. It was leaning up against the side of the shed and missing several rungs.

"Doesn't exactly look as if it's been approved by the Worker's Compensation Board!"

"André's got one he said we could borrow," offered Dave.

We set off down the trail. After a few yards Dave turned off the track, into the forest.

"Short cut," he said, ducking under some moss-laden branches. He pointed out a broken swing. "That was Jess's."

Jess is now a successful barrister in Vancouver, living in a smart city condo. Nevertheless, it was not hard to picture her here, developing her roots, moulding her formidable character. Growing up in a place like this would leave you with few fears of any courtroom.

André was a Quebecer, long displaced. He'd fallen in love with the wildness of the Charlottes and built himself a small, modern cabin, with solar panels to heat water and provide electricity. He had a water barrel, and a composting toilet that looked normal and was completely odourless. He'd given his cottage a metal roof, guaranteed to keep out the rain longer than the sturdiest Graham Island cedar. He offered us his aluminium ladder – and more importantly, he told us to take his two ladder jacks.

"These are great," said Dave. "We can set boards on them to stand on. They're almost as good as scaffolding and much more portable."

"We need two ladders in order to use the jacks," I pointed out.

"I thought you already had a ladder," André queried.

"Gerry's got one," said Dave. "We can borrow his."

Gerry lived further along the trail. He wasn't there when we got to his cabin so we took his ladder and left him a note. Gerry's place was not as smart or as modern as André's, but it had a gas cooker and a proper water pump, a polished wood floor, skylights and a couple of bedrooms.

On the way back Dave showed me Gerry's old biffy. It had been more or less flattened by a fallen tree, but it was like the Ritz compared to Dave's outhouse. When I used it later it was peaceful, and I'd sit there in the forest and listen to the ravens and the chatter of the squirrels, and watch the deer move silently among the trees.

We now had a pair of decent ladders and a substitute for scaffolding. We had even found some rope to give ourselves a bit of security on the steep roof. Dave didn't have an Exacto knife to cut the roofing felt, but I had brought one, just in case. I had also brought a small hammer. I knew I didn't want to be hanging over a thirty-foot drop swinging a heavy framing hammer just to bang in a two-inch roofing tack.

We spent the next six days suspended from the tops of ladders and dangling from the ropes, trying to keep our feet on the steep, slippery cedar wood. We got very dirty, and I used muscles and joints I didn't know I possessed.

It continued to rain, and the leaks in the roof multiplied as we removed the old shakes. At night Dave's mousetraps wreaked terrible carnage, going off like rifle shots and jerking me awake every time they claimed another victim. We had fourteen of them in use, and the peanut butter worked better than the feta.

There was no time for golf or fishing. We were up at six every morning and we went to bed with the sun. But despite the depredations, the compensations were extraordinary: an ethereal silence, a close-woven carpet of stars at night, ravens the size of eagles, eagles the size of paragliders, and sandhill cranes that flew up the slough making such strange, creaking cries that the children up there called them "rusty robots." We saw bear, deer, and ancient cedar trees hung with moss a foot thick. With almost no undergrowth the forest had the ambience of a cathedral. And some days, before things deteriorated to a miner's regimen of pork and beans, we had food to eat that you'd pay a fortune for in London or Paris: smoked Alaska Black Cod baked on the wood stove, venison, fresh crab, clams & scallops. And Dave's Dalwhinnie to wash it down.

HEART SONG

GAEL DUCHENE

I awake in the night with something stirring in my soul, as though I have been transported to another place, another time ... I slip out of my warm bed, my heart calling out to the cold night. My feet remember their way: the hard edges of the loft ladder, eight quiet steps to the door. Outside, the soft wood shavings of the porch floor, then cold damp earth. My hands part the cedar branches wrapped protectively around the small cabin. My feet feel gingerly for the first angled rock on the right, careful not to stub my toes on the rock on the left. One big step down and I enter into the sanctuary of another world.

I stand on a jutting rocky point and breathe deeply, inhaling the silent beauty of the night. Above me, dark clouds sail, revealing glimpses of the starry cosmos stretching out forever. Beneath me, the ocean is quietly ebbing. A curtain softly opens on this great stage of the mudflats at night. There is a hush in the air, but it is alive with expectation.

Then the silence offers a gentle splash. An animal, probably an otter, has slipped off the rocks below and I can hear it swimming now, softly, gently, rhythmically. I hear the blow of exhalation. A seal? I listen to my own soft sigh, then a rustling in the bushes by the water's edge. This sound is almost certainly raccoons or martens.

The gravelly cry of a heron plucks an ancient string in my soul and my body vibrates in tune with a deep primal chord. These night sounds are like an orchestra tuning up.

Clouds part and the moon peeks out as the water recedes. The rippling expanse of the mudflats with all its living treasures is exposed now, luminescent. The stage is set, the feast laid out. The night sings with hundreds of waterfowl commencing to feed.

Some time during these hours of darkness, silence again returns. It is in this deep stillness of the mudflats at night that the song of my own heart is revealed and I am filled with gratitude and love, knowing that I am not just an audience, not only bearing witness. I have a part to play in the magnificence of life.

* * * *

Time has passed and that small cabin in the wilderness of Clayoquot Sound is now gone, yet I still awaken in the quiet of the night, filled with the beautiful heart song of the mudflats, and I am deeply at peace.

A POET'S RETURN

LISA SHATZKY

The late afternoon light penetrates the forest floor in long slanting rays. A hazy softness illuminates countless tiny cobwebs suspended in the dark furrows of these giant and beautiful living columns. Patience walks with me in this space of deep splendour and a sense of timelessness prevails. Here, on the far western edges of Canada, in Clayoquot Sound, I continue to learn how to wait and listen. I am no longer running as fast as I can. I am no longer afraid of the silence. The music I have known is born out of silence and dies away into it again. Between the movements of music, I listen to the manifest silence. And it is perfectly pure, perfectly empty, perfectly giving, and everywhere at once. Sometimes, the music comes from the trees. Sometimes the entire forest sings. I am finally able to answer. Here in an ancient forest by the sea, I am home. Here is where my voice first returned. These are the trees I dreamed of a long time ago. Perhaps they, too, dreamed of me. Yes.

(Last journal entry, summer 1996)

A critically creative moment that changed my life forever came to me when I was a young child, maybe four or five years old. I lay on the grass in our back yard in Montreal in late summer and discovered that I was part of something bigger. It happened just like that, as I watched the different colours of the sky join together. Such exhilaration I felt in my small body with this discovery. No matter what was happening in the family, I knew that if I could go outside and touch the grass or a tree or look at the sky, I would be okay. I felt like I belonged to something very special, something more powerful and beautiful than anything else I knew at the time. The trees and the grass and the stones felt warm to touch and they were part of me and I was part of them. I don't know how I knew this. Maybe all children know this very simple truth, until we tell them otherwise. This was the beginning of my deep connection to the physical earth. And in this connection, I wrote words. From as early as I could remember, I played with words and sounds and rhymes and by the time I was seven I was writing little poems about the trees and the animals and the sky. Sometimes, the words would come through dreams and I remembered them easily. But the most profound dream was a recurrentone: I wander in a forest. There are birds calling. All around me are giant trees so thick and tall that the sky can hardly be seen. I am lost and can't find my brother or my parents but strangely I am not afraid. I try talking to the trees and they answer, not in words, but in song. The forest suddenly swells with a most lovely music and I can feel myself smile. There is something magical about the place and though lost, I feel that I am not alone. Then I wake up.

As a child I wrote many poems about this dream and called them all "The Land of Song." Sometimes when the dream happened, I told myself (while in the dream) that I had to remember the music. If I could somehow remember the music, the forest might actually appear in my waking life. But the music was always gone when I woke up. The image of the place itself was clear inside me yet I spoke to no one about it. I carried it like a secret hiding place I could retreat to when I needed to make myself disappear. All children learn to make themselves disappear when it feels like they are not being seen. Or so this was what I thought. Some kids know how to do it really well. The disappearing part, that is. I was one of those kids.

By the time I was six, my parents' relationship had deteriorated. Even as a very young person, even admidst the confusion and heartache of a family coming apart, I did not blame them. While my deepest wish was that my parents would see the good in each other again and maybe stay together, I somehow understood that this might never happen. So I simply craved their happiness. I longed to see my mother smile. I wanted to hear my father's laughter. Small things easily given. I wanted my brother and I to be okay. I wanted us all to be okay in the end. During difficult times, usually at night, I would lay awake in my bed and pull the blankets over my head and just breathe. And listen. I would close my eyes and imagine the forest of my dreams. Sometimes, if I was lucky, I could make myself go there. It was an odd sensation, to be awake and asleep at the same time. Suddenly the trees would appear in my room - or maybe I found a way to leave my room - and then I was in the magical world of my imagination, safe from the real world of my life

My parents divorced when I was seven and then spent the next six years fighting each other in court, a long, bitter, and drawn out custody battle over the broken pawns of their war, "the children". I wrote as much as I could in the beginning but gradually the words began to disappear. It was as if my own voice was becoming less known to myself. I continued, however, to spend time outdoors. There wasn't much nature in Montreal, but even a flower or a leaf or a stone was of comfort. I relished the warmth of the sun on my small body and the smell of new green leaves in early spring. I imagined that if I could make "contact" with the physical earth, we would all be okay. That somehow the earth had the potential to "save us" if only we listened. I'm not sure if I fully understood at the time the magnitude of these thoughts but in some small way here was the beginning of my spirituality. But the words of how to describe what I was feeling slipped away at the time.

By the time I was thirteen, the writing stopped completely. So did the dreams of that forest. So did visits with my father. I did not see him again until I was nineteen. Looking back on those years now it is no surprise that I became a therapist and the poetry seemed to fade away.

How much easier to immerse myself in the world of academics and stay far away from the world of feelings; how much safer to bear witness to other people's stories and suffering than to get close to my own. There were far worse situations than mine anyway. What right did I have to complain? I continued to read poetry even though my own words seemed gone.

At eighteen I snuck into a Montreal after-hours bar with some friends and got to meet Al Purdy and hear stories of Baffin Island. Something in me was charged again by those stories. I realized how the city was not the right environment for me and I craved a more natural setting. I longed to find a forest that resembled the one I dreamed of as a child. The next year I made my way to Baffin Island with some anthropology students from McGill and lived there for a few months. I liked being on an island as far away from the concrete and stifling city as possible. From Baffin Island I ended up in Thunder Bay for a few months and then made my way to the Gaspé. I was searching for land to belong to again. I loved the natural landscapes of the Gaspé, its people and culture, abundant wildflowers and windswept shores. I may have stayed there forever had it not been for the question that hovered along the edges of my imagination, an imagination I couldn't quite reach but sensed its presence still. I stood by the water's edge one day in early autumn with the first leaves already turning when that old question surfaced again: Is this the place of my dream?

An obsession with geography emerged for me and is still present to this day. If I could feel more connected to a physical place, to a geographical location, would the words hidden out of reach inside me return? Could I return to the child-space where the words flowed as if my whole body became a vessel connecting me to something large and beautiful, like those times I lay in the grass and looked up at the sky? It was a big question and perhaps it scared me. I returned to Montreal and continued my studies and put the question out of my mind. I even stopped reading poetry and was eventually accepted into graduate school. But one day, a few years later, I woke up in the middle of the night and felt a loneliness and brokenness so profound in me that I began to weep. All I wanted was to get in the car and drive and keep driving for as long as possible until the road ended and I could touch the Pacific Ocean. A few weeks later my boyfriend and I packed up his old beater and headed out west on the Trans-Canada Highway. No work, not much of a plan, and a five thousand dollar loan my father co-signed for us, bewildered that we were leaving. Somewhere in me a fragment of a dream remained.

In 1990, at the age of twenty-two, I set foot on Long Beach in Clayoquot Sound for the very first time. It was the beginning of spring and everything was in bloom. I was struck by the smell of the ocean, the sweet spray mixed with the flowering blossoms. There were a few surfers out and we stood there watching them rise and fall with the ocean swells and I admired their perseverance. The sun slowly melted on the horizon, changing from red to pink to bright orange gold resembling a Kumquat fruit. Afterwards we wandered in the forest along the edges of the beach for a while until a damp mist settled in the gathering darkness and the black shadows whispered in the breeze. It felt as if I had come home. I started a journal that evening. My first creative writing since I was thirteen.

How long have you lived inside me, oh deep forest of the wild edges of my heart? How good it is to finally meet you. Touch me so I may awaken and live again. Hold me so I may find the lost words. This is my first time here and yet I have known you all my life. I have been waiting to return.
(*FIRST JOURNAL ENTRY IN CLAYOQUOT SOUND, SPRING 1990*)

And the next six years were about that return. I kept a journal in which I wrote every few days. I still did not write any poetry in that time but something inside me was loosening. I don't think I realized what "return" meant, even though I used the word in my journal. Looking back, it becomes clearer now that *return* was more than just returning to a geographical location my heart had dreamed of since early childhood. Return in a larger sense was about returning to being an artist, returning to the creative magical space and source inside me that I had shut down for over a decade. The return was not easy. There were protective walls firmly in place. There were remnants of a painful childhood I had minimized or completely ignored in my paradoxical race to become a therapist. And there was my own ambivalence about poetry in general, and self-doubt about my ability to write in particular. What on earth could I say after all this time? And how? My writing voice was gone. And the speaking voice dared not speak the unspeakable.

I spent enormous amounts of time in the forests in and around Clayoquot Sound those first few years. Meares and Flores Island called to me, as one who loved islands. Hot Springs Cove and the Kennedy Lake area were also places of deep solitude and personal exploration. I would go there, a small knapsack on my back, sit, wander, then sit some more. I didn't call it meditation or anything special. It was just sitting time. Waiting. Waiting for what I did not know. I listened to the wind in the trees and the sound of the breakers on distant shores. There was something about these forests and their proximity to the ocean that awakened the part of me desperately trying to rouse itself.

There was something strangely unsettling about these trees. I was moved and absorbed and stirred by them. There was a sense of the mysterious and the sublime, and I felt a harmony with something familiar. My body relaxed. My senses opened up. I felt myself breathe more deeply and slowly. It was as if I had to come to the far ends of the earth, to a most wild and precarious and magnificent shore to find the earth's original elders: these ancient trees of the temperate rainforest. And sitting with them enabled me to sit with myself, finally. I had been running for a long time. How exhausting it had been. Here, in the sacred space of these ancient forests, I could no longer distract myself the way I had amidst the glitter of city lights. The long awaited encounter with myself could no longer be avoided. It was as if the veil had been lifted. What was that veil? I can't be sure. Even when I re-read the journal entry, I'm not completely sure what I meant but it seemed as if I could see something I hadn't seen before, even if it had not yet found a way into words.

> *I can feel something larger than what meets the naked eye here in this place. . . . I am not lonely anymore. I am in awe at the magnificent splendour of this wild coast and I will do whatever I can to protect it. I have heard of logging in this area and it frightens me to think that all the secrets and wisdom (and music!) of these trees, of this land, could be so easily lost.*
> *(JOURNAL ENTRY, SPRING 1991)*

Can one be healed through connection to geography? Can one return to being an artist as a result of such deeply embedded connection? I know the answer to both of these to be yes. I believe that one of the purposes of art is to repair the brokenness, to bring the pieces together in such a way that they are integrated back into the singular life of oneself and the collective life of all humanity. I didn't know as a child that writing poetry was my little life-line, my small way to repair the fallen pieces of my world. I could not have known that our bodies and minds and spirits are self-healing, if only we would give them even half a chance and not stand in the way. It was only much later, several years after being in Clayoquot Sound that I realized, if I did not allow what was inside me to be expressed, I would eventually be harmed by it. The geographical features of this wild coast opened something that had been shut down. The raw fury and power of the ocean broke through the protective walls. The ruggedness of the land rattled the dusty corners of my heart. And in the presence of the ancient trees in the fog-shrouded inlets, I began to hear a small voice again, and I listened well.

> *Sometimes I can hear the trees breathing. I know how silly that sounds. But alone in these forests among the sounds of insects flying about, the wind in the leaves, the songbirds, the woodpeckers, the ravens, water trickling somewhere, there is a gentle silence. In that silence I can hear the trees breathing. Or maybe it is my own breath mingled with theirs. Here in this place, the wind knows my name.*
> *(JOURNAL ENTRY, SPRING 1993)*

I have come to believe that so much of our individual and collective suffering comes from the bruised silences we carry like stones in our mouths. After a while, the unsaid and unspeakable things accumulate on the inside and the only way to keep them there is for the surface to freeze over. We can live a seemingly and outwardly productive life without knowing we are frozen. Indeed I had. Then one day the ice began to melt. Suddenly what I thought was solid softened in my hands, like humpback whales breaking the surface to come up for air. Like thousands of monarch butterflies homeward bound. Like bees dancing on the windowsill of my skin. Suddenly I could feel fully again. Everything was intensified, the colours and sounds and smells. And it hurt at first, pins and needles and icicle daggers falling. I hung onto the frozen pieces like precious lifeboats in a great storm. But the wind was silent no more, now that it knew my name. Here in the far west coast, I discovered my name again. I realized that if I wanted the poet back in my life, I would have to be able to allow the unspeakable to be spoken. All artists must be able to sit in the silence of solitude so to eventually break the toxic and bruised silences of the world. We are in this together, as painters, sculptors, musicians, writers, dancers, performers, poets, like a great symphony of colours breaking through the unspoken.

Maybe that is why so many artists, both lost and found, find themselves here on the wild untamed edges of this particular geographical place on earth. There are few distractions. The winds are fierce. The waves are ruthless. The land itself is a survivor of relentless storms. The trees race toward apical dominance so to grab as much light as they can because they know the rains will last for months. Mists and fogs and dark shadows permeate every nook and rock and moment. This is a wild land, not for the faint of heart. But to be an artist, one must be willing to leave, if only for a while, the false security of the concrete linear world and walk in the exquisite storm. And the poet must speak of that storm with eyes wide open even if the hands are trembling. I was ready to give it a try.

By the end of the summer in 1996, at age twenty-eight, I started writing poetry again. The journal writing of the past six years came to an abrupt end. The poems began to trickle back in, a long road back to the beginning. We moved to Bowen Island, a small island that was a twenty-minute ferry ride from Vancouver, but continued to visit the Clayoquot Sound area every month. Bowen was a gentler version of Clayoquot Sound and I seemed to have a need for both. From my home on Bowen I could see Vancouver Island. The presence of those ancient trees was always close, and poetry returned to being at the centre of everything else I did. The ferry travels from Bowen Island to Horseshoe Bay and then to Vancouver Island were natural rhythms from which many poems were first born. Once I started writing, I couldn't imagine how I had gone for so long without it. The words stumbled and fumbled uneasily for a while, as if being aroused out of a long and deep slumber. The poet's voice was frail in the beginning and took some years to acquire a more sure footing. But being on the coast, especially the extreme coast of Clayoquot, continued to instil a sense of patience and acceptance that things would happen in time. Control was never fully mine anyway:

many missed ferries, many power outages in the winter, few amenities compared to the big city. And the poet thrived. And remembered. The sky and its endless and evolving colours and patterns held my gaze with wonder and gratitude. Every stone told a story. My body and spirit fell into the natural rhythms of the seasons and waves. The moonlight hiding behind midnight clouds whispered the poet's return. I could hear her again.

> *And the road is littered with children who fall and can't get up. But do not give up on them. They will surprise you, their strength, their resilience, their spirits. Look closely. They are here. Beyond the concrete hallways and dreamless rooms and paved roads, they are waiting to play again. And when the children weep and the trees sigh and the wolves call, it is all the same song.*
> *(BEGINNING OF THE FIRST POEM, AUTUMN 1996)*

Perhaps ending on the words of the first poem of the poet's return is a good place to be. When I look upon these words now, I am not surprised that they still hold meaning for me. The artist and the child are one. If we are to tap into our naturally creative spirits, we must hold close the hopes and sorrows and dreams of the child inside us. It is from the child the artist emerges. And the child was always connected to the land and its magic and wonder. To the child, there were no divisions between mind and body and spirit. In the wild places, the child was filled with an effervescent sense of awe. Even children who grow up in cities marvel at the stars at night and run with reckless abandon on beaches and play outdoors until their hands and feet are frozen. They do not want to come in. The planet calls to them. And they feel more alive in direct contact with her. Perhaps the allure of Clayoquot Sound has something to do with the raw energy of that child still calling to me. The return of the poet was a return to the wisdom of the child. How do creative people prevail in a not-so-creatively oriented culture? They play. They play and they paint and they sing and they dance and they make things with their hands and they erase the walls and break the ceilings and speak the unspeakable and swim in the culverts as if their lives depended on it. And in their play, the broken pieces of themselves and a greater humanity are given voice and transformation and maybe, even sometimes, some kind of healing. In the presence of those ancient trees, I became a child, many years after the fact.

GETTING IN TUNE
SHIRLEY LANGER

I was seventy-one when I stepped out to centre stage and performed a vocal jazz concert for the first time. A case of late blooming you may surmise, but not so. I have been a registered nurse, raised a family of four, learned Spanish, and worked as the assistant to the editor of a Spanish/English newspaper in Cuba, ran a country inn, received an Honours degree in Romance languages, Spanish and Italian at age fifty, and translated seventeen of Robert Munsch's popular children's books into Spanish. Politics and civic duty enticed me, and I ran for mayor of Belleville, Ontario in 1991, and won the election. More recently I have entered the headspace and world of writing, not as a dalliance, but as a serious endeavour. My most serious writing project is a 300-pages-plus manuscript for young adults about the post-revolution Cuban Literacy campaign. Am I a karma chameleon? Perhaps. But it wasn't until 8pm on the Saturday evening of June 14, 2006 when I took centre stage of the Clayoquot Sound Community Theatre in Tofino, British Columbia, and launched into an upbeat jazz tune that I felt I was doing what I had always wanted to do. In that moment I felt more myself, more authentic, than I had ever felt before.

What took you so long? I hear you asking. The usual obstacles, both naturally-occurring and self-imposed: duty to my family, not knowing how to play an instrument, not having close association with musicians, not wanting to put myself 'out there' by beginning at the bottom where the patrons might ignore me at best, or worse, heckle me, or even worse, throw things at me. Mostly I held myself back, simply lacking the confidence or *chutzpah* to make my dream of performing jazz a reality. Although I sang occasionally at parties, I honed my chops behind closed doors. I was a closet singer singing along with all the jazz greats, mostly emulating the jazz divas Ella Fitzgerald, Sarah Vaughn, Billy Holiday, Nancy Wilson, June Christie, Carmen Macrae, and more recently, Diana Krall. I have learned hundreds of songs from the repertoire called simply, 'the jazz standards.' I started doing this when I was twelve and have never stopped. I felt most vividly alive when attending performances by jazz musicians, although afterward I always had trouble sleeping, so keenly did I feel the unrequited yearning to be one of them.

The first time I visited Tofino was in the late '70s and I was so captivated that I vowed I would live there someday. It wasn't until 1995 that I finally was able to move to this tiny wet, west coast village carved out of the temperate rainforest at the edge of the continent. From here you can go no farther. You have reached the western terminus of the Trans-Canada Highway. To leave, you can only turn around and roll back up the same road. So I settled in.

It was the fertility of Tofino's music scene that spurred me to turn my fuzzy dreams into a modest performance plan. Music, informal and staged, amateur and professional, was performed often in this difficult-to-get-to village. Despite its remoteness, celebrity performers enjoy playing here. After being showered with love by a Tofino audience, performers such as guitarist Don Ross, bluesman Harry Manx, or singer/songwriter Katherine Edwards may fall asleep to the sound of surf in some beach house, awaken to go boogey-boarding, surfing, or simply take a walk along the expanse of one of Tofino's gorgeous beaches before setting out for their next gig. Travellers often strum guitars sitting around driftwood fires on the beaches or lounging on the patio of the Common Loaf Bake Shop. Folkies and rockers entertain at house parties. Every winter a classical music series is booked at the community theatre. Music fills the air of this coastal edge.

Many of us are moved emotionally by the sounds we hear and the sounds we make. Sound lures us to move physically, to sway, clap our hands, tap our feet. As I walked the beaches, I began to sing aloud and compose songs, emotionally jazzed by the splendour resulting from the symphony of light, clouds, reflection, shadows, colours, movement and sound that every vista presented. Days of un-interrupted gray skies prompted the blues, laments about bad dudes and bad times, or the celebration of righteous women and hopeful times. On brilliant sunny days, jubilation tunes about having the world on a string and having it around your finger prevailed. The intervals of the waves breaking on the shore set the tempo. My feet scuffing the sand could sound like brushes swishing on a drum. A roiling sea surging into a cave or channel boomed like an upright bass. I imagined the voices of backup singers carried by the riffing wind. On the days it seemed I could see the very needles of hemlock trees on Meares Island, I would belt out that well-known song about seeing clearly, literally and figuratively.

Eventually I got to know some local musicians. They weren't jazz musicians, but they were open to learning some jazz tunes. That was 1998. We rehearsed twenty numbers, and called our jazz quartet *Jazzmatazz*. Guitarist and vocalist Wayne, a talented carpenter by trade, had broad musical knowledge. Erv, a tiler in his day job, played bass. The third musician I never knew by any other moniker than "Slab," which undoubtedly referred to his body type. Slab's hands were red and inflamed and often pained him because his day job con-sisted, as he explained it, of "guttin' and evisceratin'" iced fish at the local fish plant." Despite Slab's work-damaged hands, his precise drumming was the timekeeper for *Jazzmatazz*.

We gave a dozen-or-so performances, often in the lounge of a local resort. The audiences were mostly locals, with many friends among them. It was nerve-wracking, but exhilarating too. The guys looked great, dressed up in clothing they hadn't worn in years pulled from the backs of their closets. A local sax player performed with us occasionally and his improvisations were crowd pleasers.

Despite the nerves, the gaffes, some false starts, a few faked endings, we enjoyed ourselves, and audience feedback for *Jazzmatazz* was favourable. Regardless of the gratification I felt performing with the group, I realized that playing the same repertoire repeatedly in a small community like ours would become tiresome to the audience as well as to us. I told the guys it was necessary to add and rehearse new tunes, which would naturally require considerable time and effort. They were resistant, so eventually *Jazzmatazz* dissolved.

During the year we performed, I had learned some significant things about singing and delivery, the kinds of things that were not manifest when performing was just a daydream. I had learned how much stamina is required, about being an entertainer as opposed to merely singing, about collaboration with fellow musicians, about gauging the responses of a paying (and drinking) audience, and importantly, about coping with the unexpected–like singing at an open air event without amplification, for example.

Nine years passed before the itch to take the stage again became an obsession. Though musicians were around, there weren't any experienced jazz instrumentalists in the area, and I wanted to perform in a concert setting with seasoned professionals. During that time, I felt as though an earthquake, a creative eruption was slowly forming within me. The desire to perform was like the tectonic plate off the Tofino coast, slowly but inexorably grinding under the fault line. I was holding back because I told myself that it would be ridiculous for a woman my age without a critical performance history to suddenly appear on stage in concert.

Elder jazz divas still performing had started when they were young, but they had been world famous for decades. They didn't even need last names. *Ella* was enough. *Sarah* was enough. The world of convention was on a collision course with my world of unrequited satisfaction. If I didn't give expression to this need, I felt that an impending and devastating disappointment in myself would ensue. I felt completely out-of-tune, yet I needed to see what I could bring forth if I really prepared and had the backing of musicians with deep roots in jazz performance. The writer Somerset Maugham once said that every production of an artist should be the expression of an adventure of his or her soul. Getting in tune became imperative. I was one of many people in Tofino who had ventured down the corkscrew road and stayed. Surely others like me, young or not so young, were likewise inspired to develop and exhibit their creative talents within the spectacle that is Clayoquot Sound. Surely they would support me on my quest for creative expression, despite my age.

I began looking for a jazz pianist.

Though I contacted many pianists, they all declined when they heard I didn't already have professionally charted music and arrangements of the tunes. But persistence eventually paid off. An acquaintance from Victoria mentioned that a neighbour across the street played the piano. She thought it was jazz. My Jewish *chutzpah* genes surged forward again.

"Knock on the piano player's door, give him my name, get his phone number and ask if I can call him," I said. She did, and thus I came to know and collaborate with Robert.

At our initial meeting in his home, he said he would play a gig with me if, and only if, I had what he called "the chops." I sang Gershwin. Robert's next words gave me all the courage I needed from then on.

"Yep, you've got the chops."

Then a whirlwind of preparation and organizing began. As producer of the show as well as performer, I booked the Clayoquot Community Theatre in Tofino. I hired musicians from Victoria; obtained local accommodation for them; got a smashing poster designed, printed and distributed around town (and replaced them when they were taken as souvenirs); arranged for tickets to be sold at various venues (how I agonized over what I should charge); obtained a permit to serve alcoholic beverages; arranged for the food concession and servers for the intermission; decorated the theatre lobby and stage; hired a sound and light technician; arranged for the sound check and people to handle tickets; and planned the after show party.

During this time, I travelled to Shawnigan Lake where Robert now lived, so that we could work on the songs I had selected for the playlist. We had to work out keys, tempos, and arrangements. Thinking that singing lessons would be time and money well spent, I practiced breathing and vocalese exercises twice a week with Sandi, a talented local musician and singer twice a week.

"Yo-o-ee-o . . . Yo-o-ee-o . . . Let me see how low you can go!" I sung in descending scales.

"Fill up that barrel with air!" Sandi coached, referring to the expanding of my whole ribcage, front and back, to let lots of air flow into my lungs.

"Flatten your tongue! Raise your palate!" Encouraging smiles accompanied all her commands.

Two weeks before the gig, Robert threw a party and invited me and the two other musicians who would round out the trio, but whom I hadn't met yet. Robert challenged me to entertain the guests with a few tunes from the playlist. Many of the guests were accomplished musicians and artists. Would I pass muster? When Robert introduced me, they all drew chairs round like a real audience, settled in and turned their eyes to me expectantly.

Nervousness can ruin any performance, and I wanted to please these people, Robert's friends. He had already done so much for me. The few songs that I had chosen to sing were novel, and not well-known. *Just have fun,* I told myself. *They will love these tunes.* They did, and their applause was warm. As a trial run, that small performance boosted my confidence and served as good preparation for the gig itself. A few days before the gig, we gathered at Robert's again for a complete rehearsal. The only one.

At three in the afternoon the day of the show, I knew I wouldn't be singing to an empty house. Tickets to *Summertime: An Evening of Cool Jazz* sold well. The theatre looked terrific, decorated with creative arrangements of jazz album covers. The musicians were assembled on stage to run through a couple of numbers for the sound check. Robert, upbeat as always, sat before his electronic keyboard. Alex, as tall if not taller than his upright bass, was cool and collected. Gerry, the percussionist, stood before his conga drums and array of other percussion instruments.

All was as it should be prior to a show, except for me. I was feeling completely flat, flatter than a flounder, deflated of energy and enthusiasm. I sang part of one number during our sound check practice, and announced that I couldn't do anything more and left the stage.

"See you this evening," I said over my shoulder as I left the theatre, leaving everyone wondering if there would even be a show that night. Robert would tell me later that he had had to reassure Alex and Gerry that I would be just fine. And I was. A bath, something to eat, the ritual of careful dressing and application of make-up, some vocal warm-ups, a self-directed pep talk, and I was in performance mode.

Of course a singer's vocal performance is the main element for a good show. But singing isn't everything. Having presence, being able to command the stage and put people at ease plays a large part in engaging an audience. A gift of the gab is important so you can entertain the audience throughout the show in some agreeable way. And how you look cannot be underestimated. Looking good makes the performer feel good, and builds audience expectation. I would have liked to show some skin, but darn it, I'm always cold, especially when 'nerves' are affecting things. When I first emerged onstage, the audience greeted me with applause. A gratifying beginning!

I sang. I *kibitzed* with the audience. I think I may have even brought tears to some eyes with an achingly beautiful Spanish lament. I talked about the origins of some of the songs. I even flirted. I know–shameless behaviour for a mature woman! The greatest compliment regarding my performance came spontaneously from the musicians. Excited by the enthusiasm of the audience, satisfied with the gig, they kindly said, "It's hard to believe you haven't been doing this forever, Shirley!" But I know the outcome of the evening would have been far different if the musicians hadn't provided the calibre of musical support that gave me confidence and inspired me to do my best.

I remained in touch with the musicians, and two years later, on another beautiful June evening, I produced another concert, *Shades of Jazz and Blues.* The theatre had recently been bequeathed a fabulous grand piano, a Kawai. My friend Pam had decorated the stage as an elegant cabaret and almost every seat was occupied. The musicians took the stage, a quartet this time: Robert on the grand's ivories, impressive Alex on bass, the marvellous Gordon playing all the saxophones, clarinet, and flute, and the band's timekeeper, drummer Michael.

As I peeked at the audience through a slit in the curtains, I saw quite a few faces unknown to me. Tourists perhaps. I briefly wondered if they would be surprised to see a gray-haired woman (sporting a streak of burgundy red that evening) take the stage. Robert counted the tempo for the opening number and began playing. My cue. I sashayed out to the microphone and began the evening with a beloved song by Leonard Cohen, who happens to be my age.

In jazz lingo, the musicians that night were monsters, electrifying the audience with their energy and dazzling solos. Some of the tunes I had chosen were demanding: difficult melodies, sophisticated lyrics, Latin rhythms. The audience was definitely grooving. But suddenly, there was a musical mishap. A few bars into a love song promising that "The Best Is Yet To Come", I realized Robert and I were out of synch. I don't know what Ella would have done, but I stopped singing. Full stop. It took a few moments for the musicians to realize something had happened, so the music didn't simply stop, but sort of petered out. The audience remained cool and laughed heartily when Robert stood, and like a master of ceremonies announced dramatically, "Ladies and gentlemen, you have just witnessed what we in the music biz call . . . a train wreck." I reassured the audience that the best *was* yet to come, and we started the tune again, this time in synch.

When it came time to sing *Black Drawers*, a risqué blues I had composed, another gaffe occurred, but the audience never knew it. We had rehearsed this tune only once, and had set the tempo as a slow blues. Robert was waiting for me to count the band in for the tempo. I was waiting for him. Concerned with the slight lapse, and wanting to avoid another train wreck, Gord took the initiative, blowing a rousing blues sax intro. Trouble was the tempo was far too fast. I just jumped in, squeezing the mouthfuls of naughty, double entendre lyrics into racing musical lines, twisting my tongue and body with all the bravura I could muster.

> *Oh I woke up this mornin', reachin' for the telephone*
> *Yes, woke up this mornin', reachin' for the telephone*
> *Was my baby callin', this is what he said to me:*
> *Baby you must meet me, meet me when the sun goes down*
> *Oh baby you must meet me, meet me at the park in town*
> *And when you come to greet me, be sure to have your black drawers on.*
>
> *Not your red ones trimmed with lace*
> *Don't like no stripes or spots*
> *Don't want no bows or sequins*
> *And I hate polka dots*

Not blue, not pink, not brown
That just don't turn me on
Oh wear your black drawers honey
Yes wear your black drawers honey
And meet me... when the sun goes down.

When I had sung the twenty songs on the playlist, I felt utterly gratified when the audience demanded an encore. I felt embraced by a village, encouraged by that independent spirit that pervades Tofino and Tofino audiences. I felt appreciated by people who valued the performance of the performers, unhampered by conventional judgments about age appropriateness. It had indeed been a soul-satisfying adventure. I felt 'in tune' with myself, and I wondered, had I satisfied the audience's jazz-loving appetite for a good show? I hope so, for that's what counts. From the stage I invited the entire audience back to my house for the after show party and many came.

I know there will be a next time. Maybe I'll be inspired by the rainforest muse that suffuses our lives to write and perform a song about the remarkable wilderness that surrounds us. I love the poignancy of a song that Diana Krall wrote, the lyrics evocative of her hometown of Nanaimo. It is a song about place, about the fading scents of summertime, of arbutus trees and firs, of personal loss and love gained. Let's see . . . ancient cedars, lemon taste of new hemlock tips in spring, a twisting road, lacework edge of surf lapping the shore, ribbons of kelp tangled on the tide line, sharp scent of salt, the setting sun swallowed by the sea, the eye of the moon rising over Meares, the drifting fogs of August . . . Tofino, I hear a song coming on!

Acknowledgements:

Black Drawers © Shirley Langer, 2007.

WATER

THE ART OF NOTICING
MARK HOBSON

It was almost dark. The surrounding forest had lost all its detail and become a jagged wall of silhouettes against the fading sky. It was a rare calm evening in November. After a few days of basic carpentry I was preparing to spend my first night on a floating cabin I had recently purchased and towed to a remote inlet in Clayoquot Sound off the west coast of Vancouver Island. Reflections of the skyline hardly rippled in the water, separating the float house from the shoreline only twenty meters away. The smell of low tide was rich in the still air. As the darkness deepened I was looking for matches to light a Coleman lantern when suddenly from the shore there was an enormous explosion of sound. I was taken completely by surprise. For a second I thought it was someone playing a rude trick, but then realized it must be an animal, a howling wolf in fact. I had heard wolves calling on previous occasions from a distance but never did they sound like this. In a few seconds the howl was joined by another, and then another from three locations all very near.

The contrast from almost complete silence to the volume of this full throated chorus was incredible and in the coolness of the evening air it was as if they were calling right into my ear. I grabbed my largest flashlight and was rewarded by four pairs of eyes sparkling back at me. The presence of the flashlight stopped the howling for a moment but then the first wolf started up again. For several minutes their calls continued and the sound echoed and re-echoed back and forth from the surrounding forested hillsides. After a while I thought they must want to say hello to their new neighbour and felt obliged to try to respond with an answer. I am sorry I did, for no sooner had I opened my mouth in an attempt to imitate their calls than the entire group shut up instantly. I am not sure what I said in wolf jargon but my attempt was obviously something most inappropriate for in a second their reflective eyes vanished from my flashlight beam. Two years passed before I saw wolves again in that location.

That night as I lay in my sleeping bag on the floor of the bare cabin I thought of how the wolves were a good omen. I had dreamed since childhood of having a painting studio in a wilderness setting on the British Columbia coast. Having a pack of wolves as the welcoming committee epitomized everything I had imagined about finding a place where I could paint enveloped in the rhythms of the natural world.

Keeping Watch, acrylic on canvas (See page 144 Colour Insert)

The genesis of this moment had occurred sometime between the age of nine or ten. Throughout my growing up our family travelled and lived overseas interspersed with periods back in British Columbia. My father's work as an engineer took us to live in a variety of fascinating countries including Sri Lanka, Bangladesh, Nigeria and Portugal. My brother and I had spent some years at a boarding school in Northern Ireland but even though these experiences were all generally positive ones, the four years we spent back in Canada in Powell River on the inside waters of the British Columbia coast had probably the strongest impact. I was between eight and twelve years old and summers were spent puttering by boat among the archipelago of islands and inlets that occupy the northern end of Georgia Strait. I was drawing almost every day. Animals and marine life were my main fascination but scenes of abandoned homesteads and old logging camps also appeared among the dozens of sketches that have survived from those years. Even as a ten year old I imagined fixing up one of these old cabins and making it into a place from which to explore and to paint.

In November 1990, almost thirty years later, I had finally come full circle and at last had that studio in one of the most spectacular parts of the entire British Columbia coast, approximately nine kilometres north of Tofino and surrounded by the vibrant natural setting of Clayoquot Sound. The bay is leased as an oyster farm which legally permits one floating caretaker's cabin within four hundred meters of the growing oysters. The arrangement has been of mutual benefit for the oyster farmer and me.

My passion for the true west coast occurred the first time I visited Long Beach in 1971. I was with a group of friends from the University of Victoria where we were studying biology. A Volkswagen van with more beer than food bounced along the gravel logging roads and arrived in the dark the same weekend Princess Anne snipped the ribbon that marked the beginning of Pacific Rim National Park. Ceremonies were taking place somewhere down the beach but nothing could distract me from the scene that stretched in all directions before us that morning. I was in total awe. I had no idea that a place like this existed. The sheltered waters of Georgia Strait were picturesque but this outer coast had a rugged beauty beyond expectation. The steady unbroken roar of the surf, the huge piles of driftwood at the high tide line, and the dark, straight wall of Sitka spruce with eagles patrolling effortlessly in the up draughts made a tremendous first impression. The natural world was in full control here. Rain, wind, and the sea influenced everything. The sheer power of the north Pacific unleashed itself day and night on these shores and life had to abide by its rhythms or flounder. Even humans for once could not force their whims on the landscape but instead were huddled in the protection of only a few sheltered harbours along this extreme coastline.

Within a week of my first encounter with the outer coast I had bought my first set of acrylic paints and was trying to relive the experience by painting from memory a scene depicting a rocky shoreline near Radar Beach. It is still one of my favourite spots. After a few more visits the dream of living somewhere on the British Columbia coast was drawing me like a magnet towards the west side of Vancouver Island. Bamfield looked like my first choice; Ucluelet and Tofino were close seconds and even Kuyquot was a possibility. Finally a job offer to work as a park interpreter at the newly completed Wickaninnish Centre was enough for me to abandon my career as a high school science teacher and move to Tofino in 1984. Working for National Parks in the summers provided the perfect transition period since it freed up the winters for painting. After four years with an art career in its fledgling stages I decided to leave Parks Canada and paint full time.

In the years that followed I have come to appreciate Clayoquot Sound more and more. Over the years I have made numerous trips along the entire coastline and even throughout much of the Alaskan Panhandle. Everywhere one travels along this intricate network of islands, inlets and small communities there is outstanding beauty but nowhere else is there as much variety of habitat and indeed painting subjects in one location as in Clayoquot Sound. The wide swaths of sandy beaches are attractive indeed but there is a wealth of other features that culminate to make this place truly outstanding. First and foremost the land is comparatively free of the extensive clearcuts and tightly packed replanted forests that extend over the majority of Vancouver Island and other portions of the coast. For the most part Clayoquot Sound is an untouched landscape large enough to function as it has for thousands of years. The expansive 1,549 hectares of mudflats, perhaps the remnants of an ancient terminal moraine from the last ice age, provide a vital stop-over for over 100,000 shorebirds on their migration route every spring and late summer. The moist forests have over the centuries allowed some giant cedars to slowly increase their girth to attain proportions larger than any others presently found in Canada. Five main inlets with several offshoots penetrate into the steeply forested mountains of Vancouver Island, each with a wild river at its head where salmon spawn during the wet autumn months. Elusive Roosevelt elk, cougars, wolves, and black bears travel these waterways. The mountains themselves, though guarded by dense undergrowth and steep ravines, are another world to explore for those determined enough to make the effort. Even the four human communities blend into the folds of the landscape more graciously than most. With their government docks' brightly painted red railings and slimy green pilings, they are rich in history and connected to the seasonal flow of their surroundings. The wealth of painting material could never be depleted in one lifetime.

Ironically it was the might of the Pacific I found so exhilarating that almost ended me and my painting career altogether. I had bought a small house in Tofino but it was not working out as well as I had hoped as a work space. I needed more solitude and to be closer to the natural world. When friends Vicky and Patrick offered a cabin on the exposed, west side of Wickaninnish Island as a painting studio, I jumped at the offer and for three winters packed paints and easels by inflatable zodiac across the swells to an unbelievable setting. Only the curve of the earth interrupted the view out the front windows, and the open ocean often unleashed its pent up energy on the rocky shore just below the cabin's foundations. To the horizon the mood of the heaving seas could change completely every few hours and I painted seascape after seascape learning how the ocean behaved in all kinds of conditions. Travel back and forth to Tofino, however, could be precarious and one night while trying to meet a commission deadline I headed out despite a brewing storm. A huge wave came out of nowhere swamping my sixteen-foot Zodiac. I was sent, along with my art supplies and several paintings, into the icy waters of an early March night. The boat and supplies were eventually recovered but the artwork never surfaced. I was lucky to have made it ashore in the dark from the surging waters and took the lesson seriously. The ocean sets the rules on the outer coast, especially in winter, and to ignore them I realized was asking for trouble. Before the next winter I had found the floathouse and was towing it into a more sheltered section of Clayoquot Sound.

At the time of this writing, almost twenty years have passed since the first evening encounter with the howling wolves. The floathouse serves as a home and studio for as much of the year as I can possibly manage. It has come a long way from the initial lop-sided cabin that was first towed into position in November of 1990. I have a house in Tofino where telephones, computers, framing supplies, and drawers full of limited edition prints are kept out of the rain, but almost all the creating of artwork is done at the floating studio, approximately a half hour boat ride from the docks in Tofino.

I was primarily seeking a workspace free of interruptions, but being embedded in a fully functioning segment of the natural world has had rewards far greater than I could have imagined. Through daily excursions by canoe or scrambling into the undergrowth I have spent thousands of hours getting to know the bay with its surrounding hills, bogs, and forests. A fascination with the lives of plants and animals with which I share this part of the earth was a driving force in attaining a degree in Biology and is the same force that influences most of my art endeavours. All my favourite paintings come from encounters I have experienced in the wild. Spending a few days to a week on a painting is a wonderful way to prolong or relive that experience.

In twenty years dozens of notebooks have been filled with entries of the day-to-day events that occur in the inlet, and it is interesting how often a seemingly isolated occurrence has revealed itself as a pattern when several years of notes are reviewed. The first male Rufous hummingbirds, for example, have returned from their winter migration in the south with surprising precision on the 23rd or 24th of March annually while a week later every spring all the adult great blue herons depart the area leaving only a few juvenile herons to remain through the summer. Where the herons of Clayoquot Sound go to nest in early summer is still a mystery. Every few months I gather up the compiled notes and ship the information to the Biodiversity Centre for Wildlife Studies in Victoria, where computers are assembling a vast database on the natural history of British Columbia.

Noticing details of the natural world is the hallmark of both naturalist and nature artist. While sketching salal flowers in July one morning I spotted tiny mites on the stamens and inner petals of the small bell-shaped, pink flowers. These mites were identical to those that appeared on the hummingbird feeder the same week and identical to mites that live among the jewel-like feathers of adult hummingbirds. In mid-summer when young hummingbirds are learning to fly the ingenious mites have timed their own breeding cycle to coincide with the first nectar meals being taken by the newly fledged hummers. A new generation of mites crawls down the beak of their adult hosts and transfers via the salal flowers to set up housekeeping on the unsuspecting youngsters. I find information like this fascinating as it provides an insight into the interconnectedness of the lives of creatures that are all around us.

Photography can be highly rewarding, but if time allows, sketching a subject can create a far deeper sense of connection. Sketching or painting forces observation on an intimate level and is one of the best ways to get to know something well. It takes concentration to notice the dozens of visual details that eventually go into a painting. The angle an alder twig makes with a branch or the way light glows through a blade of kelp hung up over a boulder at low tide all have to be consciously seen before they can be reproduced on paper or canvas. Painting on location in "plein air" is a fabulous way to connect to the environment and to hone one's observational skills. It keeps the mind open to new concepts of compositions that might not occur in the studio. All the required visual information is usually right there, available if you simply look for it. There can be, however, a few challenges to painting out of doors. I have certainly had battles with wind, rain, bugs, and temperature but there are often unexpected encounters with wildlife when one is sitting still for a few hours. These often make up for the other inconveniences. I once had three young mink play with my shoelaces while I was painting until their mother returned with a fresh caught crab and anxiously shooed them away. Another time I was being watched by a jet black wolf on a windswept beach on Calvert Island. When I finally noticed him and slipped away to try to get his picture, a pair of ravens attacked my tubes of watercolours leaving trails of bright colours and their foot prints across the scene on which I was working.

Of course in the rainy winter months it becomes rare to find a day when it is possible to paint out of doors. I retreat to the studio and it is during this time that I do my larger and most challenging pieces. Some of the works take several weeks to complete and are nearly always attempts at capturing the mood of a particular place or particular time of day. The subject matter may vary considerably from old docks and fish boats to underwater scenes, but lighting and its play on the subject is always a crucial component. The fleeting light among fog and mist especially intrigues me. In fact it is usually in the way light falls on or through a subject that initiates the painting in the first place. For example, the light shining through the underside of a spiny leaf of Devil's Club was a relatively insignificant part in the final scene, but it was the launching point for a painting of four wolves that took two weeks to complete. I rarely feel I have done a complete work unless I have included something of the animal's lifestyle and its connection to its habitat. It is frequently just as fulfilling, if not more so, to accurately paint the plant life and supporting rocks or logs as it is to paint the creature that becomes the focal point.

Another common theme in my work is the presence of water – not surprising perhaps since I see water from all four sides of the studio. I am always amazed at how many ways the surface of the bay can look within the space of a few minutes. Moving water, calm water, tide pools, reflections, and crashing surf all have their particular challenges but they greatly assist in setting the mood in a scene from highly dynamic drama to the most peaceful serenity. Often working through trial and error, I explore the way reflections flicker in a moving stream or the way a glimpse of light shines through a wave just before it breaks. This provides a great sense of satisfaction when it is finally done successfully, adding layers of understanding as to how the world works by building one's repertoire of skills, which greatly assists in the artist's versatility and ability to problem solve.

Taking all the tangle of visual information and boiling it down to fit within the confines of a rectangular paper or canvas so that it depicts a certain feeling can be a daunting task. This is an exciting stage in a painting's journey but rarely a relaxing one. What to leave in, what to leave out, how bright or how dark, what colour and shapes. All this has to be carefully weighed and considered. The gestation period before paint ever touches the canvas can vary greatly. The composition can sometimes fall into place fairly quickly or may take several years, returning to the topic over and over with small doodles before it is finally worked out. Sometimes another artist's work will provide a breakthrough to seeing a subject from a new angle or inspire a unique solution. Once a composition is fairly well established it goes into a sketchbook and is added to a catalogue of painting ideas that may have to wait with dozens of others for a break in the list of commitments before getting a chance to see the light of day.

I am frequently asked I if use photographs when I paint. I certainly refer to photographs but a photo by itself is never the impetus that sets the painting in motion. For over fifteen years I photographed wildlife professionally for a range of magazines, calendars, and books. Hundreds of hours waiting for the right moment to get a particular image have provided rich memories. Many of the paintings I now create are inspired by those experiences. Often images I wished I had photographed, but missed become the scenes that I choose to turn into paintings. I keep an extensive file of photos from magazines, postcards, calendars, and thousands of my own slides. I gather all the available pictures I have if I am tackling a tricky subject, especially if it is for the first time. The position plants and animals will take in the composition is usually roughed out fairly early in the process independent of the file of references. Photographs are then invaluable in checking the details such as the shape of a salmonberry leaf or the way a cougar's back leg bends. The reference photos are used to fill in the gaps in the details but rarely provide the inspiration for the overall piece. As the years go on and I accumulate more experience, I frequently work from memory of the subjects that have become familiar.

It is interesting to note that what makes a good wildlife photograph, however, is not necessarily what makes a good painting. To photograph an eagle, for example, with its talons clamped around the body of a freshly caught salmon in midair would be a prize of any wildlife photographer. To paint the same subject, however, would most likely be too cliché. Searching for that fine line between a well composed natural setting and one that looks too contrived can take considerable planning.

In most cases creating a work of art is more like a journey than anything else. I often have to answer the question, "Which is your favourite painting?" Like a mountaineer who has just climbed a mountain, the best answer is often, "The next one." The journey to finishing a painting, especially a fairly major one, is full of excitement, disappointments, some failures, hard work, and eventually some sense of relief when it is all over. By the time I have been stuck in a tiny rectangular segment of canvas for two weeks I am more than ready for it to be over and nothing is more exciting than thinking of starting the next one. As it is for mountain climbers, reaching a summit is often not as exhilarating as the process of getting there.

To make a living as an artist, despite the myth that it is completely free of stress and deadlines, is in many ways very similar to running any other business. Shipments have to be carefully packaged, works have to be framed, websites updated, bookkeeping entered, prints need to be proofed and signed, and a whole range of office details need to be kept up on a day-to-day basis. In all of this work my assistant Rino ably assists me, but even with his dedication there is rarely a period longer than a week that I can be at the studio before something elsewhere requires my attention. Trips away from the bay for any reason are never done willingly. I always feel a bit anxious when I have to leave since there are always questions that are left in midair. Will the nesting eagles make a successful first flight with their new chick? Are the red-legged frogs that lost all their eggs last year to a heavy frost going to breed again this season in the same location? To be away feels very much like skipping a chapter in a thrilling mystery novel, or being pulled away from a movie and missing a few important scenes that make the rest of the story harder to follow. Life goes on of course and it is truly a privilege to be part of the comings and goings of so many interconnected species year after year in a thoroughly natural environment. I can find a degree of inspiration in almost every place I have ever visited, but in the middle of Clayoquot Sound, where wolves can be heard howling at dusk, the naturalist and the visual artist in me have found a perfect melding.

SEAFLESH

CELESTE SNOWBER

Photo: Jacqueline Dingman (See page 145 Colour Insert)

I am stilled in the presence of seascapes. The red arbutus leans towards the water. The light is changing over the bluffs. It is within the echoes of ocean I am enveloped and transformed. Here I experience the caress of island life, island *'mater.'* The matter of earth, the matter of the god/esses, I am beckoned once again to what really matters.

I grew up in Nahant, an island town on the coast of Boston, Massachusetts. I still have a deep affection for its shore, which is marked by the Atlantic. For the last twenty years it has been the Gulf Islands off the coast of Vancouver which have wooed me to their soil and salt, and it is Galiano Island in particular where I return again and again to be enfolded in the hand of beauty.

This island has a flesh. I sink into its crevice rocks, the goddess sofa as I have called it, and find a stone that not only holds my bare body in summer, but also supports my winter boots. I am endlessly captivated by this island — textures, sinews, and shapes of stone, rock, arbutus — each fabric of this seascape has managed to weave its way within my psyche, body, and leak into my words. The word has become flesh. The stone has turned to poem. Salt air has breathed its pungent smell on the pages of my world and writing in multiple ways that hold beauty, both dissonant and consonant, always constant. The elements of ocean have birthed a kind of attentiveness in seeing and being which ultimately has brought me to new eyes. Fresh eyes, ones for seeing with a beginner's sight.

I come again and again to this island as lover and in this intimate relationship I rejuvenate my love to create, and most of all my love to live. Islands are in my blood. My earliest memories are of walking on rocks by myself and with childhood friends, picking mussels for dinner, endless days at Short Beach in Nahant with my mother, kayaking the open Atlantic in front of our house with my father, eating meals by the sea, and returning to the ocean as a place for play and prayer, comfort and centring. The movement inherent in a life by the sea has mirrored the movement within my own soul. I return to my sacred spots in this west coast island to see for the first time.. First sight. TS Eliot speaks of returning to things as if seeing for the very first time. Landscapes that border the edge of sea are the lens, which brings me back to first sight.

I am reading the sea; the sea of creation reads me. The language of colour: burnt umber arbutus, deep forest green cedar, grey water, white and blue clouds, pink and lavender sky, green wet moss, brittle branch — all moistened by rain. Literacy is often equated with language. I am after a literacy, which touches beyond words, yet words are part of it; a living word, a word becoming flesh, creation as flesh, flesh becoming word — a seaflesh. Sitting at the ocean's feet, I am swooned to words, words coming from breath. My body is part of the literacy of the sea. My chest opens in evening light. Stars call me back to the glorious light of darkness, the darkness within and without. My hands long to touch every part of this oceanscape as a lover. I release my body into salt water, winter cold, and feel alive. I pick agates and grey stones with circles, hold them in my palm, massage them with a tenderness and comfort that only a lover knows. I dance on the rocks, contract towards the earth, and release my limbs toward the sky. I lean against the trunk of an arbutus and the gestures of my torso move into a duet with this tree of life. Each season beckons me to a physical connection to water, trees, wind, and breath. Every moment is a surrender of my flesh. I feel the wind in my breast and stand taller as I walk amidst arbutus, cedar, pine, and maple. I feel smaller in observing the wild ocean. I feel wider in wading in the open Pacific and feel the breezes stretch out my arms, expand my shoulders, and I become wide open.

Being wooed to be wide open. Is that not what love invites us to do? We risk. We retreat. We open and close. The landscape of ocean invites us to contract and expand with its changing weather, a brush on the canvas of the sea, a brush on the canvas of my heart. The ocean calls one to presence. It is so much larger than I; both beautiful and vicious it demands attention. I am reminded of Rilke's words, "Beauty is the beginning of terror." It is the ocean that I look at with wonder and awe, soothing my soul, and it is also the ocean that has taken lives, one after the other. I grew up with the stories of New England wives waiting for their husbands, lobstermen who never came home. The "Widows Peaks" on top of many of the houses hugging the shore always mesmerized me. I often wondered in my childhood what it would have been like to wait for your loved one to come home, only knowing that the ocean which so readily gave life, took it away. It is the ongoing narrative of loss and birth. It has its own story and it intersects with my story. What I come to know is, I really have no control. For all the ways I can organize, plan, or have intention, life has its own way of living through you and me. The sea teaches me to sit with all that comes: joy, heartache, ecstasy, loss, boredom, disappointment, accomplishment, horror, and wonder, terror and beauty. I am part of it and apart from it.

I come to the ocean and this island for refuge, but more than that, this Pacific seascape is a lover to me, a place of safety and intimacy, and a place where, in surrendering and keeping my own solitude, I come to more deeply know the wisdom of the body. The wisdom, which seeps in as salt water on the muddy shore, trickling to the textures where my body/soul becomes acutely alive is a state of being "wide awake," as Maxine Greene calls it. I hear its wooing, and creation writes me in a literacy of love.

The ocean and in particular this precious island, Galiano, is a love which has had a quality of fidelity to me. I have struggled with that word endlessly in terms of what it means in an intimate relationship, as I am prone to love more than one man, as I am prone to love more than one ocean. I have often said that I would like to be 'bi-coastal,' growing up on the Atlantic, but living on the Pacific for years, it is fierce seascapes I adore. Each has its unique qualities and I love them both, although I reside in the Pacific Northwest. I have come to Galiano Island in many forms over the years: as a part-time resident connected to a communal property, a visitor, a renter, and more recently, by the gracious hospitality of a dear friend, but always it is a first love. And of course it is here that I hold memories of my three dear sons as delighted by the terrain of island life, and its geography forming their own spirits. I could never leave it now. Its salt has seeped into my veins, and I crave it as food, as my nourishment, my sustenance, spiritually, physically, and most of all artistically. Even though I am not privileged to live on it full time and many times I only get glimpses through the months, it always resides within me, calling me back as a faithful lover.

I have been repeatedly writing about the ocean over the years, inspired by island leanings and poems that have been midwifed from the sea, and continue to reveal the ocean as lover. When any relationship dies, either by natural causes, or is lost by other reasons, I am released once more into grief, and it is the ocean at the edge of my island time that has been with me. Faithful. Constant. It is a remarkable solace in my formation. She has been with me through every critical life passage. I am still being formed and unformed and transformed in the presence of her tide. I listen at her edge and hear the voice, which resonates deep and accompanies me when I am away from her shore.

A salt lover embraces me. She breathes, rolls, and bursts in her dance of waves, and sprays her wetness in the folds of my longing. I am pulled to gravity and levity as she swooshes and softens colours of azure blue and fibrous grey. I come to her in need of tending, and her rising tones create a symphony of sound and colour, and once again I thirst for her delight and fold in the shaking of her seismic breast. The ocean has become my lover. This island is the context for her to quake me once again to a place of awe.

As I write this, I get a lovely interruption by a dear friend and enter one of those lingering phone conversations with dark coffee in hand on a Saturday morning. We talk of where we feel at home, both being transplants from other countries than Canada. She asks me if, once the children are gone, I will move where I feel more at home culturally, to the familiar east coast of lively cities. I tell her that I still don't feel at home living mostly in the suburbs; in fact the only place I am home is on the island, where the earthforms are intertwined with who I deeply am. I have thought long about what it means to feel at home, to feel a place of belonging. And belonging has the notion of be/longing within it – being in longing – where I feel much more comfortable.

I am in longing for island time always. I am a woman made up of fibres, air, and water, fire and dust. All possess capacity for great life and great destruction. Floods of water, floods of fire, and my task is to honour them all. It is the seasons of creation which enter my flesh, an internal tide of hormones echo the external rhythms of nature, and I am folded into the belonging of tidal life. The constant within me is that I feel tidal. I live a tidal life. The rises and falls are a main meal. No matter how much I endeavour to keep balanced between the demands of a life as a professor and single parent, running a household, and nurturing my artist, I create tides (not to mention the rise and fall of my hormones).

The language of wind and mist, and the language of stars is what my body aches for. I am called back to hearing the wind in my sinews, feeling the light through my nipples. It is this interplay of the seascape of islands that is intrinsically connected to my body. And here is where my body finds home and belonging. And here is where I am taught to live a life with love. To be a writer, artist, dancer, poet, mother, teacher, friend, father, one must first be a lover in the world. When we truly live as lovers in the world we spill the poetic out of our flesh, just as the salt sprays from the waves. The roles in our lives change, but our essence is sure as the moon and sun. We are swept in tidal love, in the waves of creation, and in this place we begin again, like first sight, first love.

The island's tides and seasons teach me that life cycles are bathed in mystery and yet there is a rhythm to them. Each moment is a sacrament, a mysterium, an invitation to wonder. I don't often see this in the midst of the pressures of my everyday life, which often seem overwhelming. The power and wildness of the ocean's force reminds and rebodies me that there are forces working much larger than I can see with my normal eye. The invisible is always carried within the visible.

The islands and ocean mentor me to live and celebrate from the inside out. This is something for which I have deep intrinsic values, but even as I gaze on her surface I am continually brought to the reality that it is within her surface the preciousness of life is held. Fish, plankton, molluscs, and sea creatures of all shapes, sizes, and species swim beneath and in her surfaces. She reminds me to live from the inside out, dance from the inside out, and write from the inside out. What is within continues to animate the outer life, and here I am called to honour everything, the tears and the ecstasy.

As I write this now, I come to the day greeting it with tears. I am dwelling with a lot of emotions, a returning grief, and I drive back to my house after dropping the children at school, welled up in tears. I continue to find tears close to my breath, my bone, and my face. I don't easily embrace my tears, for they slow me down. Yet our bodies are made up largely of water. We are born in fluid, conceive in fluid, and grieve in fluid. The ocean can contain all my tears, all my fluid and I bear my body to her source, and not just to let go, but to learn to let be.

In the tides of island life I am called back to honouring the soul and body. The spiral mystery beckons me back to my true nature. The flesh of shoreline, stone, wind-swept trees, bluffs, wind, rocks, sand, and water beckon me back to my true nature. Here I learn to cooperate with my nature once again, to accept it, in all its manifestations. I am drawn back to the bare truth and to come home to my own texture. A texture of relaxing into a sacred space of honouring the movement in my own life. A place of h/earth so inviting one falls into his/her own life and once again finds home.

This is a journey back to who one really is. I am once again nourished in seaflesh – the food which sustains the deeper portion.

References:

Greene, M. (1995). *Releasing the imagination: Essays on education, the arts, and social change,* SF: Jossey-Bass Publishers.

Rilke, R.M. (Trans. by S. Mitchell). (1984). *Letters to a young poet,* NY: Vintage.

ART IS A GHOST
JANET MARIE ROGERS

Art is a female. She is a ghost and she is everywhere. She takes your hand and leads you through the forest of inspiration to elements and energies you need. She feeds you with messages. You can hear her, you sometimes see her, you smell her in the earth and at the right moment, she touches you – you know then, she has blessed you. Look around, Art has been there before you. Praise her for the beauty and curious contemplations she lays in front of you. Trust her and she will stay with you, loyal as a life-long friend.

I could hardly believe my eyes. For the ninety minute drive to Nanaimo from Victoria, I was rewarded with this: pictures in stone. I had become intimate with the images through books and research and now, with a gentle swerve off Highway #1 and a few steps away from the parking lot, I would be greeted with indefinable peculiar picture etchings, ready or not.

I was preparing for an exhibition called Rock, Paper, Scissors back in 1994, the same year I arrived on Vancouver Island from the busy city of Toronto. I was able to take my research off the page and into real experience. This was an opportunity to experience tangible encounters with images created some 14,000 years ago. My love and respect for petroglyphs and pictographs deepened when I read a passage by an anthropologist confessing that he/she was not sure what the petroglyphs represented or what messages were being conveyed (if any). That same passage further informed me, even the much-referenced carbon dating method was now being questioned, leaving the stone etchings at peace with their secrets. Who were these artists, dedicating big chunks of their lives to pounding out pictures on rock? I wanted to thank them.

Looking back, as an artist, I may have 'rounded myself to the beginning of the circle' in my artistic focus. I wondered, had I exhausted all the Indian icons from the common North American native image bank and was now looking to the origins, the first arts? Stone, as much as skin, became the first canvas. My inspiration grew as I settled into Vancouver Island and gradually understood, on deep levels, the meaning of the term "very sacred place." The petroglyphs were thought to be created in areas where the forces of nature were especially strong. I could feel it. And I made it a mission to continue this research after the exhibition.

Many of the Gulf Islands host petroglyphs. Extraordinary examples can be found on Gabriola Island, Quadra Island, Salt Spring Island, as well as other parts of Vancouver Island such as Port Alberni and East Sooke Park. The most populated petroglyph site I've had the pleasure to visit was in Bella Coola, British Columbia. I was performing poetry pieces at the Discovery Coast Music Festival in July 2008 and was led to the site by a local NuXalk nation man who knew the stories of those frog images, human images, sun images and shaman images.

I now write full time, and still wonder what it was about making the permanent shift from Ontario to British Columbia that led me to writing. It wasn't part of the plan. Were the words already here, waiting for me to arrive? Did I cast something off when leaving the city, creating a void to be filled with love for words? To this day, I can't put my finger on it, but am thankful the words have befriended me and continue to take me to new levels of creativity. They take me beyond my community to share my literary work and continue to provide messages and inspiration for more. I hear Art (the ghost woman she is) the strongest when I am in the forest, or collecting sage in the interior in late May, or picking berries in August. She is a presence among the cedar trees. She rides the waves of the lagoon where I walk.

Water, the element that surrounds Vancouver Island, seems to be something I can only describe as a conduit for the writing. Sound travels on water and for me, that sound comes in the form of words. Those words come via the water in some unnatural places as well, such as the steam room and the community swimming pool. Many a verse has been lost for having nothing to write with while taking in a recreational swim or soak in the hot tub. Thankfully, many more have been captured. We are filters for our art while we learn how the muse trains us to attain her gifts. In essence, we are the biggest deterrent to natures' artistic intensions. I have received clear messages here and know in my bones I am embraced by this land, a place I call home with no disrespect intended to my people and place in the east.

Echoes of Ancient Art
messages carried in
on wild winds
scented with sage
aged by traditions
conjured by song
sung in earth tones
pulled at my soul
till it broke
tiny molecules
spread like seeds
land and rest

over long cold winters
songs wait
to be sung again

ripples expand
and come back
as rich visions
when we least expect it
everyone was there
everything was there
just as you remembered
blue plants, red prints
ebony liquid jam
of ripe berries picked at just the right time
our stories come pricey
the young can't afford them all
but buy time shares
and use lay-away plans
to help them understand
what has been lost can't be bought back

We have strong relationships to land and it is what we learn inside those relationships that become the basis for how we define all things spiritual. Our connection to the earth is spiritual and it extends to the sky and everything in between. This connection creates meaningful relationships with self and when spirit energy has no more room to move inside us, that's when we paint and write and dance and create. Art is love. Art is a female. She is a ghost and she is everywhere.

MYSTERY ELEMENT
JOANNA STREETLY

I'm feeling the whole world. I'm feeling it through my skin like a snake, and breathing it through my blood like a fish. The motorboat flies across the flat water, on and on, my hands on the wheel. The sky swoops forward to meet me and the reflections swing into a thousand images in my wake. The world is not just around me. It is in me. It is me. These moments of fullness are such that I can hardly breathe. I am too receptive. I have no filters, absorbing everything that flows towards me. How many of me are there? How much of me is there? Where do I end and where does the world begin? Oh, to be able to fly like this forever! I am a bird, on top of the water, skimming the surface, never penetrating the glass barrier, never meeting my reflection. Always avoiding what lies below – creatures of the deep – only a surface away. These are my elements: the water, the air, the land. All three of them converging, moving around me, and I move into-onto-amongst these mysterious elements that give me life and are life.

If only every journey into the wilderness could yield such a feeling! I wish it could. But there is another element, a mystery element that comes and goes as it pleases – a magical key that unlocks the barrier between person and place. It is not a key that can be found. It turns in the lock rarely and at random. When my heart flies out to greet the sky, then I know that I am in a place few ever find. I am transported, and I have to make the most of these moments and love them because they are so fleeting.

Such sensory adventures delight me, but they also frustrate me because they can never be absolutely catalogued or reproduced. They are the result of my physical response to the landscape. I cannot write them all, or paint them all, safe in the knowledge that my audience will understand the emotion that produced them.

My daughter asks what infinity looks like. "If you write all the numbers to infinity Mummy, how much space does it take up?"

I ask myself: If I try to write or paint everything Clayoquot Sound means to me, how much space would that take up? How much time? How much heart-ache? I cannot join the dots and produce the perfect representation of this place. The sound is moody, changing. The same island, the same bay, can look and feel different on every passing. Fragments of Clayoquot can be caught and held up to the light, but only for a moment before dissolving. Instead, the essence of Clayoquot fills me with words, drawings and paintings. Each one of them only a single facet, but each one inspired by the magnificence of this landscape.

And so I work with moments. When I'm perched on the rocky edge of an island, sketchbook in hand, my boat lilting at anchor, I know I am capturing a moment, or letting it capture me. Later, when I sit at my little wooden pedestal coffee table, laptop under my fingers, I draw on those moments, knowing that I am describing something that no longer exists, or rather something that exists only in my mind. If I go back there, it will be different.

When I wrote my first novel, *Silent Inlet,* I began with a map, a map of an area that doesn't exist. I drew inlets and mountains and islands. I drew north and south, forests and villages, sand and pebbles. I drew this imaginary land in black and white, and as I began to write, the colours and moods of Clayoquot Sound flooded in to fill the spaces. What moves me as an artist moves *from* me also, so that in some ways I am merely transferring information from one medium to another, tinting it along the way with my own responses. But the transfer is not always smooth, quick or easy.

Inspiration is a presence that I feel. When I am overwhelmed by it I follow where it leads. But often it must sit on my shoulder, waiting while I live out the non-stop daily routine that is my life, all the while praying that it will not evaporate.

The alarm clock buzzes and there I am, reading stories, cosy in bed with a cup of tea and a small child. Then there is the challenge of dressing a suddenly-boneless four-year old, or challenging her to dress herself. There are meals for three, activities, chores, projects to be accomplished, classes to attend, timelines to be kept. There is working-for-money, housework, gardening, shopping, family time, play time, rest time.

Born in Trinidad, I am the unexpected fifth child. When I was six months old, my forty-six-year old mother packed her paints and went to Guyana, wandering remote villages in the highlands, painting for weeks. Swamped by motherhood, she'd lost part of herself and needed to get it back. I didn't uncover this story until recently, but I can understand her. I only have one child, and as a parent, I am not as free as I used to be. I cannot idly roam the land, seeking only the dew of inspiration unless I too hire a nurse for six weeks and vanish into the wilderness.

My mother's artistic self survived and as I grew older, she began to take me with her on her forays, letting me play with charcoal and paint, or having me sit for her as a model. A creative person can find a way around anything. So if I can't always go out into the wilderness, I can bring the wilderness to my home. Living on a floathouse in Clayoquot Sound, I know that I will always be reminded of its magic. I can look up Lemmens Inlet to Mount Mariner as the golden-pink dawn creeps over the glacier and be rewarded with a feeling of icy pleasure. I can catch the moment when the rainforested slopes of Mount Colnett become in-digo and the dark and bright-green islands below it sparkle with the light of the water and the sky. I am able to feel and observe so much as I go about the tasks of living. I may not achieve moments of ultimate connection, but at least living on the water as I do, it is impossible for me to become detached. A trip in a small boat, even if it is only for five minutes, can change my day, jolt me from the banality of daily life and produce a moment of intrigue, excitement, and beauty.

The sea pulses, ebbs, and flows, pulled hither and thither by the moon. My blood pulses too, and flows with the pull of the moon. Is this elemental connection to the water the reason for my attraction to it? If so, why have I not felt the same way in other coastal areas? Why here? Why Clayoquot? Why – the first summer I came here – did I dream the orca whales, the night before their every visit? Why – the first summer I came here – was I able write poetry for the first time in years? Why – the first summer I came here – did I laugh more, smile more, throw up my arms, sing in public places, have a sure knowledge of forthcoming events that defied the concept of linear time?

It is not simply the conjunction of land and water that produces inspiration. There are places on Earth that are charged with an element that has no name, an element that is tangible, yet invisible, which pushes us to seek it, yet always, eventually eludes us. That element, if it can be called an element, is my drug of choice, the co-agent of my inspiration. It has no name because it is never the same twice. It exists here because I can feel it. Others feel it too. They may even name it. But for me, to name it would be to kill it. And in doing so, kill the very part of me that is most alive. As much as we long for explanation, it is mystery that feeds our hearts and minds. I must not question why I feel so alive here. If I ask the question, I will have to take apart the puzzle pieces, examine each shape, wonder at its purpose, seek answers and risk disappointment.

I prefer to live with the mystery. Clayoquot Sound keeps me here because I cannot consider leaving. My frustration is that I will never be able to fully represent all the ideas that come to me. They lead in so many directions! I don't wish to abandon my daily commitments: my home, my life with my family. And it would be selfish to venture only where the magic takes me. I might even lose my way.

Is it possible to compromise, to live with a foot in both worlds? I think so. I am content to trust that I can rely on the mystery to feed me flashes of connection and inspiration, enough to keep me alive. Enough so that part of me can always, in a moment of fullness, feel the whole world.

RETURN
MIKE EMME

• • •

On the island, it's always about water.

I first came to the island an immigrant adventurer,
raised in an urban coastal desert where water was
a desperate plaything that poured from lead pipes.

In that place, the spurt and hiss of cast bronze sprinkler heads kept
the St. Augustine's grass, razor-sharp and decorative
while all the excess trickled down the street
like lovers' waste
or simply evaporated into the burnt orange haze.

Surface Chemistry #11
Water Management UVic campus

"Art is great for your sister, but you need to get a job."

I followed a high school buddy who spent summers on the island.

He was going home, I was going away.
Either way, an epic journey.

The move was almost over before it started because of
a small explosion of drain cleaner at a summer job.

As it was, my first travelling to the island was three days
of refracted light and blurred impressions
produced by temporary blindness
and daily drops of belladona.

My initiation to island ferries was a Black Ball out of
Port Angeles. The ship, a heaving, Shakespearian crone with cracked
skin and a wreaking, salt-diesel musk, pushed soft cleavage through
the cold liquid border. When she docked at the inner harbour, all of
us tumbled into the arms of customs agents, stout midwives to our
adventuring who swaddled us in carbon copied permission to begin.

My first seasons on the island were an introduction to slower rhythms.
A combination of the syncopated rush to and from classes, soft staccato
rain, the hollow percussion of lovers' random footfalls balanced across
log strewn beaches. It all blended into a gentle common time measured
in 4 years.

As a newcomer, the island was all of Canada as far as I knew.

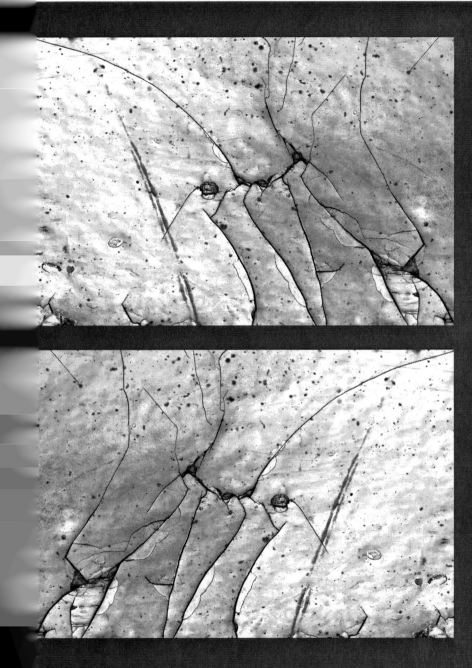

Surface Chemistry #1
Queen of Saanich - Both Ways

Then...

     ...The only way to stay was to go.

Transformed from a student to an actual immigrant. I staggered off a greyhound bus with a backpack to take a job nobody else wanted. It turned out to be a year of teaching for room and board and $75/month in a school run by volunteers. Even now I am not sure if what I walked into wasn't the last vestiges of the residential school system. A transition, maybe. About half the kids lived in dorms on campus. Before the opening of school, their elders taught us how to teach their children. Most of the kids were from Carrier villages and reserves within 100 miles or so. I was told they were sent by their parents. Some came with federal education grants. The rest, the day kids bussed in from town, were mostly white. The teachers and staff came from everywhere but there - Brits and Americans looking for adventure or in need of escape. A few (the scary ones) thought they were missionaries.

There was art:

    The kids' jean jackets with marker-penned eagles' heads and feathers carefully circled with names and phrases in Carrier. Sometimes we would sit together at night, play guitar and sing. A mixture of country songs and KISS.

    The art teacher, a Vietnam vet who had refused to end his tour by baring arms against college kids at home, served part of his dishonourable discharge teaching me jewellery-making on our weekends, when he didn't need to be alone.

    My high school habit of screen printing t-shirts helped me connect with the friendship centre and the Mormon youth group of a grade 12 girl who secretly researched
    the dirty bits in the Canterbury Tales).

I spent everything I earned and some savings on long distance calls to Mary-Jane, back on the island. My Christmas vacation that year included days in the old library in downtown Victoria, a faded monument to Andrew Carnegie's wealth, marking final exams. Muttering and shuffling crumpled papers just like everyone else in the library on a cold damp midweek.

I tasted my first real winter that year in an interior pulp town where ice-fog mixed with the thick sulphur smell of money. Come breakup, the sounds of hidden water flowing under rotted ice reminded me that I was free to choose the coast.

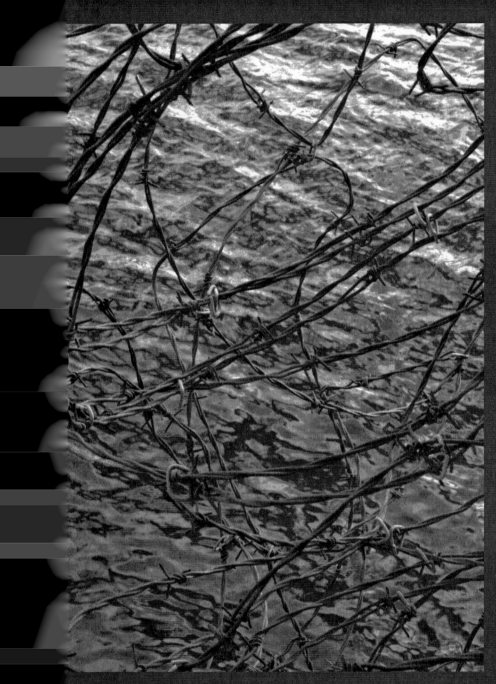

Surface Chemistry #6
Safe Moorage

As a kid, art was always a subversive activity.
Back of the classroom sort of stuff, or toxic experiments in the basement or
garage. Creativity with carcinogens. I did win
the 'patriotic poster contest' in Grade 8, a poster titled, "O say can you see!," that
gave me a chance to show my skill at drawing military hardware.
Even then I knew I was pandering for a red ribbon.

Most of what I know about art as a learned thing
came within sight the Straights. Between teaching gigs
on the Alaska Highway I spent six summers down
the Spanish Banks, expanding notions of the figure by drawing
on Wreck Beach, photographing the beginnings of coffee culture around False
Creek. During the last of those summers our son, the one who hears music
in words, was born within earshot of Expo. My last screen print, an abstract
expressionist rework of a topographic map, titled 'Nuclear Landscape' shares his
month and year.

Money took us back north for a time.
Little towns are a great place to learn. Big duck in a little pond - I photographed
people to make art and pay for equipment.
One-man shows in the community art centre.
Discovering that making pictures at weddings
is working with the temporarily insane.

Then came another two years on the urban side of the water. Ivory isolation
near a city where squalls off the sea couldn't wash away the wall art posing as
graffiti. With my back turned toward the water, it was a time to theorize about
what can't be seen in photographs. To conceptualize.

Can art still be a subversive activity when you are not a kid?

Surface Chemistry #9
Sooke

There is nothing Protestant about a port town.
East or west, the salt-funk gumbo of seawater
and over-spilling industry saturates every sense
with the detailed minutia of life and death. The body can't be denied. It's right
there. A sado-masochistic pleasure.
Catholic all the way.

Moving again. Between a classroom in Richmond, a University gig in a tiny
cow-town in Montana and a year teaching art on the island, we had half a day
to choose our next move. The choice was clear.

Our daughter, of the flaming red hair and camera vision, was born an island girl.

But, believing then that progress trumps place, skip ahead a short year from the
water bug launch and landing of the floatplanes to heavy traffic in Halifax
harbour. I learned my place at the margins of the art world at the college of art
and design. I could pass, dressing in black on the weekdays and being barbecue
neighbourly with the other nomads in a commuter suburb of that military town.

Homesickness was a new experience at 36 when I found myself 4 time zones
to the east. Not knowing whether the people in the town where you were born are
awake or asleep. When you can't imagine the time of day, you are away. The
similarities were in the air, but the downwind acid-etched patina built up over
more history than a westerner could imagine was foreign
to the 4 of us,
counting the two babies,
for two years.

Surface Chemistry #10
Ceremonial Alter - Chinese Cemetery - Victoria

Nearer and further

Working back meant working south...

...to a former land grant college in a small American town
where the cows and college kids each outnumbered the locals. Water was
everybody's little secret. It oozed down from the Cascades and filled the local
water table to the brim
in a town where it hardly ever rained.
Dry winds and flooded basements. Great for growing timothy hay. Designer
horse feed.

This move from coast to almost coast was like time travel. West coast funk
ceramics and the 'road kill school'
of neo-expressionist painting were the uniforms
that the individualists wore.

Every art community has important things to teach
and things it will never know.
I learned to wear flannel and get my hands dirty again.

The ocean was a morning's drive away.

The island half a day, plus a ferry trip.

We made it over the mountain and to the water occasionally.

Sometimes art needs to be more about people than place.
Less metaphor and more direct engagement.
Though we always imagined transporting
what was good about these moments to the island,
more and more, Mary-Jane and I focused
on what we could access,
on where we were needed.

Surface Chemistry #3
Cliffside access - Sooke

Prairie oil brought us back north, to Canada
(the big Island?).

Payday politics.
Buy your new best friends rounds until you're broke.
We can fight later.

Rig workers needing teachers for their children meant
that there was money for art classes so that their teachers could be sure the
kids didn't put out an eye with their crayons.

Unfortunately, art making can be a crime of opportunity.
For the first time, I was not connected to an art community. When I
mentioned my art life, many around me apologized
for themselves, creating a respectful distance.

In the oil town I became voyeuristic.
My children and my students grew in their art.

Except for frenzied moments
that resembled an illicit affair. Lovers' weekends.
Something about the low humidity in prairie winters. Or duty.

Just when I assumed that the island was a place only in memory I had a
search and rescue moment. A startling glimpse of peripheral vision when I
was looking in another direction.
An invitation and an opportunity. A gift from a friend.

And now...

places and people have converged.
Every stop on the journey is reflected back
in these new images of an old place that is my home. Again. Water and
rust. Surface chemistry.

On the island, the water ripples with metaphor.

Images and Text by: Michael J. Emme

Surface Chemistry #2
Arbutus Cove

Return...

A PAINTER'S TRAJECTORY

AVIS RASMUSSEN

« Victoria? »

« Oui. l'Ile du Vancouver qui est situee pres de Vancouver, Canada. »

I am visiting Normandy, painting *en plein air* the ramparts of Castle Caen built by William the Conqueror and saved by the Canadian Forces in 1944. Passers-by often think I'm American or British, or if Canadian, from Quebec. They are surprised when I tell them there are thousands of kilometres between Quebec and Vancouver Island on the west coast of Canada where I have my studio. What a distance to travel!

Since 2000, I have painted one month of every year in Europe. I went to Normandy on my latest trip in part because that is where I have roots. From Normandy, Dad's ancestors brought their art of gardening across the English Channel to Wales and along the Thames River. Dad emigrated from Reading, England to southern Vancouver Island's Saanich Peninsula in 1919. Here my world began in Sidney by the Sea, surrounded by the kaleidoscopic two-acre garden my parents called *Arbourfield*.

My earliest memories involve art making, and I soon took the crayons used for colouring books to draw my own pictures. Some of these early works recently surfaced in my mother's belongings – drawings of roses, hyacinths, cherry blossoms, and Japanese plum trees down the drive with Quila, our spaniel. To witness my first steps again I saw how my surroundings inspired me to paint what was to become my passion: the ever-changing light of the seasons. *Arbourfield's* colourful garden, through which there were glimpses of the sea, caught my imagination, my desire to express with paint how I saw my world on the far west coast. In fact, illustrations for *Charms of the Seashore, Saanich Fields,* and *Garden World,* chapbooks of poems for children I wrote about Brennan's Beach came from my sketchbooks growing up in Sidney on the Saanich Peninsula.

My connections to this place are life-long. I was born on a tiny island in Shoal Harbour, which I cycled past to attend North Saanich High School in my teens. I roamed this tip of the Saanich Peninsula in my formative years, sketching log-strewn beaches overhung by twisted arbutus trees, farms nestled in fir forests, John Dean Park, the glorious view over Sidney to the San Juan Islands, and snow-capped Mount Baker. As a young adult I commuted to Victoria, working for the British Columbia Forest Surveys making maps by looking through a stereoscope. This paid my fees for Senior Matriculation and one year of Education majoring in Art. In college I became familiar with reproductions of international paintings hung on the library walls, and I felt inspired by the many art books my brother sent from London, England. Along with exhibitions at the then recently established Victoria Art Gallery, I whetted my artist's appetite to travel to make and see art in other places.

After two years teaching elementary school, I boarded the Canadian Pacific Railway boat to Vancouver with my sister. We travelled on the CPR train to Montreal and finally onto the *Empress of Britain* for Liverpool. Seeing the vast expanse of the Canadian landscape for the first time plus a week crossing the Atlantic Ocean opened my eyes, as did seeing London's National Gallery, the British Museum and the theatre. We cycled to Cambridge, toured Britain by train and local buses, visited Denmark, Germany, Austria, and travelled with the National Union of Students by steam engine through Yugoslavia and Greece. That sketchbook survived too and looking back, I am intrigued by what I chose to draw – the stately Georgian Marden Hill where we stayed with family, Salzburg at night, and Old Corinth in Greece. All places so different from anything I had ever seen or drawn in Sidney. On my return I made a painting of Itea, a town of white buildings on the edge of an aquamarine sea, with a background of receding blue Greek hills. Although the journey gave me a fresh perspective, I eventually returned to teaching, finding ways to balance my art making, work, and family.

I have come to understand travel is an essential part of my ongoing practice and central in my artist identity. Geographically, I am isolated from major art centres and galleries of the world, as well as the landscapes painted by the Impressionists or Renaissance masters. I understand artists like Emily Carr, who was born on this island a century ago, wanting to paint elsewhere in order to study and see landscapes she had heard about but could only imagine before making the long journey abroad. She then returned here, to her passion, painting her greatest works: these forests of the west coast. On the last leg of my flight home from my most recent venture to Normandy, I was reminded of this beauty as we came to the Gulf of Georgia's scattered islands, blue-green on ultramarine, over ochre fields, multi-hued houses and bejewelled gardens in the evergreen forests of the Saanich Peninsula. I saw with a bird's eye my southern Vancouver Island west coast palette. These are the colours I have absorbed all my life.

I joined friends on a fish boat in Tsehum Harbour shortly after my return, gliding on glistening seas past those blue-green islands. I tried to catch the colour by mixing paint as the light constantly changed the landscape on Sidney Island. Clouds scampered over the sun as the day progressed. The vast surface of water rippled, undulated, and caught reflections and the sky's mood. Trees, rocks, boats, even if stationary, changed hue, created and became shadows, figures, shapes, moving colours. The process of *plein air* painting is one of rapid, innate, intuitive selection from the panorama.

In my Victoria studio these images are often transposed onto large canvases. This is a method I developed during my days as a painting major at the local university, yet my absorption of the immediate surroundings – whether by drawing linear, textural, or tonal impressions, or by painting shapes in colour, or variations of the visually fluctuating light – all began in my parents' garden. As Dad gardened, I painted. As I got older, my family gave me gifts of sketchbooks, high quality paper, brushes and paint. And by picking strawberries, raspberries, and loganberries on the local farms, I began to purchase my own art materials in Victoria, a twenty-mile bus trip along the winding East Saanich Road to the city. At that time Sidney had no art shops, no bookshops, no library, and no art galleries. Fortunately for the artist in me, the school hired an enthusiastic art teacher when I was in grade eight.

Now I see I simply painted because I liked painting. My four siblings and my five children have been amazingly supportive of my artist lifestyle. Some still live close by, others far away, but all in various ways facilitated my progress. Their understanding sustained me through my visual arts degree, where I finally took up painting and printmaking at the University of Victoria as a mature student, and their encouragement helped me participate in the first Metchosin Summer School of the Arts over twenty-five years ago. From that painting workshop emerged the large charcoal drawings of boats lying around the Pedder Bay docks of Pearson International College of the Pacific. These became a series of place-based watercolours, Japanese woodblocks, and oil paintings which, combined with oil paintings of fish boats of French Creek, were exhibited as *COASTAL LIFE* in a gallery up-island. In fact, I painted this series in an old button factory while staying with my sister, perhaps the most generous supporter of my artist life, who still lives in Waterloo, Ontario. With this series of boat paintings, I applied to the Emma Lake Artists Workshop in Saskatchewan, noted for nurturing Canadian talent and for its renowned international art faculty. That summer, thirty artists came together, and in my studio at Emma Lake, I painted a series of boats from sketches made lakeside. When accepted in 1992, I received help from my family, which made the fees, lodging, painting supplies, and flights possible.

In recent years, I was offered the great opportunity to paint in Venice, Italy, and saw with my own eyes Renaissance paintings I had studied from slides and books many years ago. I painted a series of boats, bridges, and churches reflected in the canals. The ambient light created magical colour, a transformative experience for a painter. I filled a sketchbook with drawings of sculptures, the Duomo of Florence, The Piazza del Campo of Siena, and Saint Peter's of Rome, which upon my return to Victoria I painted on canvas. These along with the watercolours of Venice were exhibited as *AMBIENT ITALY* at my alma mater. With these paintings I was accepted in residence at the International School of Drawing,

Painting, and Sculpture in Umbria, Italy. Our instructor, a New York painter of some standing, commented on my natural sense of colour and invited me to paint the next year in his art program set in another beautiful hilltop Umbrian town. Again I returned to Victoria with a renewed appreciation for setting up my easel to render Vancouver Island topography onto my panels.

Off Meares Island, oil on canvas (See page 146 Colour Insert)

This year, my trip also took me to France, and I painted in the northern towns of Rouen, Honfleur, Caen and Mont Saint Michel – places of contrast to the warm Mediterranean coastal towns of Provence where I had explored painting in the footsteps of Cezanne and Van Gogh last year. Although I painted on my own in Normandy, I visited my daughter and family in Paris, and spent time painting in the Jardin Des Plantes, visiting the Kandinsky and Calder exhibitions in the Pompidou Centre. Returning from France and enroute to family in Toronto, I also took the opportunity to see contemporary art in the new Art Gallery of Ontario, ceramics in the Gardiner Museum, and our National Gallery in Ottawa. Each centre of the arts offered me further inspiration as I now prepare for an opening of the Normandy series in Victoria. I have spent my life painting colour on paper, panel, or canvas in my studio or *en plein air*. My art has always been in movement, an exploration of seeing, literally and figuratively, sometimes close to home, sometimes far away. As a visual artist, seeing colour and light is the key to my expression, and a poem from my *Garden World* chapbook, written when visiting a painter friend on Hornby Island, captures that way of seeing:

Studio Garden
Mirror'd on your studio walls
your garden
green leaved, lush
flourishing through French pigments
on paper and panels,
pinks,
marigolds and magentas
glowing
amongst the verdant growth.

In your island coppice
you have come
to your flowering time.

THEY SAY THAT SEEING IS BELIEVING
ROLAND RASMUSSEN

I often use a guide to find what's on in the local art world, but my best insights to discovering Victoria's art scene is my mother, Avis. Mum has painted in Victoria since the early 1970s, and if you ask her questions about her artwork, she will most likely defer with humility, speaking instead of the qualities of other artists or how Vancouver Island has changed for artists in recent years. This place has become a sort of national sketchbook full of artists from across Canada who have come to paint the west coast. Many who have made Vancouver Island home have built a nurturing artistic environment, creating spaces of artistic integrity, and in the process, contributing to our society and our understandings of identity through their images, forms, and styles which come from the land around us. As her son, I have witnessed many such discussions, and I know how much Mum must paint this world in her own way. In truth, I have tried to imitate that painter's will my mother has, which is a struggle for any artist. What I see in my mother's work is a facet of colour that shades in the twilight and inspires others, including me. Not everyone is an artist, yet many can find realms within the imagination and explore all the possibilities that come with hand and eye and something that makes a mark.

Avis Rasmussen believes that art-making should be cherished by society because the creating and expressing speaks for the people of that place. And my mother has that sense of history, as many mothers do, for something passed on generation to generation. In a matriarchal family such as mine, this sense of purpose is to be cherished and respected. As a watercolour artist, Mum has a full archive of people and places throughout her life of travel, rendering many muses she discovers while moving along her interesting paths. I came to see into the world of art by watching my mother paint in her parents' garden. It all began for her as a child, free to paint without criticism, "for all little hands are artistic hands" my mother likes to say. How different it was to see her work on a beach or quickly sketch from a Gulf Island ferry. To watch Mum as the light changed, rushing to capture an image, was to realize the challenge was not as much in accuracy, but in seeing, making, and tricking the eye through illusion. I believe that for Avis, the act of painting reflects a story of shifting light and blending colours, and these are the attributes that define her life as an artist.

In my experience, it is rare to find an artist who has not travelled or found inspiration by opening up new and unfamiliar realms. Yet art is always in relation to the realities of making a life – work, family, hard choices – even though Wassily Kandinsky proclaimed, "there is no must in art because art is free." As the son of a painter, I wonder if Kandinsky's words are still true today. Can art be free? In my view, the "must" in art doesn't always exist. My mother's lifetime as an artist has always involved teaching art as well: Teaching children, teaching other artists, teaching the curious who watch her paint. It is far too common for artists to need a "real job" to be free to pursue art. And the teacher-artist is another kind of artist – someone who is social, who communicates with a generous spirit, and has the confidence and willingness to share their own process of creating. Avis has built a strong network in the regional arts community, and I feel that the infusion of energy and inspiration comes to my mother from others, and in turn, it is passed on to those who are open and willing to listen.

Looking back at her formal education, the three choices available to young women in the 1950s were secretary, teacher, or nurse, and Avis chose to be a teacher. Then came marriage and family, but unlike some, she didn't put her art aside; instead she embraced it fully while raising a family. In the 1980s, Avis finally pursued her master's degree in Art Education. It was then she took up print-making and discovered art that challenged the boundaries of her work. This marked a shift in my mother's career, and her graduate studies became a key turning point in her artistic development. Avis the painter, the print-maker, the poetess, or the activist, speaks about her education as the most precious of commodities, never to be taken for granted. "Painting first, for otherwise there would be no time," she says, just one of many expressions a lifetime as an artist has generated. Mum has always followed her artistic vision, and where 'the voice' calls from, and where it calls to, be it forest, shoreline, along wooded ridge, in front of an easel, or at practically any art festival on Vancouver Island, Avis is there. These are the moments of real value in an artist's life. And for me, it is also the memories of Mum sketching at almost every point when we travelled through nine provinces to Prince Edward Island, with five kids in a VW Van. Then she wrote a poetry book about it. That sums up the whole of Avis's 'can-do' spirit.

Dear to her heart are also sketches made throughout the years of jazz musicians, for my mother is a jazz enthusiast, perhaps not fully aware of how she has visually documented the evolution of jazz culture in our city. This is another aspect of Avis that is not conventional, but rooted in experimentation with wild reliefs and innovative mono-prints. In recent years, print-making is something she shares with inquisitive children and adults during many art fairs throughout the year. This is the 'free tenor' which comes from her 'must,' demonstrated by an artist who keeps working hard and producing an extraordinary body of work well past retirement.

Painting all her life, always close to family, and always open for conversation, perhaps the greatest of Avis's artistic skills is listening to what people see in her art, in her use of colour, or the movement in a line-sketch which might be translated to wood-cut or lino-cut. When Avis spent her seventy-third birthday with family in Rouen, her focus was on the artwork of her grandchildren, knowing that something will be passed along to them, some aspect of how art can still be 'free.' I imagine she feels lucky to have travelled for art, like Kandinsky, and to have taught by example.

This is my post-script for my mother and her reflections because so many conversations have occurred about art in the city of Victoria. There are many art works yet to come by new faces and talents. Most exciting for me is knowing that to truly live, see, and believe, one must take time to make relationships and interact with the land where we work our craft, leaving something behind for future archaeologists. We were artists. We lived along the inland waterway, behind those Olympic Mountains, sheltered in rain shadow. The conversation with art is never over, yet it is always apparent to those like Avis Rasmussen who have the freedom to see and believe.

Notes:

For further information on Wassily Kandinsky, please see: http://www.mnstate.
    edu/gracyk/courses/phil%20of%20art/kandinskytext.htm

WAKING UP IN CLAYOQUOT SOUND
SUSAN KAMMERZELL

POST-PEACECAMP BLUES

Blessed and powerful though it is
to walk and sing
alone
in these magic places
I sometimes long
to join hands with you all
to sing our soul-songs
again.

I hunger for the beauty
the healing
the power
the love
and the rising joy
that we all are
when we uncover our hearts
for each other and our home.

FOUNDATION

Oh my people
We of the many skins and
the one blood
Lay your ears to the Earth
Lay your hearts to the uplifting continents

Do you feel the voice of the home-world?
the presence of massive love
the embodiment of support
beauty always emerging

With such foundations we need not fail
to reach the bedrock within
nor are we ever far
from the power of deep intention
true-founded.

WATER QUESTION

Our birthright:
desperate, intolerable predicaments
astounding species' idiocy
accelerating

chaos.

But what about the rivers of joy?
Haven't you always heard them
in the voices
of our music?
Don't they try to catch our eyes
in every drop
of sun
moon and starlight?
Do they not
rise full in our own veins
when we reach out our arms
to each other?

Do the blessed
bounteous
beauteous
spirit-waters of our home
remind you
of the rivers of joy
flowing here
all around us?

UNDERWATER STARS
VELCROW RIPPER AND HEATHER FRISE

Heather

I had a conversation with a friend the other day and we agreed that we need to leave the city in order to grow old properly. We need, sooner or later, to leave Toronto, this cult of youth culture we live in, so that we can grow our hair long and silvery and take pride in our creased faces as if they were maps of the places we've been, dramas we have and will have survived.

Sometimes, when I am in the downtown crush, dropping my baby off at daycare on King Street, a single, new mother turning forty, I wonder how the hell I got here. I'm completely stunned that this is my life. I always vaguely imagined the coast was where I'd have babies and eventually grow into an old sea witch. This was in the spirit of Susan Musgrave, with whom I have felt an affinity since I was a teenager. She was a poet, she was bewitched by trees and the pull of tides, and she was an outsider in love with an outlaw.

Since my late teens I always wanted to go to Haida Gwaii. I'm not sure why; it might have been because of Musgrave or Thoreau or just a romantic longing for a place that was remote and undefiled. I was living in Montreal then, and I told my boyfriend at the time, Velcrow, that I was going to the Queen Charlottes and he was welcome to come. Of course I wanted him to, desperately, but I played it cool. I was, after all, fearless and committed to being a free spirit.

'Crow was game to accompany me. He had come from the west originally, but the guy I knew in Montreal was a skinny punk rocker with spiky black hair. He could barely swim, much less drive a boat or make a campfire.

Velcrow

I grew up on the mild side of the wild west coast, on the Sunshine Coast, a place that is sheltered by the protecting bulk of Vancouver Island. The storms are tempered and the sea is often slow molten calm. In this 'ecological suburb' the fecund forest, my playground of ravines and creeks, hollow logs, and mossy beds, epiphytes in my armpits, microrheyzal fungi in my veins, all nurtured me. I was part of that land. It was part of me, it was home.

But not long after finishing high school, I found myself drawn to the east, to Montreal, where I soaked up a different kind of creative energy in the frenetic, worldly flavour of the cosmopolitan city. Montreal brought me closer to double-sided, cutting-edge, old world Europe. I drank in the culture and chaos, developed my chops as an experimental filmmaker with a taste for espresso. It was a time of punk rock and Goth, of fiery rebellion and flirtation with the shadow. I wore pointy shoes, painted my face white punctuated by dark black eyeliner, and danced to *Sisters of Mercy* and *Joy Division* at Les Foufounes Electrique, "The Electric Buttocks," Montreal's version of New York's CBGBs. My first line of French, considered a sure fire pick-up phrase at the time, was a quote I paraphrased as "I have no regard for eternity. The days pass me by. I punish myself." It was all a play for me. I indulged in the juicy darkness of nihilism with recklessness and glee, a healthy counterbalance to my often sunny optimism.

Heather was a feminist '80's woman, a trouble-making McGill University student reading her Deleuze and Guattari, hanging out at *Cafe Commun Commun*, writing poetry, painting, handing in her theory essays, exploding with the need for freedom and justice. But there was a nature lover in there too, formed during her summers in the *Group of Seven* land of Georgian Bay in Ontario, and months as a canoe guide down rivers and lakes with gaggles of kids. But no salt water, not yet.

One day Heather told me she wanted to fulfill her dream of visiting Haida Gwaii (named 'The Queen Charlotte Islands' by the colonizers after some dead queen), an archipelago of islands on the west coast of Canada, bordering Alaska. It was said to be a mystical land where the enormous ancient trees were still standing – though disappearing fast – teeming with eagles, whales, and a thousand tiny islets, nothing but open ocean between you and Japan. She was going, and I could come. If I wanted to. Did I want to?

I was quick to say yes. What's more, I was beginning to feel charged with a growing awareness of an impending environmental crisis, and a convergence emerged. We decided to make a film about the last great ancient temperate rainforests on the west coast of Canada, threatened by clearcut logging. We had no money, but we did have a Nizo Super-8 camera, perfect for time-lapse nature photography. And if there wasn't always food in the fridge, there were always rolls of film, scrounged 'short ends' at the very least. It was to be an experimental poetic essay film, a forest meditation, called "Bones of the Forest."

* * * *

Not long after, we crossed the rough ocean on the Prince Rupert ferry, stepping out on the deck as we approached Skidegate Landing, finally reaching Haida

Gwaii. And just as quickly a razed mountain appeared in the pink dawn light. It was a shock.

We decided to kayak down the coast of South Moresby, now a park operated by the Haida, where locals promised we would find trees the size of the CN Tower, totem poles, and abalone at low tide. We tracked down a kayak rental shop owned by two loggers, Bill and Doug, who, upon realizing that trees were becoming less plentiful than tourists, had bought a bunch of kayaks to rent out. We booked a two-person boat from them for all the money we had.

Doug drove us out to the launch point, and kept saying Bill was the kayak expert, Bill would explain everything. We waited around the dock until Bill finally pulled up in his pickup truck.

"Well I've only been out once, for about an hour," he explained, "but it seems simple enough."

He showed us a how to steer and paddle, and then they both drove off, leaving us alone at the dock, forgetting to give us life jackets. In desperation we broke into their shed, found two sets, and spent the next hour stuck in the kayak at the dock, trying to get our spray skirts on. They were brand new and too tight.

But we learned along the way, and as the weeks of kayaking passed, we found ourselves transformed into a sea mammal, our kayak festooned with feathers and kelp, our bodies caked in salt, bronzed and freckled. Life became simple, primordial, immediate. A rhythm of paddles dipping into the ocean, following the tides, nights under the brilliant stars. We were setting out on a five-week trip, all the way down to the tip of Haida Gwaii, to the World Heritage site of Ninstints where the original Haida totems still stood. Most had been felled, tied into booms and floated down the coast to museums. All the anthropology 'colonizers' of the past left behind were the sky graves, where chiefs were interned in caskets up high on beautifully carved poles.

A seal began to tail us on the third day, popping her head up on one side of the boat, then the other, disappearing with a splash. At night we could hear her cavorting in the water near the tent. The next morning she would be waiting for us to resume the adventure. She stayed with us for days.

We had a book that taught us how to eat the wild foods of the region, and dined on chicken-of-the-woods (a kind of fungus), kelp, beach asparagus and once, a single, precious rock scallop, eaten with reverence and awe, as it was some eighty years old. Afterwards we felt guilty for days. We only tried fishing once. It was just too horrible and terrifying trying to bludgeon a writhing fish to death on the side of a sea kayak, rocking and dipping madly from side to side.

Some days would be dedicated to filming. We would set up the camera in time lapse mode and create animations out of the entire landscape, moving logs and rocks like magic into transmuting formation across the shore. Half a day's work might result in a minute of animation. It was laborious, but creative and inspiring, a collaboration with nature herself. And we had lots of time. Our only timepiece was the sun and stars, the moon and tides.

When we finally arrived at Ninstints, we had to wait at dawn for the tide to rise enough to let us through the narrow opening into the bay. A fellow kayaker arrived, and to pass the time he started telling us stories about kayaking accidents. He had ordered a report of case studies before he left on his trip and knew all the variations. His favourites were the sudden endings: *Tom and Judy set out on what seemed like a clear day, when a storm came up out of nowhere, capsizing their over-loaded boat. They drowned in minutes.* He had so terrified himself that he'd done his entire two-week trip from Sandspit to Ninstints in four hard days of paddling, because he was afraid the good weather would change. Now he was here, and was just going to wait for ten days until a float plane came to pick him up.

That afternoon we met the Haida watchmen, locals who took turns staying in longhouses at several key locations throughout the park. When South Moresby was saved from logging, the land was turned into a federal park. After years of struggle with the federal government, the Haida were granted custody of their lands.

Andy, one of the watchmen on Ninstints, was friendly and happy to share his knowledge with us. He appreciated the fact that we'd come down the hard way, under our own steam. He had less appreciation for the tourists who flew in by helicopter for an hour-long visit, and would wander into the longhouse asking where they could buy some film and ice cream. He would direct them out into the forest, "Just go past that stump, turn right at the cedar tree, over that stream and you'll find it." They had no idea they were a two-week paddle from the nearest store.

A few days later, we decided to go a little further, to the very tip of Haida Gwaii. By the time the kayak was loaded it was starting to get dark and there were threatening clouds on the horizon. Heather suggested we wait another day, but I talked her into leaving and she relented, despite her misgivings about my foolhardiness. An hour out to sea the sky darkened, thunder boomed, and a storm erupted. The tide had started to turn and we found ourselves surrounded by standing waves, ten-foot walls that came from all directions. Heather was in the rear steering, and had to constantly reorient the bow so we could avoid capsizing. We were in trouble. We could die. I started whooping each time we crashed down into a gully between the waves.

"Stop that!" Heather shouted.

I refused, whooping only louder: "If I'm going to die, I'm going to die happy!"

"You're not respecting the ocean."

"I am respecting the ocean. The ocean doesn't need me to be terrified."

As the storm unleashed its power we shouted and argued, whooped and screamed about the merits of respectful terror versus adrenaline-stoked ecstasy in the face of impending doom. Our argument ceased when an enormous light appeared in the darkness. It was a ship, heading straight for us. We blew our whistles, a pathetic peep against the rolling thunder. I gaffer-taped my waterproof Maglite flashlight to the end of my paddle, and began waving it frantically, no longer whooping, as the ship continued to bear down on us, refusing to change its course, not seeing us. Moments before we were crushed to death, its full bulk came into view. We discovered it was a lighthouse.

We were paddling straight for our doom, all the while thinking our doom was chasing us. We back-paddled desperately against the force of ocean as it tried to suck us into the rocky shore and we got lucky at the last moment. Out in the open ocean again, we relaxed slightly. The storm alone seemed less challenging than storm plus rocky shore plus the mirage of a ship. Then our paddles dug into a small island suddenly below us. But it wasn't an island, it was softer, too soft. It was moving. It was a whale.

Heather

Thunder booming, our hearts still racing, suddenly the kayak was rising. Out of the black ocean a huge orb of light appeared, lifting us; it was a whale illuminated by bioluminescence. It seemed we might rise up off the ocean's surface into the night sky on this giant ship of light. Instead, we watched it descend and drift westward underwater, the bioluminescence trailing off into the black night sea. It was like the night sky was suddenly below us, a slow motion meteorite colliding gently, and then drifting away. As if a magic talisman had just blessed us, the storm slowed, quieted, stopped. All was calm and the stars came out again, up above this time.

A few days later, as we approached the end of our journey, I spent the afternoon napping on the beach, with a newborn fawn curled up in the sun a few feet away from me. A sense of peace infused me, leaving a residue that I can still taste to this day.

* * * *

Back in Sandspit we met a woman who was tending the local thrift shop. Her hair swept up into a bun, her eyes a bright green. She was lithe and delicate looking and yet there was a ruggedness in her face, in her hands. She was breastfeeding her baby and talking a blue streak. Her name was Tamara and she was clearly hungry for conversation with off-islanders.

Tamara said she was an outsider in the town, shunned even. "All my kids have different fathers... one night stands with guys in town."

When we told her that we'd just come from kayaking down Moresby, she said casually that she'd done the same trip with her one-year-old daughter, just the two of them, about twelve years ago.

She let me have the cardigan I was going to buy gratis, and a pair of orthopaedic granny shoes. She asked us if we wanted to come and have dinner at her cabin. Sure, we said, we'd love to. We left our packs at the ferry terminal, tucked in a corner behind a couple of beat up chairs.

We all hitchhiked together, clambering into an old pick-up truck, and disembarking again at the side of the road, her little cabin visible through the trees. Tamara explained that she had built the cabin on hydro land and was essentially squatting. Her two older children were picking vegetables from a row of raised garden beds overflowing with leaves and vines and flowers.

We had salmon for dinner and heaps of vegetables from the garden. Her daughter had made blackberry fruit leather for dessert. Then we smoked some pot.

"It's getting late. You might as well sleep over." We slept in a bunk in the one-room cabin, the distant sound of waves crashing all night.

I woke up at one point and Tamara was bathing her little baby in a basin by candlelight. It was a strange yet magical scene, so quiet, an almost solemn ritual. She made being a mother look serene and effortless.

The next morning Tamara was still sleeping and her ethereal daughter was wearing an incredible party dress with crinoline and sequins. She was busy making bread.

'Crow and I hitched back to the ferry terminal to catch the boat back to the mainland only to discover that our packs had been stolen. We had our tickets and nothing else now.

The film that we had made, and laboured on so intensely, was gone.

We searched the roadsides, hoping they had perhaps kept the goods but thrown away the rolls of film. We put up notices, we asked everyone we met for clues and then we stood in defeat on the ferry's car deck, looking back on the island as it grew smaller and smaller, holding each other in tears. We had the shirts on our backs, a huge bag of home-grown pot that Tamara had given us, and the clothes we had culled from the thrift shop – the moss green cardigan, a hunting vest, granny shoes, a bandana.

We had come to the coast not to retrieve what we'd lost but to begin again, and to make something that would tell a deeper story. The memory of the images we made, those precious rolls of film, formed the blueprint for *Bones of the Forest*, the film we would spend the next ten years dreaming into existence.

I often think about the west coast of Vancouver Island and of Haida Gwaii. That odyssey was the wellspring from which so much of my work has flowed. There is something to be found in a person's formative years, a kernel of who we are and what we are to become. So when I wonder about how the hell I wound up alone, with a baby (not Velcrow's), I think back to Tamara, a beautiful, strident misfit. And my secret aspirations to be like her, alone with a brood of babies, vegetables, and seaweed on the table, hitching rides in old pick-up trucks.

And yet looking back I wonder about that wildness in her face, if it was the wildness of the bush, the ancient forests, or the sexual freedom of a woman who had one night stands, or motherhood and the madness that motherhood unleashes and the profound loneliness that attends it. When I'm walking in the downtown corridors, looking for some place to get a decent cup of coffee, I think about Susan Musgrave, my teenage heroine, living on Haida Gwaii, and I feel that same pull, the sea witch in me that yearns to live on the coast, in that wildness, in the midst of all that giganticness and haunting beauty.

THE CORTES CURE
MELODY HESSING

May 14

When I moved to British Columbia from Montreal in 1970, Vancouver *was* the west coast. Back then, watercress grew in the ditches, foxgloves flowered the alleys, and blackberry thickets encroached on stucco bungalows. Today, concrete towers replace the fir and cedar giants and 'nature' has been reduced to pocket parks. 'Extreme' west coast today means gang murders and escalating condo prices.

Every year about this time, when I'm in the grip of traffic or crowds, I am desperate for the feral, tangled coast, ready to shuck the gridlock like a crab sheds its shell. I want to *be* Peter Pan. I've spent too long being Wendy.

I register for a nature writing class on Cortes Island.

* * * *

My tent is pitched on the margins of this continent, where islands puddle in the Salish Sea. The Cortes aura is textbook new age, with cedar buildings and fences and a garden laid out like an organic Versailles.

I brace myself for spiritual cleansing. In the bowl of Georgia Strait, Savary Island pancakes to the south, a terminal moraine deposited by retreating glaciers. Our first field trip to Easter Bluff is a baptism in saxifrage and shore pines, purple camas, and umbrellas of maidenhair and sword ferns, all spouting from rock. On the porch for our afternoon discussion, our teacher Don talks about nature writing. I think he's got my number. Overwritten descriptions. "Nature alone isn't enough to sustain our interest," he says, in a slow, deep voice, his gaze loping around the deck at our sprawling forms.

Hmm. Right now I could spend days just looking at the view.

Do flowers *need* a narrative line?

Don shifts his lanky legs and continues, "We need story, human drama."

I'm sick of human drama. If all the world's a stage, why do we focus on one species? Ambulance sirens, the evening news, jumpers on the Port Mann Bridge; right now, nature grabs my attention, and I see a western tanager, red and yellow with black wings, perching in a leafing maple like an errant parrot. That's theatre enough.

May 15

Manson's Lagoon, our venue for field trip #2 is awash in intertidal drama. Gulls squawk and crows rasp in the wispy wind; water gurgles with the receding tide. Beneath my feet sprawls a tangerine-coloured sunflower sea star, a Ferris wheel of eighteen legs! Clamshells peek open in a soft sunrise pink. To my right, the exposed shell of a moonsnail rounds like a bagel above its muddy keep.

Bill, our nature guide, provides a running commentary, "See this clamshell?" He waves a small bivalve with two small holes in front of us. "It's been predated, probably by a moonsnail."

Then he climbs above the tide pool in his gumboots and gestures, "Have a look at the macro-algae."

A green slime of sea lettuce and sea wrack coats the exposed rock. In the tide pool, small crabs float across the sand. Sculpins dart above black sand dollars stacked tight like mushroom gills. A green crab scuttles sideways, bony finger-legs probing spider-like through the tangle of eelgrass.

Here, the laws of intertidal ecology govern everything I see.

I already worry about the social drama, about development and the encroachment of urbanism. I know about the ecological legacy of resource exploitation, about clearcuts and leased shorelines. I'm complicit in this. For now, I want to observe the web of the natural world, to savour its novelty. I want to forget the origins of my species.

Maybe writing about nature is a 'soft' predation on the wild.

Back in the workshop, I can't write. I'm saturated with visual images and biological creation myths, but there is no story. Plunk in the middle of the Salish Sea, I am between tides, at the beginning of the north coast and the end of middle age.

May 16

After the final meeting of the writing course, Laurent, one of the other older students in the group, ambles over to me, "We're going to take our boat over to Mitlenatch, if you'd like to come." Mitlenatch is a nature reserve in the middle of Georgia Strait, a sanctuary for migratory birds and wildlife.

I meet the others at Squirrel Cove. Laurent, white hair wisping in all directions from his toque, scuttles down the gangway with extra gear. His partner Julie and our guides Bill and Don clamber after him. The aluminium boat floats like a toy dinghy at the bottom of the steep gangplank. The tide is out. I edge my way down gingerly, my hands tightly gripping the railings.

As we load, the boat rocks back and forth in the bottomless dark water, against steel-gray mountains that bulge into the skyline of Desolation Sound. The wind picks up as we head across the Strait to Mitlenatch. I count the life jackets, flotation cushions, anything that looks like it might stay afloat, just in case. At times the boat shudders, slamming down so hard between waves that we can hardly hold on. We're all on edge.

Nearing Mitlenatch, a bald eagle soars above the rocky cliffs, harassed by shrieking glaucous-winged gulls. Pelagic cormorants line the rock face; the purple-green of their coats gleams like starling sheen. As the boat putters around the coast, an eagle nest comes into sight, a basket of woven pick-up sticks. Dog-faced sea lions and harbour seals bob near the rocky bluffs. Harlequin ducks feed just offshore. Nesting oystercatchers probe for dinner, their red beaks vacuuming the rocks. The boat gurgles towards the soft curve of a sandy beach on the lee side. As the wind softens, Laurent cuts back the throttle. The water is boulder-ridden, a dark rich green as we approach the shore. Sea wrack dribbles past, emerald flags translucent with sunlight. We ease into the Mitlenatch anchorage, but we're in too close, and the propeller grates against the rocks. Bill grabs the pitch pole, pushes off, and we drift in towards the rocky headland on the eastern side of the cove.

We stumble off the boat into the soft muck of draining soil. The blooms are at their peak. Hot pink and buttery yellow mimulus decorate the seeps. Hyacinth blues of meadow camas sprinkle scented beds of pink sea blush; chocolate lilies dangle above fields of yellow buttercups. We slog uphill through the sloppy drainage. I scan the island: chickweed, avens, nodding onions, blue-eyed Mary, frothy white death camas, wild rose, alum root, starflower, Saskatoon and woolly eriophyllum. Oh my, there are gulls in the midst of mating. Bill gives a running commentary:

Now he's fanning his tail. But nothing's happening.
There! Now, see her fan her tail, and then he catches it.
There, now he's at it, and on the left.
Uh, off again, no, still fanning, back on her, fanning to the right this time.
He's on her! Uh-oh, they're finished.

He sounds like a sports announcer on television. Around us the wind howls, mixing with the shrill of hundreds, maybe thousands of gulls. Below us, sea lions bark and grunt from their haul-outs.

* * * *

That evening, safely back on Cortes, we tuck into Julie's little caravan house. A washer and dryer twin the back porch, with a rusty old fridge perched to the side. A square of curtain hangs demurely in front of the toilet seat in the outhouse. Julie chops onion and garlic for sauce while Laurent scrambles pots of steaming, simmering seafood around the stove. Don claws barnacles from the oyster shells. We've built a kitchen midden of shells with just one meal.

Laurent turns redder and redder, like the prawns simmering in the pot. Kettles boil. We drink too much beer, and roar with laughter, euphoric to have survived the white-capped Strait.

May 18

Two days later, back in Vancouver, I can still smell the sea, as if it's draining out of my pores. My mind is submerged on an oyster string in Desolation Sound.

I wander through Stanley Park. Herons nest above the tennis courts. Yellow trumpets of skunk cabbage funnel from swampy soil. Hot-pink blooms of salmonberries dazzle woody stalks; raspberry-red currants unfurl in the sun.

Spring is here, on the west coast, even in Vancouver.

LIVING AND WRITING ON THE EDGE
HEATHER KELLERHALS-STEWART

For me, this conversation begins while sitting in my kayak, bow pointing seaward, past the last, rocky islet of Quadra Island. Surf sound lets me know I'm perched on the outer edge. Beyond is where my imagination navigates.

I ask my daughter why she likes living on our small island. After a moment of hesitation, she replies, "Because I like living on the edge. It feels like wilderness when I step out my door. I never know what will be waiting there."

I nod in agreement.

Living on the edge, or as some might say, *in the boonies,* allows time to sniff out the essence of a landscape. Not that there aren't distractions. A small community is one neighbourhood and there is intense social pressure to join all sorts of groups, the do-good groups, feel-good groups, you-name-it groups. Still, there is enough quiet and space to become embedded in this landscape, and to reflect on its story, a story I dare to try describing in words.

After many years of living on our island I know the turkey vultures arrive in early March each year. I welcome the chatter of violet-green swallows and, later, the barn swallows' rapturous return to the nest above our door. Seasonal returnees are greeted with joy: the first succulent asparagus spears in April, the burst of artichoke heads or with occasional dismay, the cabbage butterfly sniffing out my unsuspecting plants, the perennial caterpillars that munch on my gooseberry and currant bushes. If, as occasionally happens, the usual chain is broken, one feels a sense of foreboding. Why was our bay so barren of seabirds this last winter? We missed the melancholy murmur of murres that ease us through the dark days.

For me, living on the edge means expecting the unexpected. I walk out my door one morning and find myself encompassed in a coming-out party of newly fledged swallows. The feathered missiles shoot around me, filling the air with chatter. One lands on my shoulder, eyes me as if to say, '*I didn't know you were invited,'* and takes off again. The party lasts perhaps five minutes. I'm privileged to have taken part, however small my role.

Cities are filled with sounds and smells and stirrings that overwhelm the senses. In the depth and darkness of winter I sometimes yearn for those bright lights, the conferences and writers' meetings. But I rejoice in being around the fellow creatures that I keep, or perhaps I should say, that keep me. Whether they are our cattle, turkeys, geese, or ducks, these are my capable teachers. And the learning curve is often proverbially steep. I'm reminded of the urban reviewer who, when criticizing a children's book for being anthropomorphic, stated that *animals do not mourn*. Hmm ... two days after losing his mate our gander is still hiding in a shed, head buried under one wing.

Living on the edge over the years transforms the self. It offers rare glimpses into how people adapt to a landscape. I remember the first time I heard a raven calling, unseen overhead. I wondered, was that a dog barking? A bell sounding somewhere? No, it was the trickster raven, who speaks like all of these and more. My writing is inspired by such moments. On a hike through old growth forest, an isolated beach lies ahead. Long before catching sight of the ocean, I hear the roar of surf chewing at the continent's edge. Muffled at first by the tangle of cedar, hemlock, and salal around me, the roar mutates into individual waves reaching and departing the beach in enticing whispers. I'm pulled forward. The forest opens and I stumble onto the sand and the eternity beyond.

I return to my desk and write of the ephemeral moments that record the passing of the year. It has been snowing all night, something that rarely happens on our edge of the world. In the morning I put on skis and head into the forest. My tracks merge with other tracks, some hurrying, some wandering in seemingly aimless circles before diving underground. I discover padded cougar tracks leading along the path ahead. But I'm not turning back. I follow the tracks until I reach a depression in the snow where the animal was lying. How long ago? I lean over and let my fingers caress the melted snow, imagining the warmth left by that body. The forest is very still.

The First Peoples who lived here were superbly adept at living on the edge. Their art, stories and dramatic dances filled and gave meaning to the mysteries of the far west coast. We more recent *edgers* gather in local community halls for films and potluck feasts. We quilt and weave and paint and write, striving to capture the intriguing twists and turns of living on the edge in our own ways.

I bend over my computer, wrestling with the opening paragraph of a new project. For relief I glance out my window. A northwest wind has cleared the morning mist and the last scraps of yesterday's snow away. Swollen with melt water, the waterfall is surging over the bluffs. Camas is there too, lapping up the warmth of sun-touched rock. Spring! So much still to write, but the garden is calling, no, demanding my shoulders and a shovel. A knock comes at the door. *Yes, a cup of tea might be nice.* When a friend has travelled the long and pothole-filled road to reach our doorstep, there is no turning away. I shut down the computer, leave the troublesome paragraph for another day. Nothing like living on the edge to put the world into perspective, to nudge me towards what is important.

THE WET AND ROTTING REALM OF NANG SDINS, SGANG GWAAY LLNAGAAY, HAIDA GWAII

SUSAN MUSGRAVE

It has taken me nearly forty years from the first time I heard of Sgang Gwaay to this day when I leap from our Zodiac and scuttle up the beach. I'd even uprooted myself from the west of Ireland to move to Haida Gwaii in the early '70s because I felt so strong a pull to visit this mystical place where the fiercest of the Haida lived in their invincible stronghold. What's taken me so long to get here? The usual suspects, time and money, plus the fact that this 2000-year-old village is one of the most remote and difficult to access.

My friend, the writer Doug Coupland, had chartered a plane to fly him and his guests to Rose Harbour, from which point they hired a guide to take them by boat to the Island. I emailed him to see if he had any tips for me about getting to Sgang Gwaay. "The German guy who runs you in and out is kind of weird," Doug wrote. "We call him 'The Dentist' because he kept on talking about how, if he'd stayed in Cologne, he'd have been a dentist, but instead of speaking to captive prisoners in a dentist's chair, he speaks to captive prisoners in his Zodiac. He went on about nature and how much he was a friend of the planet, so I volunteered that I was glad about native otter populations returning after near extinction, and he went ballistic and started screaming about how bad they were for the abalone industry."

Being held captive in a dentist's chair wasn't how I had envisioned my first visit to this sacred site. My friend Claire told me she'd sea-kayaked through Gwaii Haanas to Sgang Gwaay and she was the one who convinced me it was now or never. "Before it's too late," she said. "Those poles aren't going to be around for that much longer."

Since I had to make the trip there and back the same day, I called the sole charter company operating on the Islands. "It's only the rich and famous who can afford to fly to Sgang Gwaay these days," the owner joked, when I flinched at the going rate of $2500 for the day trip (this includes the hour-long flight each way and the twenty minute crossing by Zodiac). John suggested I put my name on a list at the Visitor's Centre in Queen Charlotte and split the cost with others looking to share a ride. Two days later I got the call. A plane would be leaving at noon the next day. I packed a picnic lunch, and drove down to Queen Charlotte on a rare cloudless blue-sky morning. It had taken me nearly forty years, but as long as my truck didn't break down on me (the odometer read 666 as I pulled out of the driveway) I was finally going to make it.

I meet my fellow passengers at the Inland Air Office – Pat and Carol from Vancouver, Alvin and Kathleen from Ontario – where we are given brochures telling us the Island's history. The village itself, Sgang Gwaay Llnagaay, is on the protected east side of the island of Sgang Gwaay, shown on charts as Anthony Island, located off the far southern tip of Moresby Island and west of Kunghit Island. The village is also named Nang Sdins Llnagaay (Ninstints) after one of the most renowned chiefs.

In 1957 before the resurgence of contemporary Haida culture, eleven of the best-preserved poles of Sgang Gwaay Llnagaay were removed and floated down to museums in Victoria and Vancouver. Twenty-three years later, UNESCO declared Sgang Gwaay a World Heritage Site, making this the only example on our Earth of a traditional Northwest Coast First Nations site, with over two dozen still-standing poles as well as the posts and pits of several massive cedar long-houses. In 1995, after consultation with chiefs and elders, a number of the poles were straightened to prolong the period before they lose their struggle with gravity, and return naturally to the earth.

Some archaeologists would like to rescue those remaining tilting Nang Sdins Llnagaay poles from gravity's constant tug, to remove them for preservation, straighten them to standing tall, save them for posterity, but that isn't going to happen. The Haida want those mosses and lichens and the salal to continue growing on the tall wooden poles carved by their warrior ancestors. In fact, they'd like to see the other eleven "museum pieces" returned to their village of origin, the wet and rotting realm of Nang Sdins, where they rightfully belong. (Reading this makes me think of two lines from a poem by John Corsiglia: "yes, children, grave robbers and archaeologists are as different as night and day, which is when they work").

Today, we won't be the only foreigners visiting the Island. A Japanese film crew will be making the trip in their own plane, and I overhear them explain to the young woman at the desk how they would need to take the door off their plane as they circle the village site taking aerial shots.

Marvin, our pilot, helps us on board the six-seater Beaver, a no-nonsense bush plane equipped with floats for landing on water. Marvin straps me into the co-pilot's seat in the rustic cockpit, and gives each of us a set of headphones, with microphones attached. The microphone turns out to be useful in more ways than one. It impedes access to my mouth and stops me from biting my nails: Yes, I'm a nervous flyer.

The plane ride down to Sgang Gwaay alone is worth the price of the ticket. We fly over Hot Springs Island, Burnaby Narrows, and the tiny, solitary island known as All Alone Stone. The scenery distracts me enough that I don't even start hyperventilating as we put down in a sheltered cove on Kunghit Island and then ride a Zodiac across a stretch of open rolling water to Sgang Gwaay (which translates from the Haida as "Wailing Island" because of the wailing sound the winds make pushing through a hole in the rocks at a particular tide), in the misty distance.

The Zodiac lets us off at the north end of the island and we follow a boardwalk trail over the thick emerald moss that carpets the ground and makes you feel like you are in an enchanted forest where everything – the caves, rocky outcrops, the jumble of lush vegetation – is keeping an eye on you. I've heard people who've visited this place speak of hearing the laughter of children, or, more often, the cries of the sick and dying. Smallpox epidemics nearly wiped out Sgang Gwaay's population in the late 1800's and the hundreds who died here were buried in caves, in mortuary poles, and in the earth. Whichever way you turn you can feel the presences of these spirits.

Today I can hear rap music through the trees, a sign, I figure, that we are nearing the Watchmen's cabin, where three young Haida, who serve as guardians of the site, spend their summer. The one in charge of the ghetto blaster, who wears a baggy T-shirt that says JORDAN across the front, and white shorts down to his knees, invites us to sign the Visitor's Book with an eagle-quill pen. Watchman Steven Yeltatzie volunteers to give us an artist's perspective of the site, and we set off along another trail to the village where at one time twenty longhouses lined the bay. My first glimpse of the poles is through the trees, and I slip away from the rest of my group down onto the crescent beach, feeling shy about taking photographs in this numinous place. It is low tide and I can see the ancient canoe runs – areas deliberately cleared of rocks – still clearly visible in the sand. I think of my friend Claire who landed on this same beach in her kayak. Confronted by the row of massive, weathered mortuary poles carved more than 150 years ago with the bear, eagle and whale crests of the powerful families of this village, she said her whole body started shaking, and then she broke down sobbing, and couldn't stop.

After I've taken my few photographs – and even though I have seen hundreds of images of the totem poles losing their struggle with gravity, and the places where huge cedar plank houses fell and lie rotting beneath the moss – none has captured the strong medicine-magic. I am standing humbled before the Bear Mother Pole as Steven explains how her tongue reaches into her cub's head, symbolizing the passing on of the oral tradition, just as the Japanese film crew, and their plane *sans* door, buzzes the village. Minutes later they radio-telephone to give Steven and the Watchmen their profound thanks.

I hardly remember leaving the Island. We'd been a talkative bunch on the way down to Sgang Gwaay but now it is as if we have been stunned into silence.

"I won't ever see *that* again," Kathleen says, as we board for the trip back to "real life" as it is so often called. For many people, it is true: this will be a once-in-a-lifetime experience. On our trip home Marvin takes a detour up the east coast, so we can get a bird's-eye view of the humpback whales, at least a dozen of them. The water is so clear, you can see their entire mammoth bodies, surrounded by aquamarine light, as they twist and turn beneath the surface of Hecate Strait. I can't speak for hours when I get off the plane in Queen Charlotte, and it takes me two days to come back down to earth, as if I had travelled to a faraway supernatural realm, and returned, changed. I console myself: I'll go back to Sgang Gwaay again before I die, even if it takes me another forty years to get there.

References:

Yates, J. M. (1970). *Contemporary poetry of British Columbia*. Vancouver: Sono Nis Press.

A BEAUTIFUL IMPOSITION
CHRISTINE LOWTHER

Here nature dwarfs the human. The environment is alternately a place that overwhelms and destroys people, a place of refuge, and a place of revelation. The space and grandeur of this place decentres humans and so requires a re-thinking of the meaning of the human person.

Patricia O'Connell Killen

There are things I dislike about Tofino, the village where I live. Visitors and residents alike think it's better than the city, but we have no fudge shop. No music store. A choice of only two pubs. Not even one nightclub. No optometrist, no surgeons; no M.R.I. or C.T. scanners, no births in the little hospital; no lasting tattoo parlour. No meditation centre; too much yoga. No art supply store.

Something I do like is how artists take up challenges and find innovative ways to create. Many carvers and sculptors of wood thrive on the 100-mile diet, setting a bioregional example by improvising with salvaged lumber, burls, or drift-wood. Other artists make baskets and jewellery from kelp and beach glass. Quite a few of us write.

When author Sharon Butala came to Tofino, gave a workshop, and expressed belief in my ability as a prose writer, I felt a deep, resolved exhalation. It appeared I would not be letting go the literary grindstone. First, however, I had to face up to the healing there was to be done. Not only was poetry how I healed my youth, but nature was the conveyor of the poetry. Together, nature and poem-writing conspired to heal me, like an art therapy. Living in a wild place, where every leaf is its own poem, brought healing process and poetry together. They became one fierce beast, and then they became a book.

Poetry, says Marilyn Bowering, "takes us out of the chaos, lets us stand back and understand even while we are deeply involved in the process of living terrible contradictions." I think of this in everyday moments. Smiling back at acquaintances in the post office, answering, "I'm fine, thank you." In truth I sometimes feel poison behind these upturned lips because I'm not fine, not really. Poetic expression, for me, continues to equal repair, restoration, and growth. Despite violent origins – the big bang, or an exploding apart of family – evolution occurs. Despite, or because of it, as Cormac McCarthy said:

> Creative work is often driven by pain. It may be that if you don't have something in the back of your head driving you nuts, you may not do anything. It's not a good arrangement. If I were God, I wouldn't have done it that way.

* * *

The mystery of the natural world lies in its power to evoke a human response, and in the variety of the potential responses.

Fred Kaplan

For ten years after the birth of my first poetry book, I kept mainly to non-fiction, pooh-poohing anyone who introduced me as a poet. The poems had dried up. Yet reading poetry eventually renewed my fascination with it. In time, while living close to Schooner Cove in Pacific Rim National Park for two months, poems sprouted inside me, seeded there by the outdoors. (Admittedly, it helped that I had just been dumped). I was suddenly living the miraculous: writing a poem a day.

My method of practice is, as my teenaged nephew likes to say, "random." I go for walks or bike rides in nature to find inspiration, as the splintering rain, gale-blown trees, and reaching, crashing waves reflect how I feel more often than not.

This season
is all about motion, begs response from us,
wails against polite sunset-viewing. Caught
between roiling ocean, statues of shore rock
and standing stick-humans, no wonder

the self bleeds out my eyes.

In part the question becomes, does *geology* influence writers? Susan Musgrave wrote twenty meditations on stones. Pat Lowther was "madly in love" with stone, writing books called *Milk Stone* and *A Stone Diary*. Sharon Butala wrote *Wild Stone Heart*. In the Tofino area an island of rock at the end of a tombolo on Chesterman Beach is a favourite place, even a magical place for many. This is an excerpt from a poem written during a productive autumn:

> They say the place is a ley-line intersection:
> peak of planetary pressure points,
> the lure behind every Pacific coast pilgrimage.
> There I've witnessed the wretched

as they cried and clung to veined stone.
I've seen them kissing and caressing jagged rock.
Whether returning on dry sand or wading through incoming tide,
their faces come down the tombolo blazing with newfound peace.

Rock, stone, bedrock, these are the foundation of place, even land that is unstable in the face of soft sand, extreme tides, and miles of boot-sucking mud-flats. Clayoquot Sound is a coastal place of plenty. Oystercatchers and marbled murrelets, unlogged mountains, oyster farms, solid weeks of rain, waterspouts, seals, whales, shaggy thousand-year-old cedars, boats and surfboards and kayaks; there is almost too much to write about. Drinking island-brewed beer at the Maquinna on karaoke night and stumbling to a party at Tonquin Beach without a flashlight.

For me, writing about nature demands constant vigilance against sentimen-tality; the poet must blast any hint of a cliché off the page. Ruthless, driven and excitable describes me in this process, like the weather, like the environment. If we take ourselves with us wherever we walk, I wonder, if I were walking in a pastoral setting rather than on a windy wild beach fringed with grizzled forest, would my poems be softer? I hope not.

Some locals, artists included, suffer from Seasonal Affective Disorder. The only time of year it affects me that way is tourist season. I welcome foul weather. It means grounded, undistracted hours of writing and pitching, rewriting and editing. Winter is essential for catching up to one's dreams and goals. It allows a pajama-clad holing up with one's projects. I resent too many nice days in a win-ter. And when the storms cause power outages, I take my walks and bicycle rides in search of my muse. Even a winter storm on my coast is comparatively mild. When the rest of Canada is buried under deep snow in January, men have been seen topless and barefoot on Tofino's beaches, throwing a frisbee. The wild-yet-mild polarity can only be a boon to the artful mind.

> [T]he natural world is an inexhaustible source of meaning, directly available
> to us if we allow our contemplative attention to rest there . . .
>
> Jan Zwicky

Where is the support for the creatively inclined out here? Where is the stimula-tion? In a fudgeless locale, where can I turn? To books, writers' groups, reading clubs, visiting authors, the theatre society, disc jockeys, and live bands. We even boast a highly organized Pacific Rim Arts Society. Still, a writer is always isolated. Sometimes the group doesn't meet for a long while. My own struggle has to do with juggling three day-jobs with alone time — my time for creating. Having enough energy to deeply focus, to find the acutely awake state required for poem-making, the uninterrupted hours required for prose writing. Busy season in a tourist town allows precious little of this writer's most coveted tool. When time presents itself at last, my energy is often too drained to make use of it.

Most helpful in my aspiration to prevail and thrive has been particular individuals who believe in me so doggedly that they are able, sometimes, to break down the barriers I consistently throw up with equal determination. A recent reminder from one of them that writers and artists *suffer* was far from stereotyping. She was allowing me a crucial affirmation. Suddenly, I was not a sour, resentful curmudgeon curtailed by writers' block. I was an artist! A long-suffering artist!

I have a 1950s photograph of eleven women and two children. Pat Lowther, my late poet-mother, is one of the women. Unlike any of the others, she looks uncomfortable. I always wondered if she was in a lousy mood at the time of the photo, or whether she didn't like the photographer. Maybe she was miffed at her Mum who sits beside her, grinning widely. One day a filmmaker, Anne Henderson, was studying this picture in her preparation for the documentary *Water Marks*.

"Look at her face," Anne said. "She knows she doesn't fit in. See? She was an *artist*."

True, someone else might interpret the expression differently. They might say, "She was a feminist." Her sister, my aunt, who is also in the picture, might explain, "She was exhausted and had one of her migraines coming on." Perhaps the pain in my mother's face is there because she wishes she could be happy and content with her lot, as the other women seem to be. The two children are hers, my elder brother and sister. Today, I can't help but wonder if, in an era of traditional gender roles, she was longing for time and energy to write, and for acceptance of such yearning.

Mine is a different era with new freedoms and new constraints. I envy the hell out of those who don't call themselves artists or writers. They are the free ones. Work, play, family, friends. Can't I be grateful for all I have? Oh, no. I have to write. A normal life could never be enough.

I am never enough. I require the support of my fellow writers along with ample outings to forest, beach, and mudflat.

* * *

In my experience, west coast places cause art. They demand expression. Their beauty imposes itself upon our consciousness, and what imposes necessitates response. Poet Greg Simison offers that, for British Columbia poets, a poetry *of place* "is impossible for most of us to ignore when we live where the geography is so dominant."

Does this invite open-mindedness and experimentation? Does the mild climate lower fears and soften conservatism? We may have a right-wing government in British Columbia but not compared to Alberta and other places worldwide. What gave birth to the bush dweller living off the grid, making crafts to sell at a Gulf Island weekend market? We're not hemmed in here. The ocean is open; we can breathe freely all the way to Japan. So a new question emerges: When writing under the influence of my natural surroundings, what blocks my creative process?

In a word, fears. I have fears of laziness, emptiness, and writing with clichés. There is also the freezing fear of judgment. It has been said that nature writers are too often sentimentalists, a core dread of mine I mentioned earlier. That my work will be deemed soft, anthropomorphic, oblivious to privilege, irrelevant to urban readers, in denial of gritty realism. Yet is there not some wisdom in embracing the inescapable? More "than what can be counted and measured," there is "what the meditative [artist] mind brings to bear in its attempt to find human significance in natural phenomena." So wrote author Fred Kaplan. I close my eyes, centre on my gut and write what I experience … judge me as you will. In the words of poet Maleea Acker, "I try to attend to small pieces of southern Vancouver Island ecosystems, in words or by action," while asking, "what could possibly be an adequate response to the landscapes around me?" The challenge sustains me – here comes another baggage-encumbered word – spiritually. I hope I receive this sustenance without deafness to the voices that were here before me.

Up until very recently I feared that nature did my work for me, that I was no poet without it. Then I went to Europe for an entirely urban holiday, attending a music festival in Glasgow, visiting a friend in Amsterdam, exploring art and architecture in Milan, Florence, and Rome. I did not write poems, just kept my journal as usual. Months later, back on my floathouse in the Sound, I finished up a manuscript of nature poems, yet still felt chagrined to have created nothing out of so much legendary Italian art, the trip now fading in my memory. So I went through my journal and drafted two 'Europe' poems. Two entirely non-nature poems! No lichen, no rocks, no jellyfish! I swelled with pride and relief.

It is healthy to keep asking myself questions that push my practice as a writer. Whether it is with tunnel vision or focussed response, I have to write what I know, while facing the fears of unconsciousness and exclusivity. I fear to write without attending to others' experience, blind to my own ignorance and advantage. I fear to exclude other realities, classes, ethnicities, those who are not wanting or able to live under the imposing beauty of the far west coast.

In closing I think back to Bowering's quote about terrible contradictions. The wild-yet-mild is not merely a fact about the place I live; it can mean exhilaration or depression, even life or death. I often feel deeply polarized within myself. This can seem healthy and balanced and unpredictable. Other times it feels stressful. Nature has no need of me, but I cannot live without it. Summers I'm in a floathouse, off the grid, away from civilization, gasping from my forays for work and groceries into the tourist hub. Winters I'm in Tofino, gleefully connected to as many wires as a townie can be connected to. Half the year I am sedentary, the other, fixatedly fit. I've been stamped both "nature girl" and punk rocker. Lately I am a roller derby girl with a bruised, butterfly heart. I am industrious and rebelliously distracted, productive and procrastinating, both damaged and healing. I am not sure what this sea-sick, pendulous way of life does for my art. So far, writing happens without structure, without routine, but obsessively. Place imposes itself at random; creative response is obligatory. My plan is to follow the art, try to keep up with it, in whatever season.

References:

O'Connell Killen, P. (2008). *Memory, Novelty and Possibility in This Place*, Douglas Todd (Ed.), *CASCADIA: The Elusive Utopia*. Vancouver: Ronsdale Press.

Ed. Fertig, Mona and Rhenisch, Harold. *ROCKSALT: An Anthology of Contemporary BC Poetry*. Mother Tongue Publishing Ltd, Salt Spring, 2008.

Hollywood's Favorite Cowboy: Author Cormac McCarthy interviewed by John Jurgensen in *The Wall Street Journal* on-line at http://online.wsj.com/article/SB10001424052748704576204574529703577274572.html

Kaplan Fred. *Lincoln: The Biography of a Writer*. quoted in *Sky* magazine, Feb 09, page 88.

Zwicky, Jan. *Lyric Realism: Nature Poetry, Silence, and Ontology; The Malahat Review* # 165/Dec 08, University of Victoria.

CONTRIBUTOR BIOGRAPHIES

ROBERT AMOS is a painter and art writer for the *Victoria Times Colonist*. He has published six books of his paintings, writing and photographs and *Artists In Their Studios* is the only book on the artists of southern Vancouver Island. His new book, *Inside Chinatown* was published by TouchWood Editions in September, 2009. See: www.robertamos.com

GREG BLANCHETTE (a.k.a. greg blee) moved to Vancouver Island's west coast 13 years ago. His published work includes magazine articles, essays, short stories, chapbooks and on-line pieces. He is active in the local arts and environmental scenes, nurtures an interest in music and performance poetry, and takes his community seriously.

KAREN CHARLESON is a mother and grandmother, married to Stephen Charleson. She and her family are members of the House of Kinquashtacumlth and the Hesquiaht First Nation. Karen is a long-time resident of Hesquiaht traditional territories, where she and her husband operate Hooksum Outdoor School. Karen has an MA in Integrated Studies.

PETER CRESSEY is a furniture maker (naturaledges.ca) who lives in Victoria with his partner Sonya and daughter Fern. He has been involved in the non-profit bookstore Camas (camas.ca) and in helping to organise a twenty-year Walbran blockade reunion (walbranvalleyreunion@blogspot.com)

MICHAEL SCOTT CURNES, author of the novel *Val* (1996 Brownell & Carroll) spent eight years living, working, writing, and loving in Clayoquot Sound (1995-2003). Today he is Western Canada Planned Giving Coordinator for Nature Conservancy of Canada in Vancouver. In his spare time he writes, sings, acts, and dances in local productions. His latest novel is *For the Love of Mother*.

ROBERT DALTON is an Associate Professor in Art Education at the University of Victoria. His studio practice supports and is supported by his research in children's art-making in diverse cultures. Having lived on the prairies for forty years, he has a special appreciation for the climate, geography, flora and fauna of the west coast as a "magical place."

ADRIAN DORST is a long time Tofino resident whose careers have varied widely during his life, from industrial painter and steeple-jack in his youth, to taxidermist, field-ornithologist, and nature photographer. While his photographs have been seen widely, less well known is the fact that he is also an accomplished wood carver and sculptor.

KEVEN DREWS shut down the Westcoaster.ca in early 2011, but remains a journalist. Keven says he is still dealing with his Dad's death, and wonders, like many sons, how he could have had a better relationship with his father.

GAEL DUCHENE has lived in Clayoquot Sound for twenty-four years. On her wood lathe, Gael turns burls from local wood that industry has discarded, and then adds hand carving and other artistic embellishments. "Heart Song," Gael's first writing attempt, won first prize in the *More Than Just Mud Contest of Words* in 2008.

MICHAEL J. EMME is an exhibiting photographer, printmaker and art educator. Born in California, he has co-created comic books, gallery art, installations and performance works with elementary students, educators and fine arts graduate students across BC, in Nova Scotia, Ellensburg, across Alberta, and he now teaches at UVic near the water.

MIKE EMME's pursuit of photography, printmaking, publication design and writing along with work as a classroom performance artist has taken him across North America. He has marked his return to Victoria with work in a graphic novel-esque form intended to provoke a collaborative-creative environment where lines between reader/author/artist/designer blur.

DAVID FLOODY is late: late to Clayoquot Sound, late to writing novels, late to return library books. But his desk overlooks the busy 'Gibson Path,' and early on he learned that this daily flow of village life represents narratives in embryo. If the village ever decides to push Gibson Street through and asphalt his inspiration, David will be the first to throw himself in front of the bulldozers.

For over fifteen years HEATHER FRISE has made documentary films, including the Genie award-winning *Bones of the Forest*. She has worked extensively as a freelance documentary film editor and educator, and has taught at Access to Media Education Society, Emily Carr University and Toronto's Ontario College of Art and Design.

KIM GOLDBERG's latest book, *RED ZONE*, documents homelessness and urban decay in downtown Nanaimo through poetry and photography. Her previous poetry collection, *Ride Backwards on Dragon*, was a finalist for Canada's Lampert Memorial Award. She is the publisher of Pig Squash Press, www.pigsquashpress.com.

KIT GRAUER will soon be Professor Emerita of the University of British Columbia where she taught for 27 years. She will be found walking on the beaches at Boundary Bay and Galiano and pursuing her art making, research and time with her family, friends and menageries.

SANDRA GWYNNE MARTIN is a poet living on the west coast, snug in the Gulf Islands between the mainland and Vancouver Island. She recently left the city pace behind in search of a lifestyle where she needed neither a watch nor a daytimer. She is loving country life and relishing the wisdom of donkeys.

KEITH HARRISON, born in Vancouver, has written seven books, including Eyemouth, Crossing the Gulf, Furry Creek, and Elliot & Me, and has edited Islands West: Stories from the Coast. He teaches film, creative writing, and Shakespeare at Vancouver Island University and lives on Hornby Island.

MELODY HESSING lives in Vancouver, and has taught and published sociology for most of her working life. She now scribes more creatively in non-fiction and has been published in several literary anthologies and journals. Her creative non-fiction book, *Up Chute Creek: An Okanagan Idyll*, was published in 2009.

MARK HOBSON lives in Tofino, on the rugged west coast of Vancouver Island, where he has painted for over twenty years. A diverse artist in both subject and media, he is equally comfortable in watercolour, oils, and acrylics. Mark's work has won awards in the United States, Canada and Europe.

WANDA HURREN is a poetic photographer/cartographer living in Victoria. Her artwork has been featured in several exhibitions of text and image. She is a member of *Crossgrain*, one of the few remaining darkroom societies, and she is an Associate Professor at the University of Victoria.

JAN JANZEN lives in a cedar driftwood and glass cabin shaped like a mushroom with a clamshell cap at the edge of a small grove of gigantic old-growth trees at the edge of space and time, in the heart of Oneness. His book, *Rumours and Other Truths about the Indescribable*, is available in Tofino.

SUSAN KAMMERZELL is riveted by the massive changes in the world around and within us, and is using the strengths gained during her coastal decades to create a life that lies within the budget of our planetary biosphere. She is learning, gardening and building her new village homestead in BC's interior.

SHIRLEY LANGER began writing about Tofino soon after moving there. The result was *Road's End: Tales of Tofino*. An historical fiction novel, *Anita's Revolution*, about the 1961 Cuban Literacy Campaign will soon be available on Amazon.com. Shirley volunteers teaching literacy at Literacy Victoria, and oh!–Shirley loves to sing.

BERNICE LEVER, born in Smithers, retired to Bowen Island, BC in 2001, after decades around Toronto. Her 10th poetry book is "Imagining Lives", Black Moss, spring 2012. She has written a college English textbook. Now a freelance editor, she enjoys helping others get published. www.colourofwords.com

CHRISTINE LOWTHER is the author of *Half-Blood Poems, My Nature, New Power*, and *A Cabin in Clayoquot*; co-editor and co-author of *Writing the West Coast: In Love with Place*. She admits to sometimes writing 'soft' poems about bees and flowers. Just to break things up.

SHARON MCINNES writes a monthly column, *Just for the Birds*, for The Flying Shingle on Gabriola Island. Her first book, *Up Close & Personal*, is a compilation of those columns with colour photos. She has also written articles for several magazines. Currently Sharon is working on a novel.

MARY ANN MOORE is a poet and freelance writer based in Nanaimo where she leads Writing Life, a weekly circle. She is as happy writing her own poetry and personal essays as she is mentoring others in their own writing practice. See www.maryannmoore.ca for Writing Home: A Whole Life Practice.

LIBBIE MORIN's inspiration stems from growing up in downtown Toronto, living in isolation on Vancouver Island and being immersed in the beauty and magic of Tofino. She won the E. Bickle Award at North Island College. Her work appears in NIC's *Zeitgiest* and in the E-zine, *Pages of Stories*.

MARGARET MURPHY is passionate about sharing stories and helping others find their storytelling voice. A co-founder of the *Around Town Tellers* in Nanaimo, Margaret helps build community through story, whether in the classroom or boardroom or spaces in between.

SUSAN MUSGRAVE lives and writes on Haida Gwaii. She teaches in the University of British Columbia's Optional Residency in Creative Writing MFA Programme. Her last collection of poems was *Origami Dove* (McClelland & Stewart) and a novel, *Given*, will be published by Thistledown in the fall of 2013.

AVIS RASMUSSEN is a painter, printmaker, and poet-illustrator of chapbooks *Charms of the Seashore, Take Five Coast To Coast, Saanich Fields and Garden World*. She paints around Sidney, her birthplace, and Victoria where she lives, and on her travels. Winchester Galleries of Oak Bay exhibits her paintings. With a BFA and MEd, she is currently on the University of Victoria Alumni Board. She is a CARFAC-BC artist.

ROLAND RASMUSSEN, painter, poet, and writer, born on Vancouver Island in 1966, is chiefly interested in the building of artistic communities within Victoria. A painter at an early age, he has sought to document our western Canadian landscape and provide new ways to use image and colour to bring his subjects to a curious eye.

VELCROW RIPPER is an award-winning director of dozens of films and videos, including *Bones of the Forest*, an environmental film co-directed with Heather Frise which received nine major film awards, including a Genie award for best feature-length documentary. His non-fiction writing has appeared in anthologies and magazines, and he is currently developing part three of the Fierce Light Trilogy: http://www.facebook.com/l/f6506; www.fiercelight.org

JANET MARIE ROGERS is a Mohawk/Tuscarora writer performance, recording and video poet. She has been living on traditional Coast Salish territory (Victoria) since 1994. Janet is a radio host on Native Waves Radio CFUV fm and CBC's Tribal Clefs. She is Victoria's current poet laureate; present to 2015.

AHAVA SHIRA completed her PhD in Language & Literacy Education from the University of British Columbia, where she developed the arts-based practice of loving inquiry. Author of a new poetry CD, *Love is Like This* (2010), Ahava now works as a creative mentor, helping youth & adults to follow their h*earts*. Visit ahavashira.com.

LISA SHATZKY's poetry has been published across Canada and the U.S. in magazines, journals, books, and anthologies. Her poetry book *"Do Not Call Me By My Name"* (Black Moss Press, 2011) was short-listed for the 2012 Gerald Lampert Poetry Award in Canada. When not writing she works as a psychotherapist on Bowen Island, B.C.

ANITA SINNER has been an exhibiting artist in the Sooke region for fifteen years. She is an Assistant Professor in Art Education at Concordia University, Montreal, and her research interests include life writing, arts-based research, community art education and digital media.

CELESTE SNOWBER is a dancer, writer and educator who is an Associate Professor in the Faculty of Education at Simon Fraser University. A well published author, she also creates site-specific performances of her poetry and dance in seascapes. Celeste is the mother of three sons, all a tribe of artists. Her website is www.celestesnowber.com.

HEATHER KELLERHALS-STEWART lives on one of the original Quadra Island homesteads where she and her family manage a farm and woodlot. Depending on weather you can find her working in a garden gone wild or writing - picture books, novels for young people, sometimes poetry and essays.

JOANNA STREETLY is a freelance writer, illustrator and editor living afloat near Tofino. She is the author of *Silent Inlet* (Oolichan) and *Paddling Through Time* (Raincoast). Her current work-in-progress is historical fiction set in 1919 both at Lennard Island Lighthouse (Clayoquot Sound) and on the Isle of Wight.

MARLA THIRSK, known as "Ucluelet's Artist," has lived in the region for almost thirty years, painting many of the town's murals and playing an active role in all aspects of the arts. Working in several different mediums, her style is eclectic and her art has gone all over the world: www.marlathirsk.com

JANINE WOOD was born in Kamloops in 1966. She has lived on Vancouver Island for more than twenty years, and has travelled extensively to Australia, New Zealand, Europe and the UK. Janine has worked in the restaurant industry, studied dance, and attended university until moving to the far west coast where she now resides.

JOHANNA VANDERPOL is the author of *Honouring Your Emotions: Why It Matters* and a positive psychology coach who enjoys helping clients live their best life. She is grateful to live in a home overlooking Cowichan Bay with her eighteen-year-old son. She can be reached at www.johannavanderpol.com

BILL ZUK is Professor Emeritus in Art Education at the University of Victoria. He is co-editor of the *BC Art Teachers' Association Journal* and curates the *Art in Public Places* program. Bill received the national Gaitskell Award for Excellence in 2007 and was Artist-in-Residence at Num-ti-jah in the Canadian Rockies in 2009. He is currently collaborating on a visual arts project with Ballet Victoria.